I0815246

THE CARS OF THE 70S

Charger 770
CHARGER 770
Charger

THE CARS OF THE 70S

A HISTORY OF CARS MANUFACTURED AND ASSEMBLED IN AUSTRALIA DURING THE 1970S

GAVIN FARMER

Published in 2024 by New Holland Publishers
Sydney

Level 1, 178 Fox Valley Road, Wahroonga, NSW 2076, Australia

newhollandpublishers.com

For image credits see page 222

A record of this book is held at the National Library of Australia.

ISBN 9781760792527

Managing Director: Fiona Schultz
Designer: Andrew Davies
Production Director: Arlene Gippert
Printed in China

Keep up with New Holland Publishers:

NewHollandPublishers
@newhollandpublishers

CONTENTS

ACKNOWLEDGEMENTS

This book would not have been possible without the assistance of a great many people, all enthusiasts for their particular marque or model. Included in this illustrious group were people from the Chevrolet Club, the Triumph Owners Club, the Vauxhall Club, the Humber Car Club, Chrysler Restorers Car Club, the Chrysler Car Club, Rootes Group Club, Austin Car Club and the Morris Register.

From a personal point of view I would like to thank Simon Fitzpatrick (Renault, Peugeot), Stewart Underwood (Holden), Brenton Thomas and Jim Quigley (Studebaker), Bob Freeman and Colin Main (Rambler), Ian Webber (Chrysler), John Lowe (Bolwell), Rod and Lloyd Davies, Phil Matthews and Carl Moll from the VW Car Club, Michael Bowen from *Jeep Action* magazine.

For checking my work for accuracy I would like to thank the late Max Gregory and general counsel for information on the decade Pedr Davis, Ted O'Brien, John Regan and Kenneth Wright Jnr; Robert Simpson for the registration figures and Richard Johns from Australian Automotive Intelligence in Melbourne, and Michele Cook and Doug Wallace from the Ford Motor Company.

I would also like to express my thanks to the folks at the Library at the Sporting Car Club as well as the National Motor Museum, Birdwood.

INTRODUCTION

The Seventies was a decade of mixed blessings for the local automobile industry. It was a time when for the first time in decades the country had to get used to having a Federal Labour Government led by Gough Whitlam and it became a time of great difficulties for the business world. This was because one of the first things the new Federal Government did was to begin the process of dismantling the tariff system. The effects of this were not immediately felt but as the years rolled on it was obvious that Australian industry was competing on anything but a level playing field despite the words of assurance from our former Treasurer. In addition, the ACTU led by future prime minister, Bob Hawke, became extremely militant and demanded (and received) massive pay rises for all and sundry.

In many respects the Seventies could be divided into two parts, the period from 1970-through-1974 and then 1975-through-1980. The first period was when the local content policy from the Federal Government was enacted where GM-Holden, Ford, Chrysler, VW and BMCA (later to be renamed Leyland Australia) agreed to Plan A which meant that they had to have 95 per cent local content in each and every car that rolled off their respective assembly lines. Reaching 60 per cent local content was relatively easy, to get to the levels required in Plan A meant that body panels had to be stamped here and items such as engines, transmissions and rear axle assemblies also had to be manufactured here.

Both Toyota and Nissan wanted to be a part of the local manufacturing industry and so the Government came up with Plans B, C and D so that the two Japanese companies would invest in their local operations, Toyota with AMI and Nissan with Motor Producers. Plan B allowed a company to assemble up to 7500 vehicles a year with at least 60 per cent local content, Plan C was for between 2501 and 5000 vehicles a year with up to 50 per cent content, and Plan D was for up to 2500 cars per year at up to 40 per cent local content. AMI, Renault, Peugeot, Nissan and Toyota were all operating on the lower volume Plans with GM-H, Ford, Chrysler, Leyland and Volkswagen all on Plan A.

By 1973 the Government's plans were collapsing. The then Minister for Trade and Industry, Dr Jim Cairns, had initiated across-the-board tariff reductions of 25 per cent for all imported goods (not just vehicles) and this was followed soon afterwards by the OPEC fuel crisis that had a disastrous effect on world trade, not just Australia's. By November 1974 the tariff rates on cars was back to 44 per cent, just below where it had been for years. Linked in with this was the fixed-rate currency exchange rates – floating exchange rates did not arrive until 1983–84 – that had the value of the Australian dollar rising as a result of UK and US devaluations; Australia was at the time in the middle of a mining boom with associated pressure to revalue the dollar upwards. At the end of 1972 the Whitlam Government revalued our dollar by 17½ per cent(!) but by mid-1974 it was heading down again.

By the mid-70s the Government revised Plan A by reducing the requirement down to 85 per cent local content so that the existing manufacturers could average their content over all their model lines because apart from the Kingswood, Falcon and Valiant they were struggling to meet the original requirements. The other aspect of this move was to encourage Toyota and Nissan to move up from 60 per cent content. At this time quotas were brought in to avert the flooding of the market by importers.

And in July 1974 the Industries Assistance Commission announced its inquiry results in a 1300-page document that involved every company and organisation having made submissions before the panel which ultimately would make recommendations to the Federal Government.

The decade also saw the arrival of mandated emission and crash safety requirements – Australian Design Rules (ADR) – for all manufacturers, requirements that were non-negotiable. And just to make things awkward the local ADRs were slightly different from the rest of the world. Why? Go figure …

It would be fair to say that the Seventies was a decade of turmoil in Australia's industrial history – tumultuous I think is possibly the word to describe what happened. The Seventies saw the power of the trade unions at its zenith. Not a week went by without some industrial dispute hitting the headlines in the media. With rampant inflation reducing the buying power of worker's pay packets there were strikes for more money and so the spiral went on and on. Was there a winner out of all of this? I think not. As former MD at Chrysler, Ian Webber, said, "It was a slow motion train crash heading for destruction!"

With rampant inflation and spiralling costs the new car prices rose dramatically through the 70s although the manufacturers were forced to negotiate with the newly established Prices Justification Tribunal before applying any increase in price. The PJT was another bureaucracy established by the Whitlam Government in a futile effort to keep a handle on things but in reality all it did was to rubber stamp any and every price increase. It was eventually disbanded.

Until then GM-Holden, Ford and Chrysler had successfully marketed their idea of what the average Australian family wanted in motoring terms – the Holden Kingswood, Ford Falcon and Chrysler Valiant. They were merely going with the flow, so to speak. Technical refinement, interior fittings and quality of assembly were an anathema. And in 1973 Leyland Australia entered the same market with their uniquely Australian car, the Leyland P76. A sub-market evolved at the time populated by the Holden Torana, Ford Cortina, Chrysler Centura and the Leyland Marina Six. All were compact family sedans originally designed around four-cylinder engines but for the Australian market they had six-cylinder engines transplanted into their engine bays.

In the meantime came the inexorable rise and rise of the Japanese manufacturers, in particular Toyota and Nissan, followed by Mitsubishi in 1971 with assembly of the Galant sedan and wagon under license with Chrysler.

VW pulled back from Plan A to Plan B during the 70s and then took on assembling and painting Nissans and Volvos while across town Renault Australia had committed itself to local assembly of the R12 and the brilliant R16 under Plan B as well as the assembly of the Peugeot 504, one of the world's great family sedans. Also in Melbourne, AMI was quietly assembling the Triumph 2500 saloons and various models from the US Rambler range as well as various Toyotas.

Towards the end of the decade there were rumblings from the Federal Government about a common industry four-cylinder engine. Many pointless meetings were held with representatives from Holden, Ford, Chrysler, Toyota, Mitsubishi and Nissan but it gradually became more irrelevant and the idea was finally dropped.

Along with this growth in the manufacture and assembly of vehicles was that of the supplier group. After the war GM-Holden struggled to increase its production levels because the few local suppliers were not able, or willing, to invest in the machinery required to build parts in the volumes GM-H needed. Gradually, however, that changed as international companies like Bosch, Hella, Yazaki, Nippon Denso, Bridgestone and others invested in new facilities to meet the growing needs of our automobile industry.

The power war that began in 1967 with the release of the Ford Falcon GT was followed by the Holden Monaro GTS 327 and continued with unabated enthusiasm into the Seventies with Chrysler joining the fray in 1971 with its Charger E38. These were cars sporting engines with up to 300bhp and top speeds in the vicinity of 140mph. Admittedly they were to some extent homologation cars for motor sport although all three manufacturers agreed that they would build them to demand. This blew up in their faces on June 25, 1972 when a headline from the *Sydney Sun-Herald* screamed out "160MPH Super Cars Soon: Minister Horrified." Overnight the rules were changed under political pressure but the inexorable rise in power and performance from Holden and Ford was resumed after the dust had settled.

By the end of the Seventies the juggernaut that was the Australian motor industry had been derailed as the effects of poorly planned Government edicts and interference took their toll. We lost Leyland Australia in 1974, Chrysler Australia had become Mitsubishi Australia in 1980, VW and Nissan faded from the local scene in the 80s and as we now know Ford ceased manufacturing in 2016, Holden and Toyota in 2017. It was all rather sad and unnecessary really. A monument to political stupidity.

Gavin Farmer

CHAPTER 1

HOLDEN

The Seventies opened with Holden announcing the hastily prepared HG range of sedans, station wagons, coupes, panel vans and utilities. These were in reality stop-gap models that came about because the release of the forthcoming HQ range was running a long way behind schedule. Apart from a differently textured grille, slightly different taillights and badging the HG was virtually indistinguishable from the HT it superseded.

Holden had to wait until July 1971 to announce the quite different HQ range of sedans and station wagons. The HQ was by GM-H standards a radical design and was almost all-new apart from the carry-over engines and gearboxes. From 1967 the chief engineer at GM-Holden was George Roberts – he succeeded the well-respected Bill Steinhagen – who was a man who had come from Cadillac and who had some very different (and fixed) ideas as to how a car should be engineered. Perhaps his greatest contribution to the HQ was the inclusion of the half-frame under the front of the body. This was near and dear to his heart as he had created exactly the same half-frame for the Camaro/Firebird twins in America and he was determined that he would include it in the HQ's specifications. On this subject he would brook no argument. Mounted on the forward part of this sub-frame was the steering box (the usual Holden recirculating ball system) which put the steering arms forward of the front wheel centreline, something new for Holden. If power steering was ordered it was now integrated into the steering box.

Besides a group of talented Australian stylists, Holden also had several experienced American stylists who were out here on rotation and it was one of them, John Schinella, who became the lead stylist for the HQ. He had gained favour within GM for his designs of the late 60s Pontiacs that featured blisters over each wheel arch. Schinella, in collaboration with Peter Nankervis, Phil Zmood, Chris Emmerson and others honed the concept until what we know as the HQ was approved. Apart from the distinctive wheel arch blisters the other notable achievement of the HQ was to appear to be much smaller physically than it actually was. Careful management of body contours together with generous glass areas combined to make it look smaller and lighter. In reality, it was as physically large and heavy as the rival Falcon and Valiant!

Two clever touches were evident – the front slightly vee-shaped clip was detachable for easy replacement after a minor accident and it also facilitated easy differentiation between various models – Belmont and Kingwood had single headlights, Premier and Statesman had four headlights, for example – and the A-pillars were unusually thin which meant that a driver could 'see through' them when looking for other motorists, especially at intersections. Large chromed pressed steel bumpers were fitted front and rear, those at the front having the amber indicator lenses in them and with the sedans the taillights and indicator lenses were in the rear bumper. Station wagons (and the utilities and the Statesman) had distinctive large vertical taillight units set into a recess at the end of the rear quarter panel and continued down into the bumpers. The sedans all had a sloping boot line that limited the depth of the boot (especially when compared with Falcon and Valiant) but if you look at mainstream GM models from the US from that time, the sloping rear was apparently a corporate theme.

The floorpan for HQ was new, it having to accommodate the new half-frame chassis that Roberts incorporated into the engineering of it to give better noise, vibration and harshness (NVH) qualities. Many local senior GM-H engineers loathed the concept because the trade-off was 'loose' or imprecise handling compared with previous generation of Holdens. Built on a 2819mm (111-ins) wheelbase, the HQ sedan was 4762mm (187.5-ins) long overall by 1880mm (74-ins) wide and 1372mm (54-ins) high, the wagons sat on a 2896mm (114-ins) wheelbase for better load spacing and were consequently three-inches longer. The front and rear tracks had been widened (from HG) and were now 1529mm (60.2-ins) each for greater stability. Kerb weight varied tremendously depending on engine, transmission and equipment levels but a Belmont six-cylinder manual sedan weighed around 1340kgs (2950lbs) for example, a Premier automatic weighed around 1410kgs (3100lbs), the wagons coming in around 68kgs (150lbs) more and if the V8 engine box was ticked that would add another 40–45kgs (90–100lbs).

Carried over from the HG were the two 'red' cast iron sixes now in 173- and 202-cid capacities, three V8 engines in 253-, 308- and 350-cid capacities, three- and four-speed manual gearboxes and the two automatics – Trimatic and Turbo-Hydramatic – and little else. Power outputs from the six-cylinder engines were up ever-so-slightly because of a minor rise in compression (9.4 from 9.2:1) so the 173 had 88kW (118bhp) at 4400rpm and the 202 had 100Kw (135bhp) at 4400rpm, torque outputs were similarly marginally increased. V8 engine outputs remained unchanged.

The front suspension continued with upper-and-lower wishbones and coil springs with concentric dampers but it was a new design and attached to either side of the front of the half-frame; a thick stabiliser bar joined both sides, and the steering arms were in front of the wheel centre line.

In line with GM divisions around the world, with HQ Holden at last dispensed with the ancient semi-elliptic leaf springs and went to a coil spring rear suspension allied to a live axle with robust trailing links and oblique upper links to minimise sideways movement. With the six-cylinder versions Holden developed new, larger and heavier cast iron drum brakes – one has to wonder why – although if the V8 engine was ordered then 279mm (11-ins) diameter disc brakes were standard, optional with the sixes.

New, too, for HQ was an integrated split-level ventilation system with the plenum chamber in the scuttle with the electric fan body at the rear of the engine bay; extractor vents were hidden in the rear door jambs where a one-way plastic flap allowed the air to exit and prevented outside gases and dust from coming in. On the dashboard were adjustable air vents and the system was designed to allow an air conditioning system to be integrated. This was a first among the Big Three in this country.

Inside were bench seats front and rear upholstered in long-wearing vinyl; Belmonts were very plain inside, Kingswoods had a little more equipment including front door armrests while Premier and Statesman had bucket front seats and floor carpets. The actual dashboard was a massive plastic moulding with a recessed section on the driver's side (about 60 per cent of the dash width) in which were mounted two large diameter square 'circles' that housed the speedometer on the right and fuel gauge on the left plus warning lights, between them on Belmont and Kingswood; rhere was a recess for the clock but generally it had a filler with the name 'Holden' on its. A vertical air vent was on the far right with a pull-on light switch between vent and speedo, the heater/demister controls (if fitted) were below that. The wiper/washer buttons were directly under the speedo where they were difficult to reach and use. On the other side of the column was provision for a radio. The positioning of the switches and the action needed to use them (particularly the wiper/washers) was more to do with aesthetics than ergonomics I'm afraid.

If a bench seat was ordered, the gearshift lever or automatic selector

GTS
MONARO GTS

Sandman
LUZ·155

was on the steering column, if buckets seats were ordered the shifter or selector was in a console on the floor; the hand brake was on the right between the seat and door sill and would drop to the floor when applied so it did not catch on clothing when the driver was getting in or out of the car. The trap for the inexperienced was to try and drive off with it applied!

The HQ was as close as Holden would get to a 'clean sheet' design since the original 48/215. Its styling has stood the test of time, the Monaro versions in particular still looking modern today more than half a century later.

Wheels carried out a three-car comparison test in its October 1971 issue, comparing an HQ Kingswood 202-cid six-cylinder engine, with an XY Falcon 500 with a 250-cid six-cylinder engine and a VH Valiant powered by a 245 Hemi six. All three cars had a three-speed manual gearbox with a steering column shift. The trio were what Mr Average Australian Buyer was apparently looking for in 1971. Not particularly exciting motoring but apparently adequate for the times. Very early in the report they wrote, where the body was concerned, "This is the controversial issue. From a practicality point of view the HQ wins easily, but it doesn't have the impressive big-car styling of the Valiant or the solid no-nonsense look of the Falcon." What needed to be remembered was that the XY Falcon was the last of the second generation of the model, the restyled XA was still some months into the future. Looking at the luggage space, the HQ rated third here because of the sloping boot line that reduced its depth and the spare tyre was stored on the floor – there was nowhere else to put it because the fuel tank occupied all the space under the boot floor.

As for seating comfort, the *Wheels* team felt the Holden front bench was located far too low and it was poorly padded – in fact, it was considered the worst of the three. Roominess inside was not an issue with any of them, it was just that the Holden seats could (and should) have been better. Rather surprisingly, the HQ was the only car with flow-through ventilation. Even though the VH Valiant was equally new, it did not have this feature. And only the HQ had an articulated wiper arm on the driver's side that swept all the way to the windscreen pillar.

Power was where the HQ really fell down. Its 202-cid six-cylinder engine dated back to 1963 and was, in comparison, dated and lacked power especially in the 1340kgs (2950lbs) Kingswood in its most basic form. This showed against the clock where the HQ took 13.4 seconds for the 0–96km/h (60mph) sprint whereas the Falcon took 12.2 seconds and the Valiant 10.0 seconds. Maximum speeds were 145.6km/h (91mph) for the Holden, 163.2km/h (102mph) for the Falcon and 164.8km/h (103mph) for the Valiant.

Within just over a year of its release the HQ had new rivals in the form of the Chrysler Valiant VH range plus the XA Ford Falcon range and in 1973 came the Leyland P76 that was a very serious attempt by BMCA/Leyland Australia to compete with 'Australia's Own.' Unlike the HQ, the VH and XA were essentially new bodies over existing and not very refined mechanical components. The P76, of course, was totally new.

Motor Manual carried out a full comparison test between the HQ Kingswood sedan, XA Falcon 500 sedan and VH Valiant Ranger sedan – it was a meeting of three very similar sedans all aimed at the same buyer demographic. All three were powered by six-cylinder engines – 202-cid for the Holden, 200-cid for the Falcon and 215-cid for the Valiant – and all had a three-speed automatic gearbox, Trimatic in the Holden and Borg Warner 35 in the other two. As for options, the Kingswood and Falcon had disc front brakes and all three had a radio fitted; pricing ranged from $3320 for the Valiant, to $3396 for the Falcon and $3405 for the Holden.

So you'll see it all, a big, wide back window.
Seats come in all shapes and styles. And every one of them's been redesigned to keep you comfortable longer.
Holden's Acrylic Lacquer finish. To make your car look shinier, longer.
More glass all round. For better view all round.
The heater/demister. It lets you mix air to just the temperature you want.
Two windshield washer jets are here, and two more for the other wiper. You'll never have a clearer view.
The GM energy-abso steering column. It w
Up here, away from exhaust fumes and dust, is where fresh air enters the flow-through ventilation system.
Dual circuit braking. So if one goes, you've still got one left.
The badge that means the most i reliability, service and resale value
entilators here air to leave the ugh ventilation make room for air coming in.
ur new coil springs that er, 'big car' ride, a quieter a surer ride.
door handles doesn't just make them also gets them out of people's way.
Ready to use but out of the way. The handbrake that knows its place.
Less windscreen pillar means more windscreen, and a better view.
This is where the ignition key goes in. When it comes out, it also locks the steering.
Holden's exclusive new chassis design. It stops road bumps and engine noise reaching you in the passenger compartment. And helps make for a softer ride.
Kingswood
Choose your power. From two big new sixes. Or three V8's.
Putting the steering box here, front of the cross-member, means better handling, more accurate steering control.
Heavier front brake drums on sixes. New ventilated power disc brakes on V8's. To stop you safer.
Wheels that track a full five feet apart. For more stability, and better handling.

Both magazines, *Wheels* and *Motor Manual*, expressed disquiet about the heaviness of the steering and the amount of understeer in the HQ's handling although its dirt road handling was regarded as better than its two rivals. This looseness and heavy understeer characteristics would become a long-standing point of contention between George Roberts and two journalists in particular – Peter Robinson from *Wheels* and Peter Wherrett from the ABC television program *Torque*.

Holden kept the HQ in production from July 1971 until October 1974, the longest for any Holden model, by which time the company had built and sold more than 485,000 units, quite remarkable. It was replaced by the HJ. This new model was easily distinguished from its predecessor by the new front clip that now had the indicator and side light lenses upright on each corner, a new front bumper and new raised grille texture. At the rear there was another new bumper and the taillight units were now triangular in shape above the bumper, this restyle requiring new rear quarter panels. This visually raised the rear of the cars because, as the Director of Styling Leo Pruneau said, "Feedback we got on the HQ was that it looked 'weak' from the rear because of the way the bootlid sloped down to the bumper so we decided to raise it within the very limited budget that we had to work with." As he somewhat wryly commented to the author many years later, "You know, we had no need to do that because right up to the close of HQ production we were selling every one we could produce!" Additional changes from the HQ included full-foam seats, revised instruments and ventilation system and upgraded equipment levels.

Nevertheless, until July 1976 Holden produced a further 176,000 units and replaced the HJ with the HX that month of which a further 111,000 were produced. Distinguishing an HX from an HJ amounted to a different grille texture, badges and restyled hubcaps, it being something of an interim model; what was significant was the introduction of a steering column stalk on the right of the column that operated the two-speed wipers, windscreen washers, high-low beam as well as the indicators. That last item could almost be regarded as revolutionary!

The big news with the HX was the arrival of anti-pollution gear on all Holden engines under the requirements of ADR27A. It was not a happy period of Holden ownership despite the enormous amount of time and resources spent on complying. The carburettor was reset for a leaner fuel-air mix, an idle stop solenoid was fitted to close the throttle valve immediately on engine shut-off, the exhaust gases were recirculated to lower oxides of nitrogen, the coil had a higher voltage output for a hotter spark in the combustion process, the ignition timing was retarded slightly and there was now exhaust heating of the intake manifold for better vaporisation. In addition, there was a charcoal container in the engine bay as well as a fuel tank breather to collect petrol fumes and feed them to the carburettor. From an owner's point of view HX's were hard to start (hot or cold), idled poorly and inconsistently even though the manual said it should idle at 1000rpm (up from 600rpm pre-ADR27A), the engine ran much hotter than previously and its fuel economy plummeted to the point where 15–16mpg became the norm with the sixes, it was worse with the V8s. And from road tests the comments about the HQ wandering at speed on the highway, wallowing when pushed hard through corners and with steering that lacked any precision kept on coming …

The final flowering of this body for the mainstream models was the HZ that arrived in October 1977. From an external recognition point of view the signs were another grille texture, RTS badges and a slightly higher bootlid pressing; inside were new graphics on the instruments. However, by now Holden had a new managing director – he arrived in 1976 – who had come from Opel in Germany and a new chief engineer, Charles 'Chuck' Chapman who hailed from Detroit. The new MD was

Peter Hanenberger and he was very much a car enthusiast and very capable driver who on arrival instigated a program that we came to know as Radial Tuned Suspension or RTS. This involved revised spring and damper rates along with revised geometry (castor and camber) at the front wheels, new suspension bushes, thicker stabiliser bar and the fitting of radial ply tyres and four-wheel disc brakes on all models. Overnight Holden went from a sloppy barge to a car that motoring enthusiasts could enjoy driving hard and fast.

The Belmont was dropped from the range and the Kingswood SL added and there was now a GTS sports sedan. There was some re-aligning of the model range and with equipment with HZ, apart from the RTS. Four-wheel disc brakes were standard on the GTS (and Statesman) and were optional on the rest of the range, the SL had a radio as a standard fitting (the influence of the Japanese!) along with quartz halogen headlights and a heated rear window. Bucket seats were also standard although a bench front seat was available to order. And steel-belt radial tyres were now fitted across the range.

Wheels published an article headed "The General Builds a Proper Car" as their introduction to the release of the HZ. And as they wrote, "Have no doubts, the Radial Tuned Suspension version of The General's big car range turns them into decent-handling cars for the first time. The tragedy, for The General and past Holden owners, is that it took so long to happen." Understeer was now a thing of the past and in their opinion the GTS had roadholding that went close to matching Europe's best. Those words had never been uttered before about a Holden!

GM-H built 154,000 HZ cars before quietly pulling the plug on their production as the company focussed on the new Commodore range, having scrapped their development of a large car replacement.

STATESMAN/CAPRICE

Having failed dismally with the Brougham to challenge Ford's dominance of the luxury car segment with its Fairlane, the designers, engineers and marketing people went back to the drawing boards and re-thought their next luxury model. The first item on the agenda was a wheelbase that stretched to 114-inches, up from 111-ins under the Kingswood, an overall length that would be nearly a foot longer and styling touches that would immediately distinguish the luxury Holden from its plebeian siblings. And a change of names was thought to be wise even though many wanted to continue with the Brougham badge – thankfully wiser heads ruled and the new model would be badged as a Statesman Custom or Statesman de Ville depending on equipment levels. In fact, after the release in August 1971 GM-Holden applied to the registration authorities for the Statesman to be recognised as a *separate* brand.

When compared with the Kingswood the Statesman featured many styling differences and consequently new exterior panels. At the front was a distinctive front clip with an upright split grille with a wide divider, egg-crate pattern plastic grille inserts flanked by dual headlights, the indicator/parking light lens being in the hefty chromed bumper. The roofline was more formal with the rear window being slightly more upright and flatter (than on a Kingswood) and the rear door window frame and glass was also unique to Statesman. All the rear panel-work was also unique to the Statesman being ten-inches longer and having higher quarter panels housing tall vertical taillight units surrounded by a chromed trim; the ends of the substantial rear bumper had cut-outs to accommodate the lower part of the taillights and on either side of the license plate were mini-grilles a la Cadillac. Side marker lights were positioned in front of the rear bumper ends each side although they were not required by law here in Australia.

Inside the Statesman shared the basic dashboard design with the Kingswood and Premier, but the instruments had squared-off bezels and the facia surrounding them was covered with simulated burl walnut; the actual instruments on the Custom comprised speedometer and fuel contents (a la Kingswood) while in the de Ville there were water

temperature and oil pressure gauges and a clock included. On the floor was thick pile carpet and the doors had full length door armrest and on the de Ville burl walnut inserts. Seating was either by a full-width bench with central armrest or in the de Ville buyers could order separate front seats with either 'leather grained vinyl' or Diamond Weave cloth with central armrests front and rear. Flow-through ventilation together with an effective heater/demister was a standard fitting with integrated air conditioning as an option.

If the Custom was ordered buyers had the choice of either the asthmatic 202-cid OHV six-cylinder engine developing 100kW (135bhp) at 4400rpm and 263Nm (194lbs-ft) of torque at 2000rpm or one of two V8 engines that were available – the 253-cid unit developing 138kW (185bhp) at 4400rpm and 355Nm (262lbs-ft) at 2400rpm or the 308-cid unit developing 180kW (240bhp) at 4800rpm and 427Nm (315lbs-ft) of torque at 3000rpm. De Ville buyers could also select the imported 350-cid Chevrolet engine that developed 205kW (275bhp) at 4800rpm and 488Nm (360lbs-ft) at 3200rpm.

Several gearboxes were available: in the Custom there was a three-speed all-synchromesh manual with column shift, four-speed manual with a floor shift or the Trimatic three-speed automatic with either a column shift or floor selector. In the de Ville buyers had the choice of the Trimatic with column or floor selector or when the 350-cid V8 was chosen the Turbo-Hydramatic three-speed with floor selector.

Depending on what equipment was fitted, a Custom weighed upwards from 1377kgs (3029lbs), the de Ville from 1504kGs (3308lbs) – they were no shrinking violets!

Amazingly, Custom buyers could actually specify their sedan with the 202-cid six-cylinder engine hooked up to the three-speed manual gearbox with a column shift! It was in reality a long wheelbase and expensive Belmont ... I wonder how many were actually built and sold?

Modern Motor carried out a full test of a Custom fitted with the 202-cid engine, Trimatic automatic, radio and power steering in the October 1971 issue and came away convinced GM had upstaged the Fairlane with the HQ Statesman. The base price was $3800 but with the extras it finished up costing $4270, slightly more expensive than a similarly equipped Ford.

Despite weighing 1377kgs (3029lbs) and having only 100kW (135bhp) at its disposal the *MM* crew managed a top speed of 155km/h (97mph) with a best one-way of 163km/h (102mph) and it took only 11.5 seconds to run the 0–96km/h (0–60mph) sprint. However, they did

VIC
LKA-264

Caprice

comment on passing on the highway by saying "overtaking manoeuvres at any speeds should be handled with caution as the car simply doesn't wind out quickly." They also said the Statesman possessed an excellent ride that was complimented by first-class handling, the best power steering system made in Australia and good sustained high speed cruising ability. As for the levels of silence, quality of finish and other attributes they felt that Ford had been eclipsed. Their only real gripe was Holden's retention of the antiquated floor-mounted dip switch.

Wheels tested a De Ville and was most disappointed with the standard of finish, its ride, handling (far too much understeer) and the front seating which lacked lateral support. Tested again a year later they found most of their criticisms attended to and found it a far nicer car to use on long distance cruises.

The same magazine tested a Statesman De Ville five months later and was even more impressed because it answered the problem of a comparative lack of power – the 308-cid V8 packed a 180kW (240bhp) punch along with 427Nm (315lbs-ft) of torque. Mind you, with air conditioning at $430, power windows at $90, push button radio at $110, vinyl roof at $80, cloth trim at $15, tinted and laminated windscreen at $50 and rear speakers for the radio at $15 the De Ville cost a hefty $6450 before on-road charges. However, it provided owners with a definite sense of style, the car had a presence on the road and it was quick if thirsty – 172.8km/h (108mph) top speed, 11.2 seconds for the 0–96km/h (0–60mph) dash, 6.8 seconds for the 64–96km/h (40–60mph) passing dash but averaged just 16.8 litres per 100km (17mpg) for the test. You needed the 75-litre (16.5 imp gallon) tank!

In October 1974 a revised Statesman became available, the HJ. Gone was the Custom as a part of the upward mobility of the name to be replaced by the Statesman De Ville and Statesman Caprice priced at $6365 and $9233 respectively. By local standards the Caprice was really something – fully integrated air conditioning was standard along with leather upholstery, heated rear window, central locking, power windows and courtesy lights everywhere – and from an appearance point of view it had a Cadillac-like fine vertical bar grille and bumper over-riders, fluted hubcaps, white sidewall tyres and a special bonnet ornament.

The new grille was a one-piece unit which meant the front clip was

a new pressing flanked by four headlights, the parking/indicator light units were on each front corner, and the bumper was new; at the rear were new (smaller) taillight units on the end of each quarter panel and, again, a new bumper. None of the changes were significant on their own but combined they contributed to the HJ looking to be a far more refined and handsome motor car. It was a car that GM-H hoped buyers would 'move up' to. And it was one which their advertising agency compared to Mercedes-Benz, Rolls-Royce, Jaguar, Volvo and even Cadillac.

The only driveline available with HJ was the 308-cid V8 developing 180kW (240bhp) mated to a Turbo-Hydramatic three-speed automatic gearbox to a 2.78:1 rear axle. With the added equipment kerb weights had crept up to 1540kgs (3385lbs) for the De Ville and 1645kgs (3619lbs) for the Caprice.

Inside improvements had been made in a number of ways, the most obvious being the redesign of the dashboard. It adopted the cockpit style that embraced the driver's environment and had a squared-off moulded safety surround with the face of it sloping to match the downward curve of the edges of the surround; the whole surface was treated to a wood grained appliqué. The instruments now resided in deeply hooded square nacelles with the speedometer on the right matched to a clock on the left – analogue in the De Ville and digital in the Caprice – with a smaller rectangular unit to the left housing the fuel and oil pressure dials; the warning lights were in a bank between the two main gauges. A flat panel at the base of the dash housed the heater/demister/air conditioning controls to the right of the steering column, radio and cigar lighter to the left, while the wiper/washer switches were on the right under the air vent.

A detailed road test was published in *Wheels*, February 1975 and the tone of the article would have pleased GM-H executives immensely. Important for buyers in this class of car was that it was quiet and as *Wheels* said, "The silence of the car while it's in motion is more relevant to its buyer appeal than its level of performance. It is a very quiet car even by Mercedes-Benz and XJ12 standards, and is at least as good that way as the Ford LTD." The test drivers felt there was still too much understeer and body lean when cornering briskly but countered that by saying Caprice buyers were more concerned with the ride aspect, which was superb. Against the clock the big Caprice ran to 185km/h (115mph), did the 0–110km/h (0–70mph) sprint in 12.5 seconds, took 17.4 seconds for the 400-metre sprint and returned anywhere between 20 and 17.5km per 100-litres (14 and 16mpg) – ouch! Still, with all that luxury equipment on board it was no wonder that it weighed 1645kgs (3620lbs).

A minor revision appeared in July 1976 in the form of the HX. It was just in time for the implementation of ADR-27A which had to do with engine exhaust emissions and in this GM-H dropped the ball when compared with Ford and Chrysler. Where Chrysler went with its 'Lean Burn' technology and Ford developed a new cross-flow cylinder head, Holden engineers fiddled with the ignition and carburettor settings, compression ratio and one or two other minor tuning tricks to get the engines through ADR 27A; the results were awful for owners with engines that were lumpy at idle (if they idled at all!) and lacked any responsiveness to the accelerator, in addition to which they were no longer economical in their use of fuel. This was not a period the GM-H engineers and Holden owners remember with any affection!

New with HX was a most welcome, and overdue, fitment of a multi-function steering column stalk that covered hi-lo beam changes, indicators and wipe/wash for the two-speed electric wipers with an intermittent phase – almost a revolution! There was the obligatory new grille texture, different wheel trims and more sound deadening material.

The final iteration of this body was the HZ that appeared in November 1977 and lasted until May 1980. The really big news item with HZ was the availability of Radial Tuned Suspension (RTS) about which Holden created much noise in the media. Compared with pre-RTS Holdens the HZ was a revelation for dedicated drivers who had been complaining about the loose and sloppy handling from early days of the HQ! Released in July 1979 was the Statesman SL/E that carried a retail price of $13,909 compared with $17,056 for the Caprice. Its specifications included air conditioning, power steering, power brakes, power windows, power antenna, AM/FM stereo system and cassette player, central locking plus a 'Sports Package' interior that added a tachometer to the instruments and a sports three-spoke steering wheel and distinctive alloy wheels. And to add to the cachet it was only available in three colours – Mulberry (dark red), Nutmeg (brown) and Cypress (green). In its publicity materials GM-H were now comparing the Statesman with the Jaguar XJ6/12 and Mercedes-Benz S-Class. True! So, to test out their claims *Wheels* conducted a four-car comparison between a Caprice, Ford LTD, Jaguar XJ12 and a Mercedes-Benz 450SEL. It was $16,129 for the Caprice, $16,121 for the LTD versus $31,600 for the Jag and $42,791 for the Merc. They were hardly comparing apples with apples.

The Caprice was the smallest and lightest of the quartet and the slowest against the clock – it took 15.7 seconds to dash from 0–110km/h (68mph) when the LTD took 11.9 seconds, the Jag 10.8 seconds and the Merc 15.1 seconds; top speeds were 165km/h (103mph) for the Caprice, 180km/h (112mph) for the LTD, 213km/h (133mph) for the Jag and 190km/h (118mph) for the Merc. Certainly the Caprice performed well in subjective assessments of finish, passenger comfort, roadholding and handling – it was far from disgraced despite the price differential and market perception. When it came down to a choice, the *Wheels* guys chose the Jaguar XJ12 as their winner followed by the Mercedes-Benz 450SEL with the Caprice in a well-deserved third place.

By this time it was common knowledge within the industry that the Belmont/Kingswood/Premier were to be discontinued in favour of the Commodore while the Caprice would continue as the company's flagship until the arrival of the WB Statesman in 1980. Times were indeed a'changin' at Holden!

KINGSWOOD

MONARO

Running in parallel with the Kingswood and Statesman ranges was the Monaro, Initially as a two-door coupe but from March 1973 the badge was applied to the four-door Kingswood body. All the body panels in front of the bulkhead were shared with the Kingswood but every other exterior panel was unique to the Monaro coupe. And it was quite beautiful then and still is today – an all-time Australian classic.

Styling apart, the range of Monaros available paralleled that of the Kingswood so far as engines, gearboxes and interior fittings were concerned. The exception was the Monaro LS, the letters standing for Luxury Sport. Sadly, it was far more 'luxury' than it was 'sport.'

Sales of Monaro coupes were slow during the HQ period which is why Holden's marketing people introduced the Monaro GTS four-door sedan and it quickly became a strong seller. By late 1975 Holden had a problem. Parked in part of the production area were 600* Monaro two-door bodies. Leo Pruneau tells the story of how John Bagshaw came into his office one day and suggest to Leo that they organise a 'white goods sale' as Bagshaw apparently said. Without communicating his inner thoughts to Bagshaw Leo agreed to mock-up an example for management to view over the next week or so. What Leo envisaged but did not tell anyone was a far cry from what was asked!

When senior management, including Bagshaw, came into the Styling department they were greeted by Leo and his small team proudly displaying what amounted to a two-door Statesman Caprice. It was badged LX, and featured an unusual metallic red exterior paint colour and wheels imported from Pontiac plus a series of delicate gold stripes. This was not what management was expecting and as Leo recounted to the author some years later, "They were very quiet as they slowly walked around the car. I was pointing out all the benefits but initially they weren't buying it. Then John Bagshaw turned to me and said, 'Leo, I think this is great, let's run with it!' "

What Leo had created was the most expensive Holden ever and a car that is now very collectable!

* Figures vary depending on who is telling the story. I have read of numbers as high as 620 but Leo always says it was 600.

TORANA

Arriving in October 1969 was the LC range of Toranas with a new uniquely Australian-styled body and the availability of six-cylinder engines as an option. This came about because the marketing people at Holden wanted to be able to offer a model that approximated the EH Holden in size and performance, and because with the EH the company had captured the imagination and wallets of thousands of motorists and they wanted to recreate that situation. A slightly enlarged Torana was the perfect starting point.

The marketing plan was quite simple – build the Torana with two wheelbases, 2433mm (95.8-ins) for the four-cylinder versions and 2540mm (100-ins) for the six-cylinder models; the 106.6mm (4.2 extra inches) were all in front of the bulkhead to accommodate the longer six-cylinder engines. The LC range was a totally Australian design, the four-cylinder variants having a blunt(ish) nose with a nondescript grille while the vastly more popular six-cylinder models had a longer front with a pointy 'beak' nose and a more interesting grille that featured a wide horizontal band across it (painted body colour) with the Holden lion badge in the centre and 7-ins headlights each end, a thin chromed bumper and indicator lights underneath. The Torana's styling was characterised by a suggestion of a Coke bottle hip near the C-pillar and a sloping rear that appeared to be a fastback but was not – 'drop-back' was the term coined by Holden. At the rear were broad ribbed horizontal taillight units each side flanking the Holden badge, a straight chromed blade bumper with the license plate underneath. It was really quite a neat and pleasing-to-the-eye if unadventurous design.

Where the fours ran on 4.00J x 12-ins rims and 5.50 x 12 tyres (6.20 x 12 for the 1600) the sixes used 4.50JJ x 13 ventilated steel rims shod with A78L by 13 tubeless tyres while the GTR ran 5.50JJ x 13 rims and B70H by 13 sports tyres with slim red sidewalls.

Physically the six-cylinder LC Torana was 4386mm (172.7-ins) overall by 1600mm (63-ins) wide and 1354mm (53.3-ins) high and weighed 1060kgs (2331lbs) for the four-door; by comparison an EH 149 sedan had a wheelbase of 2667mm (105-ins) and was 4496mm (177-ins) in length by 1727mm (68-ins) wide, 1473mm (58-ins) high and weighed 1133kgs (2492lbs). The four-cylinder Toranas were obviously the same width and height but were 254mm (10-ins) shorter (all at the front) and 184kgs (406lbs) lighter at 875kgs (1925lbs) for the four-door 1200 sedan.

On the surface it seemed as if both versions shared most of their mechanical components, engines apart, but that was not the case. Yes they both had an upper-and-lower wishbone front suspension with coil springs but the components on the four-cylinder models were much lighter than those under the six-cylinder models and the rear axle assembly was far stronger on the sixes. The specifications said the rear suspension was by four links rubber bushed to the body and live axle housing with coil springs and telescopic dampers but again the links were more substantial on the sixes. For the four-cylinder models the standard brakes were dual circuit 203mm (8-ins) diameter drums all round and for the regular sixes the drums were 228mm (9-ins) in diameter while available as an option were vacuum-boosted front discs of 213mm (8.4-ins) diameter on the fours and 254mm (10-ins) diameter

TORANA
6
HOLDEN
RALLY
CONTROL
GTR

on the sixes; the high performance GTR had a disc/drum system as standard.

Under the bonnet of the fours was the choice of two engines, both from Vauxhall in the UK – the asthmatic 1159cc OHV unit from the Viva that developed 42kW (56bhp) at 5400rpm and 90Nm (66.5lbs-ft) at 3000rpm, 51kW (69bhp) at 5800rpm and 92Nm (68lbs-ft) at 4200rpm in the SL. There was also a new slant four of 1599cc that powered the Vauxhall Victor in the UK. This engine had a bore and stroke of 85.7 x 69.2mm and developed 60kW (80bhp) at 5500rpm, 130Nm (96lbs-ft) of torque at 3200rpm, had a five-bearing crankshaft, cast iron block and a cross-flow alloy cylinder head that featured a belt-driven single overhead camshaft. This engine's claim to fame came from Lotus who used the cylinder block as the basis for its DOHC engine that powered the Jensen-Healey sports cars as well as various Lotuses over the decades.

Three six-cylinder engines were available beginning with the Torana-only 138-cid red six (3.125 x 3.00-ins, 79.3 x 76.2mm, 2262cc) that developed 71kW (95bhp) at 4600rpm and 163Nm (120lbs-ft) at 1600rpm; then came the 161-cid six that was also used in the Belmont/Kingswood range that developed 85kW (114bhp) at 4400rpm and 212Nm (157lbs-ft) of torque at 2000rpm. A special version of the 161-cid six was available only in the GTR and it developed 93kW (125bhp) at 4800rpm and 203Nm (150lbs-ft) of torque at 2800rpm through the use of dual-throat Bendix Stromberg WW carburettor, a water-heated intake manifold, different camshaft profile, a 9.2:1 compression and twin exhaust manifolds. Between July 1971 and January 1972, towards the end of LC production, the 161S engine was replaced by the 173S engine in the GTR.

Transmissions varied, the two four-cylinder engines being bolted to either a four-speed all synchromesh manual with a short floor-mounted shifter or the new Trimatic three-speed automatic with either a column or floor shift depending on trim level; the sixes offered either a three- or four-speed manual all synchromesh gearbox with column and floor shift respectively or as an option the Trimatic three-speed automatic again with either column or floor shift. The GTR came with only one transmission – the four-speed all synchromesh manual with floor shift. Rear axle ratios available were either 3.89 or 4.125:1 with the fours, 3.08:1 for sixes with a manual gearbox and 2.78:1 for those with the automatic.

The LC Torana presented buyers with a wide choice of options – two- or four-door bodies, S or SL trim packages, bench or bucket seats, manual or automatic plus a variety of engines. The GTR featured a complete set of round instruments in front of the driver – large speedo and tacho in the centre with two smaller dials each side covering fuel, temperature, oil pressure and volts; the instrument layout came straight from the Viva GT in the UK.

So enamoured with the new model range was *Wheels* magazine that it voted it Car of the Year for 1969. In its February 1970 issue it carried a full road test of a Torana GTR versus a Capri GT. It was not exactly comparing apples with apples because the Capri GT carried the 1599cc Kent cross-flow engine and not the 3.0-litre Essex V6 that came a little later. With the GTR Holden had created a niche that they had never previously acknowledged and as time would show, it became a very popular and profitable niche.

On test the GTR achieved a top speed of 168km/h (105mph), ran the 0–80km/h (50mph) dash in 7.5 seconds, the quarter mile in 17.2 seconds and returned 12.8 litres per 100km (22mpg). Speeds in the gears were 51km/h (32mph) in first, 94km/h (56mph) in second and 144km/h (90mph) in third. Typically Torana (nee Vauxhall ...) the GTR continued with the steering column and foot pedals being slightly askew to each other and there was no flow-through ventilation and equipment levels were sparse but as a package it was thought to be spot-on.

In August 1970 GM-H released the Torana GTR XU-1 powered by a special edition of the 186-cid six-cylinder engine. It was fitted with triple Zenith-Stromberg CD-150 carburettors, cast iron exhaust headers on a high compression (10.05:1) cylinder head and a special camshaft to develop 119kW (160bhp) at 5200rpm and 258Nm (190lbs-ft) at 3600rpm. Carried over from the regular GTR was the two-door body, front disc brakes and full instrumentation on the dashboard; new to the XU-1 version were fluted front guards, rear spoiler and wider wheel rims.

The XU-1 successfully replaced the Monaro GTS as the company's front line competition machine and was successful in winning many races and rallies, but not Bathurst. For that the company developed the 186 Bathurst version that appeared in September 1971 (just in time), its engine developed 134kW (180bhp) at 6000rpm and 264Nm (195lbs-ft) at 4200rpm.

February 1972 saw the introduction of the LJ series Torana which was really a mild facelift of the LC. At the front was a wide, rectangular opening filled with a plastic moulded grille with an egg-crate pattern and separate headlights that visually linked it to the HQ series. At the rear the taillights were now three small separate square units each side giving the same information as before.

With the four-cylinder models Holden introduced an enlarged version of the ex-Viva engine, its capacity now being 1256cc from a bore and stroke of 80.9 by 61mm, power went up slightly to 47kW (62.5bhp) at 5400rpm and torque was up to 96Nm (71lbs-ft) at 3600rpm. These Toranas were badged either as 1300 or (carry-over) 1600 depending on which engine was fitted.

Where the six-cylinder models were concerned, the badges now read 2250 or 2850 and for the GTR it was 3300. The GTR XU-1 had a high-performance version of the 3.3-litre 'red' six that with the assistance of triple 1.5-in Stromberg CD carburettors and 10.3:1 compression developed 142kW (190bhp) at 5000rpm and 271Nm (200lbs-ft) at 4000rpm. The Bathurst XU-1 used 1.75-in CD carburettors to develop 149kW (200bhp) and was fitted with a close ratio M21 four-speed manual gearbox; its ratios were 2.54:1 for first gear, 1.83 in second, 1.25 in third and 1.00 in top and reverse being 2.54:1 with the rear axle ratio being 3.36:1 with limited slip as standard – it was optional on the other models – and a taller 3.08 was also available. Ford had won with the GT HO in 1970 and 1971 but Holden was able to wrest the podium from Ford in 1972 when a Holden Dealer Team XU-1 crossed the line first with Peter Brock at the wheel.

In the April 1972 edition of *Wheels* there was a full test of an XU-1 and it proved to be a surprise performer, a real stormer in fact. The basic package was fine in LC form but the engineers (no doubt with 'help' from Harry Firth) tweaked the front spring rates – they were ever so slightly softer – and the rebound rate for the dampers was strengthened to eliminate the familiar LC bounce at the front and the spring rates in the front seats were also softened to bring them 'in-sync' with the road springs and so give the car's occupants a far better ride.

As for its handling it was still basically an understeerer although there was ample power to be able to flick the tail as and when desired; braking was fine although when really pushed they were marginal. As a family car it worked because it would easily carry two adults and two children and a modicum of luggage.

With 142kW (190bhp) available and running the standard 3.36:1 rear axle through a four-speed all synchromesh gearbox the XU-1 raced through the standing quarter mile in 16.0 seconds (15.8 seconds was its quickest run), dashed from 0–96, 112 and 128km/h (0–60-, 70- and 80mph) in 8.4, 10.7 and 14.3 seconds respectively, and at the 6000rpm redline it ran to 88km/h (55mph) in first gear, 115km/h (72mph) in second, 156.8km/h (98mph) in third and on to 193.6km/h (121mph) in top; fuel consumption worked out at 19–15 litres per 100km (15–19mpg) for the test so the fast touring range with the 75-litre (17-gallon) tank was limited. And at $3455 it was a performance bargain.

Incidentally, Harry Firth was well on the way with the development of a V8-powered XU-1 (it was going to be called XU-2 but apparently Firth wanted another name) when the supercar scare hit the headlines in mid-72 and the media and political frenzy that that uncorked put an end to the project. It would be revived two years later after all the hullaballoo had died down …

In its October 1972 issue *Wheels* published a four-car comparison in which four mainstream Toranas were compared – unusual that. The surprise package proved to be the 1300, especially for urban commuting where its nippiness, reasonable acceleration and light steering came to the fore. On long cruises and in hilly country it fared less well. They recorded a top speed of 128km/h (80mph) with 0–96km/h (0–60mph) coming up in 20.6 seconds and the 64–96km/h (40–60mph) passing time of 14.3 seconds. By comparison the 1600 was felt to have been something of a disappointment. While it bettered the 1300's acceleration times – no great hardship – it seemed to lack the other car's flexibility and once past the mid-range performance dropped off markedly They said, "Despite the promise, the Torana 1600 lacked the sparkle of comparable engines such as the Galant 1500, Datsun and Mazda 1600s which surpass its overall acceleration and flexibility." Top speed for the 1600 was 136km/h (85mph), with 17.4 seconds needed for the 0–96km/h (0–60mph) dash and 9.5 seconds for the 64–96km/h (40–60mph) sprint.

While the 2250 had an extra 16km/h (10mph) in top speed on the 1600 and took 3 seconds less to reach 96km/h (60mph) from rest, it was slower by a second from 64–96km/h (40–60mph) and had braking instability issues that caused much consternation to the test crew. The 2850 ran to 155.2km/h (97mph), took 13.5 seconds for the 0–96km/h (0–60mph) run and needed 9.0 seconds from 64–96km/h (40–60mph). None of the quartet returned particularly good fuel economy figures – less

Look at what you get with HOLDEN TORANA 6/v8.

outside

- ☐ Wide doors for easy entry
- ☐ Low, wide stance for stability
- ☐ Electric windscreen washers
- ☐ Bolt-on front fenders
- ☐ Full-length body wide-line protector strips (standard on SL model)
- ☐ Bumber bars strong enough to jack the car up on
- ☐ Protective rubber bumper inserts (standard on SL, SLR and SLR 5000; optional on S)
- ☐ Wrap around rear tailights
- ☐ "Rustgard" body protection
- ☐ "Magic-Mirror" acrylic lacquer finish
- ☐ Glare reduced outside rear view mirror
- ☐ Concealed fuel filler cap
- ☐ Flush mounted door handles
- ☐ Wide-sweep 2-speed windscreen wipers

inside

- ☐ Full-foam contoured seats
- ☐ 2-speed fan-boosted ventilation system
- ☐ Anti-theft steering column lock
- ☐ Foot operated parking brake
- ☐ International symbols on low-profile control knobs
- ☐ Low profile door locks
- ☐ Energy-absorbing steering column
- ☐ Six seat belts with bench seat vehicles, five with vehicles fitted with front bucket seats
- ☐ Stalk-type bucket seat belt fasteners
- ☐ Integral front seat head restraints
- ☐ Combined parking brake and brake failure warning light
- ☐ Instrument panel lockable glove box
- ☐ Safety padded dash
- ☐ Safety cargo barrier
- ☐ Safety door latches
- ☐ Padded sun visors
- ☐ Wide view, shatter-resistant interior rear view mirror
- ☐ Best glass viewing area of any car in its class
- ☐ Deep pile carpeting
- ☐ Easy-to-read recessed instruments
- ☐ Inside hood latch release
- ☐ Boot capacity 10.8 cubic feet

underneath

- ☐ Your choice of 2 six-cylinder and 2 V8 engines
- ☐ Four coil suspension with rubber bushes
- ☐ Direct double-acting shock absorbers
- ☐ 101.8" (2586 mm) wheelbase for improved ride
- ☐ Precise rack and pinion steering, 16.5:1 ratio
- ☐ Independent front suspension
- ☐ 55.1" (1400 mm) track for greater stability
- ☐ Double sided safety rims on whee
- ☐ Fuel tank holds 12.0 gallons
- ☐ The safety of a dual circuit brake system
- ☐ Rubber cushioned front cross member for an even quieter ride

BODY SPECIFICATIONS

	S Model	SL, SLR Models
Wheelbase	101.8" (2586 mm)	101.8" (2586 mm)
Track—front	55.1" (1400 mm)	55.1" (1400 mm)
Track—rear	54.0" (1372 mm)	54.0" (1372 mm)
Overall length	176.9" (4493 mm)	177.5" (4509 mm)
Overall height	52.3" (1328 mm)	52.6" (1336 mm)
Overall width	67.1" (1704 mm)	67.1" (1704 mm)
Approx. kerb weights	S 2520 lbs. (1143 kg)	SL 2584 lbs. (1172 kg) SLR 2609 lbs. (1183 kg)

ALL-NEW HOLDEN TORANA 6/v8
The car for its time

than 20mpg on test for the sixes – which further put them behind their Japanese rivals making the 45-litre (10-gallon) tank seem unnecessarily small for long distance cruising.

March 1974 saw the release of the much bigger bodied LH series Torana that was initially available as a four-door sedan only. To fill in the time between that release and the forthcoming Gemini, Holden produced the fill-in TA series Torana that was the short wheelbase LJ body with a mild facelift and besides the choice of body – two-door or four – it gave buyers a choice of engines, 1.3-litre OHV or a 1.8-litre (85.73 x 76.2, 1759cc) derivative of the 1600 SOHC engine. The TA was only built between February and December 1974. Although few in numbers built, it is definitely *not* a collectable car!

LH was an entirely new ball game from Holden because within the one body style – four-door sedan – it was the only car at that time in the GM world to be available with the option of a four-, six- or V8-cylinder engine. Back in the 60s the Chevy II made the same claim to fame but it was a US-only model. Essentially LH was built off the LJ platform but there were many differences. And interestingly while the LH would have been conceived during George Roberts's time at Holden it was not the recipient of his half-frame chassis. The wheelbase was 2586mm (101.8-ins, longer by 46mm/1.8-ins), overall length was now 4493mm (176.9-ins, up by 101.6mm/4-ins), width was 1704mm (67.1-ins, an increase of 101.6mm/4-ins) and height was 1328mm (52.3-ins), down by 25.4mm (an inch) with the wheel tracks being 1399mm (55.1-ins) at the front and 1371mm (54-ins) at the rear, an increase of nearly four-inches at the front and three-inches at the rear. As for kerb weights, a six-cylinder LJ in S trim weighed 1059kgs (2331lbs) as a four-door while the equivalent LH weighed 1145kgs (2520lbs). To cater for the wide range of engines Holden fitted the LH with a 55-litre (12-gallon) fuel tank mounted outside the body at the rear with the filler behind the rear number plate.

As with the outgoing LJ Torana, the steering was by a rack and pinion system mounted in front of the front wheel centre line but it lacked power assistance, even on the V8-engined models. Front disc brakes were not standard except for the SL and SL/R editions which put the LH behind the eight ball in relation with most of its Japanese rivals that were also generally less expensive to purchase.

The four-cylinder engine was now sourced from Opel rather than Vauxhall, it had a bore and stroke of 93 x 69.8mm for a capacity of 1897cc and with a single Stromberg carburettor developed 76kW (102bhp) at 5400rpm and 156Nm (115lbs-ft) of torque at 2800rpm. The engine was unusual insofar as it was listed as an overhead valve design in the brochures even though the camshaft was in the cylinder head mainly because the manifolding was all on one side (the right) of the cylinder head. In manual SL form the Torana 1900 weighed 1121kgs (2466lbs) to be the lightest of the family.

The six-cylinder engines were well-known to Holden fans – the 2.85- and 3.3-litre OHV red sixes that developed 87kW (117bhp) and 100kW (134bhp) respectively – as were the two V8s in the form of the 4.2- and 5.0-litre units from the HQ range. Both the sixes were 11 years old by the time of the LH and it showed in their relative lack of refinement. A six-cylinder Torana was only 164kgs (360lbs) lighter than a comparably equipped Kingswood but that did not make it a quick sedan.

From a styling point of view the best you could say about the LH was that it was inoffensive – it was sooo conservative in every way compared with big brother the HQ Kingswood. This might surprise those who know the man under whose direction it was created – Leo Pruneau – and who was anything but conservative! However, as he said, "We were directed to design a car that was bigger than the existing Torana but to keep it basically simple and clean. There was no way any design that did not conform to that demand would be approved so that is what we did." The front had a slightly W-look in profile with square headlights either side of a rectangular opening containing a plastic egg-crate pattern grille that continued below the substantial front bumper; indicator lights were below the bumper. Like its HQ brother, the LH had a bolt-on front clip. At the rear was a simple box-like style with horizontal taillight units either side with a chrome divider – top was the amber indicator lights, bottom was the red tail/stop lights – with the license plate between them, a high lip for luggage to be lifted over and another substantial bumper. The bumpers had to be strong because the jack supplied with the car was a bumper jack.

Inside were seats with full foam cushioning over Z-springs with built-in head restraints and upholstered with Sadlon leather grained vinyl. All models had reclining front bucket seats with built-in head restraints except the base four- and six-cylinder cars that had a bench front seat with headrests; carpets were on the floor of all but the lowliest Torana S four-cylinder. If a column gearchange was specified the front seat was a bench but if a floor change was ordered then two bucket seats were provided, in back was a bench. An interesting 'innovation' with LH was the foot-operated parking brake with finger release on the dash that met with a mixed reception by both the media and buyers.

The dash was a simple straight-across rectangular affair – some critics described it as bland – with three dials set in deep recesses in front of the driver to avoid reflections, multi-directional air vents were fitted either end and there was an inset panel below the main dials for various switches and the heater/demister slides. It was made from moulded plastic and was fully deformable in a major accident. Holden designed the dash to accept a fully integrated Frigidaire air conditioning system as well as designed a completely new heater/demister system for LH.

Holden used internationally recognised symbols on its various controls but the fact remained that they were not on the steering column close to the driver's fingertips, they were on the dash and had to be reached for when needed; and the hi-lo beam dipswitch was *still on the floor!* In this respect LH was quite a way off the pace.

Model differentiation was quite simple; the four-cylinder versions all had round headlights and the grille featured four rectangular sections each with six horizontal bars and the name Torana in the left segment, the standard road wheels were ventilated 4.5 x 13 with a chromed hub cap; the six-cylinder S and SL editions featured the above-mentioned square headlights and textured grille with either the letter S or SL on the lower far left. The SL/R, whether powered by the 4.2- or 5.0-litre V8, had a black stripe along the top of the front fenders that blended into the black painted door frames, black sill panels, an SL/R badge on the lower right corner of the bootlid and 5.5J x 13 sports wheels with 175SR13 steel radial tyres; the SL/R 5000 L34 option was quite a deal more extrovert with its bolt-on wheel arch flares, rear bootlid spoiler with a black rear surface that had the SL/R 5000 decal attached, a similar one being placed on the front of each front fender, just behind the headlights, it also had sports wheels of 14-ins diameter taken from the HQ range.

From a Marketing point of view the four-cylinder and six-cylinder S and SL models were to cater for the needs of mums and dads who put family practicality first, performance second. This was well illustrated in the *Wheels* road test of the 1900 in its September 1974 issue. The opening lines told the story, "It looks good … and it will sell well … but the new Torana 1900 is not the car it could be or should be." They summed up the car in just one word – disappointing. Up against mainly Japanese rivals it lacked refinement and performance in almost every aspect. The Torana was roomier inside as it should have been because it was much bigger than the Datsun 180B and Toyota Corona but it was not as well equipped and both the Japanese cars left it far behind in the performance stakes. *Wheels* published a top speed of 144km/h (90mph) for a manual version, 0–96km/h (0–60mph) coming up in 15 seconds. Handling, too, was vague by comparison – this was pre-RTS time.

A Torana SL with the 3.3-litre six-cylinder engine was not a lot more money and far better value; it also did not have such a competitive market segment to cope with because its two main rivals were the Ford Cortina Six and Leyland Marina Six, the Chrysler Centura not yet on the market. It was not much faster – 148.8km/h (93mph) top speed – but it was significantly quicker in acceleration at 12.6 seconds from 0–96km/h (0–60mph) and would return better than 12.8 litres per 100km (22mpg) on a long run. And as the *Wheels* people commented, the handling was much less precise than in LJ and understeer was always present, only the extent of it changed with the application (or not) of power. It was all part of the general softening of the model.

The performance Torana was the SL/R but surprisingly that badge did not automatically mean the engine was a V8. No, you could buy a Torana SL/R powered by the 3300 six-cylinder engine which made it neither a luxury car nor a sports sedan. If performance was what was wanted and, after all, that was what the SL/R was all about, then the buyer had to specify at least the 4.2-litre V8 engine. For those who selected the 5.0-litre engine option – the SL/R 5000 – they also received for their money a front air dam and boot lip spoiler, extensive blackout panels, 15.5-inch diameter three-spoke steering wheel, full instrumentation, five-slot ventilated steel wheels and stabiliser bars front and rear.

When released and tested by the media there was quite a deal of negative reaction to the SL/R in both 4.2- and 5.0-litre form. GM-H had introduced the SL/R as 'the new contender' but few in the media were convinced because they were not as 'hard' in their general character as the outgoing LJ XU-1s. In the opinion of many in the media GM-H had erred on the side of ride comfort with its suspension settings and not on handling. 'Lack-lustre' was a word used often in reference to the LH SL/R.

Wheels carried out a twin test of SL/Rs in its July 1974 edition – a 4.2 and 5.0 – and found there to be very little difference in their on-road performance despite the large difference in engine capacity. Both ran four-speed manual gearboxes, which in the 4.2 was a wide ratio unit and that in the 5.0 being a close ratio unit, and their diff ratios were 2.78 for the 4.2 and 3.08 for the 5.0. The high ratio in the 4.2 blunted its acceleration but conversely made it a relaxed long distance cruiser. By comparison the 3.08 axle allowed the testers to rev the 5.0 engine to 5500rpm with alacrity, and it ran to 192km/h (120mph) with ease; the 4.2 by comparison took a long stretch of road to wind out to its top speed of 179.2km/h (112mph). Comparative acceleration times for 0–96, 112 and 128km/h (0–60, 70 and 80mph) were 8.8/7.7, 12.3/10.0

and 16.5/13.0 seconds, speeds through the gears were 67/77km/h (42/48mph) in first, 93/106km/h (58/66mph) in second, 136/139km/h (85/87mph) in third and 179.2/193.6km/h (112/121mph) flat out in top.

Where they both were found wanting was in their dynamics. While the harsh feedback of the LJ XU-1 was gone, in its place was a rubbery feel and lack of precision. There was little feel in the steering and self-centring was poor. Both cars understeered strongly and both leaned far more than their predecessor when cornering. The braking system was felt to be marginal – "We never felt really comfortable about the brakes. They worked well, but were not up to continual use at high speeds." – they wrote.

As for the interior, most media scribes thought it was a vast improvement over the LJ with its off-centre steering wheel – it was now parallel with the car's centreline – and the seats were very good.

An additional model was announced in July 1974, some five months after the model's release, and that was the L34 option based on the SL/R 5000 package. It was with this package that Holden, and especially the Holden Racing Team, was going to get serious about winning Bathurst and wresting the marketing advantage away from Ford.

The L34 optioned Toranas were instantly recognisable by their bolted-on fender extensions to cover the wider wheels and tyres and the widened wheel tracks. Suspension spring rates were revised along with stiffer damper rates, front ventilated rotor disc brakes were fitted (276mm diameter) that were ex-HQ in origin but the rumoured rear disc brakes did not materialise.

Under the bonnet was a much-modified V8 engine, although from appearances it looked very little different from a regular 5-litre V8. However, the cylinder block was a stronger Repco casting (still in iron) that had an affinity to the Formula 5000 engines the company was successfully building. It was fitted with special pistons, roller rockers, larger inlet and exhaust valves, exhaust headers, baffled sump, twin-point distributor and a higher compression ratio that had been raised to 9.8:1. Power output was listed at 260kW (345bhp) at 6000rpm and 380–400Nm (280–295lbs-ft) of torque at 3000rpm. Keen buyers who perhaps had racing in mind spent an additional $1500 on some very necessary options for their engine. These included an oil cooler, solid valve lifters, competition pistons, modified exhaust system, Crane roller rockers, Holley 780cfm carburettor, a reprofiled camshaft – the so-called 'Bathurst cam.'

At its first challenge on the Mountain in 1974 the L34s dominated the race for more than sixty per cent of the time but in the crucial final hours they succumbed to the Ford Falcon Hardtop of Goss and Bartlett. The fact that L34s came home in second and third places – Forbes/Negus second, Richards/Coppins third – was beside the point. The fact is it did not win! In 1975 and 1976 it did win but it was always susceptible to its small rear drum brakes and fragile differential.

Interestingly Holden tried hard to prevent the media from driving an L34 but *Wheels* managed to persuade racer Don Holland to allow them some time behind the wheel at the old Oran Park track. Apart from more responsive handling and the much higher limits of roadholding they felt there was not a lot of difference between an SL/R 5000 and the L34.

From its release the LH sold extremely well and complemented the HQ rather nicely. In February 1976 LH was replaced by the LX Torana which was in many ways more of the same with minor updates. It was not unexpected but there were other events going on behind the scenes where four-cylinder engines and Holden were concerned. Only a Holden Torana anorak could pick the model differences – round headlights for all models, the side window frames were now painted black (they were body colour in LH) and the Holden badge at the front was larger. Under the bonnet, however, more substantial changes had to be made to make the engines comply with ADR 27A that was all about emissions from the exhaust.

In November 1976 the four-cylinder Torana was relaunched as the Holden Sunbird powered by the Opel-sourced 1.9-litre cam-in-head engine driving through either a four-speed all-synchromesh manual gearbox or Trimatic 3-speed automatic. What was big news with Sunbird was the re-engineering of the suspension that was called Radial Tuned Suspension – RTS – that showed that with the right leadership

HOLDEN
SUNBIRD
DEDICATED TO THE DRIVER IN EVERY FAMILY
STARFIRE 4
SL/E
SLE

the engineers at Holden could produce a family sedan that handled with precision. While its performance was no better its ride and handling were a revelation and once the media had driven it they were full of praise for the improvement which spread progressively across the whole Holden range.

The really big news with LX was the availability of a Hatchback version, an Australian first only because the Leyland Force 7 was killed off at birth. Mechanically the Hatch was pure LX sedan and up to the A-pillar shared body panels – it was a little like the Charger as a derivative of the VH sedan – and at the rear were the usual Torana taillights. At the back was a smoothly flowing roofline that swept down to a cut-off with just the faintest suggestion of a lip. Inside was the normal Torana dashboard and front bucket seats that now had a fold-forward facility to allow entry to the rear seat which folded down 50:50 depending on need while the lift-up hatch was supported by a large gas strut each side. Standard on both models of the hatch – SL and SS – was a centre console around the gearshift lever/selector that included a push-button radio (Holden had at last learned from the Japanese!), floor vent outlets, and switches for the heated rear window, driving lights and power antenna when fitted. Both models came rather well equipped for a locally-built car; gone were the days of bare interiors and a lengthy (and expensive) options list. A radio in the centre console, floor carpets, flow-through ventilation and heater/demister with fan boost, cigarette lighter, and reclining bucket seats in front come with both with the SS having a full set of instruments – speedo and tacho each in their own large dial plus volts, temperature, fuel and oil pressure in the other. The SL had a clock in place of the SS's tacho.

The base engine for the Hatch was the venerable 3.3-litre OHV red six mated to a wide-ratio four-speed all-synchromesh manual gearbox or the Trimatic three-speed automatic. In the SL the only engine option was the 4.2-litre V8 while for the SS buyers could select either the 4.2- or 5.0-litre V8 engine, again with either manual or automatic gearbox. Options at the time included air conditioning at $700, Trimatic at $403, radial tyres on 6-inch rims cost $112, a tinted and laminated windscreen added $71 and the 4.2-litre engine was an extra $300 over the six.

Wheels tested an LX Hatch fitted with the 4.2-litre V8 engine, Trimatic automatic gearbox, integrated air conditioning and the 'hatch hutch' and found that the showroom floor sticker price had risen from $5683 to a whopping $7340 to which you had to add the on-road costs. Hatch ownership was not inexpensive. Leaving money aside, the hatch impressed the testers. The flexibility was appreciated (it was great for a young couple with no kids (DINKS) who wanted a car that looked smart and would supplement their lifestyle) but apart from heavy steering at low speeds (no power assist) the driving experience was all positive with the caveat that if the brakes (power assisted discs/drums) were punished they caused rear wheel lockup which caused the hatch to flick sideways quite quickly, especially in the wet. The dials were easy to read, the hatch having yellow graphics on the instruments instead of the previous white. From a performance aspect, they recorded a top speed of 165kmh (103mph) with 0–70, 90 and 110kmh acceleration times of 6.8, 10.0 and 14.5 seconds respectively, fuel economy worked out at 17.6mpg (15.7 litres/100km!) for the test making the 52.5-litre tank too small for long distance touring.

Motor Manual tested an SS Hatchback (June 1976 issue) and came away with acceleration figures of 5.6, 7.7 and 11.3 seconds for the 0–80, 100 and 120kmh sprints and an average fuel economy of 17.7 litres per 100km or 15.9mpg. And the retail price of their test car was $8111 from a base of $6088 to which such options as the 5.0-litre V8 was added along with the Trimatic automatic gearbox, air conditioning, laminated windscreen, power aerial, 6-inch wheel rims with BR 70 13 radial tyres.

Perhaps the most iconic car to have been designed and developed in Australia – it's up there with the Charger E49 and Phase III Falcon GT HO – was the A9X derivative that was available in either sedan or Hatchback form and was introduced in August 1977, in time for the Sandown 500 endurance race. Intriguingly, Holden released the A9X without any fanfare and described it as a 'Performance Equipment Package' option and not as a model in its own right and was only available with the LX SS or SL/R models with the 5.0-litre V8 engine. The A9X option code was similar to the L34 designation used for the LH but added a rearward facing bonnet scoop designed to increase airflow through the engine compartment, rear disc brakes, heavy duty axle shafts and 10-bolt differential. All were built between August and December 1977 with a single example being built in January 1978.

The A9X and L34 were the result of Holden's need to comply with the Group C Touring Car requirements of the time which meant that car manufacturers had to produce a certain number of road legal examples of their competition cars fitted with all the components that were required for racing – in other words, to homologate the model.

Many improvements were made for the A9X package to make it a more competitive and reliable race car than the L34. Stopping the car was always a huge issue, particularly at Bathurst, so it became imperative that rear disc brakes be added. The only economical way this could be done was to use the stronger Salisbury rear axle assembly that came with disc brakes. And the only way that could be achieved from a manufacturing point of view was to blend the rear section of the forthcoming UC Torana's floor pan under the body and that brought with it Radial Tuned Suspension. A benefit of using the Salisbury axle was the availability of a 2.60:1 rear axle ratio.

Front brakes were similar to the L34 but now had alloy calipers, a tandem master cylinder and there was a brake proportioning valve in the rear circuit; new upper control arms for the front suspension came from the RTS program and there were new steering arms connected to a solidly mounted steering rack (the previous ones were rubber bushed), and there was a new front spoiler with air ducts to cool the front brakes.

All engines now had to meet ADR 27A requirements where exhaust emissions were concerned and the A9X was caught in that net. No A9X was ever fitted with the L34 engine option from the factory, only the L31 5.0-litre V8, even though the L34 option had been homologated. For the A9X the only differences were to be found with the engine cooling fan which was a single thermo-electric fan behind a heavy duty radiator.

Holden produced 405 A9X cars, 305 four-door sedans plus 100 two-door Hatches plus a further 52 body shells for competition purposes made up of 11 sedans and 41 Hatches. The various teams purchased bodies from Holden and then proceeded to rebuild them with the L34 engine option, T10 gearbox, interior roll cage, wide wheels and long range fuel tanks (35-gallons) and any other parts needed for that competitive advantage.

The A9X was a successful racing car having taken out the Australian Touring Car Championship in 1978 driven by Peter Brock and 1979 with Bob Morris winning in front of Peter Brock plus it won three consecutive Sandown 500s in 1977, 1978 and 1979, a feat that has never been matched since.

In each of those three races the driver was, you guessed, Peter Brock driving for the Marlboro Holden Dealer Team.

The Holden Torana A9X has gone down in Australian motoring folklore as one of the best supercars of all time.

The Torana story, however, had one more chapter to go. Released in March 1978 were the UC Torana and Sunbird in both sedan and hatchback body formats. Only four- and six-cylinder engines were on offer, the V8s being discontinued. The UC featured a new plastic grille with square headlights each end and the parking/indicator lights squeezed into the outer edge each end, new bumpers, new taillights, new dashboard that was a far more modern design than hitherto, bigger fuel tank, multi-function stalk on the steering column – that ancient foot dip switch was at long last thrown in the rubbish bin and of course, it inherited the Radial Tuned Suspension. Unbelievably, four-wheel disc brakes were an option!

Later in the year the 1.9-litre Opel-sourced four-cylinder engine was replaced by the only Australian-designed four-cylinder engine – I'm referring of course to the infamous Starfire Four that was developed out of the 2850cc red six. Its capacity was 1.9-litres, its overhead valves were hydraulically operated and it had a five-bearing crankshaft. Power output was 60kW at 4800rpm and torque was 140Nm at 2600rpm. A world-class best practice engine it was not. But it did the job and even powered the Toyota Corona for a short time …

A full test of the Sunbird was published in the March 1979 edition of *Wheels* and was headed with the words 'Starfire Misfire?' A somewhat ominous start to an article. There was one very telling paragraph early in the test report that gave readers a big clue as to how the *Wheels* guys felt about the engine. They wrote, "If you come to the new Sunbird from a Sigma or a Corona or a Cortina or even a Datsun 200B then the engine – just the engine, let's not get it confused with the rest of the car – will be a disappointment. If this is state of the art of four-cylinder engines in 1979 then a new dark age is upon us." The Philippines-built manual gearbox, too, came in for some stick from the testers.

Against the clock the Sunbird ran to 154km/h (96mph) at 5400rpm, with 55km/h (34mph) in first, 83km/h (52mph) in second and 119km/h (74mph) in third, all at an excruciating 6000rpm. Acceleration from rest to 90km/h (56mph) and 110km/h (68mph) took12.7 and 20.1 seconds respectively so it was no ball of fire when compared with its Japanese rivals.

BATHURST RESULTS FOR THE TORANA

Year	Drivers	Position
1970	D Holland/L Little	3rd in a GTR XU-1
1971	C Bond P Brock	1st in Class D in an XU-1 3rd in Class D in an XU-1
1972	P Brock	1st in an XU-1
1973	P Brock/D Chivas C Bond/L Geoghegan	2nd in an XU-1 3rd in an XU-1
1974	R Forbes/W Negus J Richards/J Coppins	2nd in an SLR5000 3rd in an SLR5000
1975	P Brock/B Sampson R Morris/F Gardner C Bond/J Walker	1st in an SLR5000 2nd in an SLR5000 3rd in an SLR5000
1976	R Morris/J Fitzpatrick C Bond/J Harvey P Brock/P Brock	1st in an L34 2nd in an L34 3rd in an L34
1977	P Janson/L Perkins C O'Brien/R Harrop P Brock/P Brock	3rd in an A9X 4th in an A9X 5th in an A9X
1978	P Brock/J Richards A Grice/J Leffler G Cooke/D Chivas	1st in an A9X 2nd in an A9X 4th in an A9X
1979	P Brock/J Richards P Janson/L Perkins R Radburn/J Smith	1st in an A9X 2nd in an A9X 3rd in an A9X

GEMINI

With the Torana having successfully created a new niche in the local market place with its six-cylinder models and (soon) V8 versions, Holden needed to fill the void left by the demise of the four-cylinder models. Once the six-cylinder Toranas became available sales of the fours were by comparison minuscule mainly because of their dismal performance in comparison with the plethora of Japanese models available. A lot of this had to do with the engines GM-Holden used – the anaemic little 1.2- and 1.3-litre OHV fours from Vauxhall which were supplemented in a half-hearted way by the 1.6- and 1.8-litre SOHC fours also from Vauxhall.

A concept that was sweeping through the halls of power at GM back in those days was that of a so-called 'world car.' The decision was made for the German-designed Opel Kadett to become a world car (or T-car as it was referred to at GM) and so it was additionally badged as a Vauxhall, Isuzu, Daewoo, Buick and Holden. Interestingly, all measurements for the Kadett were metric, not Imperial as was the way for the rest of the GM world. The Germans were unmoved by such *diktats*! It did not bother the engineers at Isuzu either because Japan was a metric zone anyway but it did create a few headaches for the people at Holden even though Australia had converted totally to the metric system.

Isuzu and Holden collaborated on the project, Isuzu making the Gemini initially in 4-door sedan, 2-door coupe and later adding a 3-door wagon and a light van version. All were powered by a 1.6-litre SOHC in-line four-cylinder engine that had powered a wide range of Isuzu cars over the years. It was well-proven and ruggedly reliable as were most Japanese engines in comparison with their English counterparts. Like most Isuzu car petrol engines it was a distant derivative of the OHV Rootes four-cylinder engine from the mid-50s, and early versions powered the Isuzu Bellett and Florian here in Australia.

For the market Holden had in mind, the Gemini was perfect – right size, right specification, right performance, right price, right everything. It was perceived as a Japanese car (which was not incorrect) which in the 70s gave it added kudos. At first GM-Holden assembled the car from CKD kits at its Acacia Ridge plant in Brisbane in four-door sedan and two-door coupe bodies in S and SL trim.

It was built on a floorpan that had a wheelbase of 2405mm (94.7-ins)

IGL-423

and it was 4135mm long (162.8-ins), by 1570mm wide (61.8-ins) by 1360mm high (53.5-ins) for the sedan, 1335mm (52.6-ins) for the coupe; the sedan weighed 895kgs (1973lbs) and the coupe was 20kgs lighter. Under the bonnet was the Isuzu G161Z engine with a bore and stroke of 82 x 75mm for a capacity of 1584cc and it developed 63kW (85bhp) at 5000rpm and 135Nm (100lbs-ft) of torque at 4000rpm using a Stromberg two-barrel downdraught carburettor and an 8.7:1 compression. Unusually for a Holden badged car at the time was the fact that the engine featured an aluminium alloy crossflow cylinder head with a single chain-driven overhead camshaft. The block was an iron casting, the crankshaft had five main bearings and the exhaust manifold was a two-into-one design although this was changed in November 1976 to a single outlet to comply with ADR 27A requirements.

At the front was an upper-and-lower wishbone system with the coil spring mounted at an angle on the lower wishbone and the telescopic damper rubber bushed onto the upper wishbone with the top mount high up in the wheel well; the brochure talked of negative steering roll radius. At the rear was a live axle with the variable rate coil springs mounted in deep 'buckets,' the dampers being positioned behind the axle while the axle's movement was controlled by two forward-facing links, a transverse Panhard rod and a torque tube as the rearward part of the drive shaft. Rounding out the Gemini's specifications were rack and pinion steering (non-boosted), a disc/drum (238mm/9.4-ins disc rotors, 228mm/9-ins drums) dual circuit braking system with a vacuum booster and the choice of a four-speed all-synchromesh manual gearbox with a neat floor shift or a three-speed Trimatic automatic. The early cars had the MSE-type manual gearbox with reverse left-and-back but by November 1975 that had been replaced by the MSG-type where reverse was right-and-back.

The Gemini sedan was described in brochures as a family car but the fact remains that legroom in particular in the back seat was very tight – OK for young kids but not so great for adults. Front passengers sat on well-shaped bucket seats with tombstone style headrests and adjustable seat backs. The dashboard was a plain moulding with the instrument binnacle set back at an angle, the instruments consisting of a speedometer, combination gauge with fuel and temperature dials plus warning lights and on the SL a clock. A very effective heater/demister was standard on the S and SL and there was a good flow-through ventilation system into which an integrated air conditioning system could be fitted for a modest outlay. On a stalk on the left of the steering column was the control for the two-speed wipers and electric washers, the stalk on the right controlled the indicators and hi-lo beam. On the outside it wore Gemini badges plus one that read Holden-Isuzu.

Released onto the Australian market in March 1975 the TX Gemini soon became the best-selling four-cylinder car Holden had ever marketed. Probably not surprising when there were more than 500 Holden dealers around the nation selling it. Its assembly took place at Holden's Acacia Ridge factory in Queensland with a reasonably high local content. As Steve Cropley wrote in the road test published in *Wheels*, May 1975 issue, "We think the all-new Holden Gemini, the small car which will probably re-affirm GMH as 'top manufacturer' in Australia, is a strong, appealing, nimble, noisy little Japanese car. It is fast for a 1.6, comfortable enough in small car terms and its prices are competitive. But it is no soft, sophisticated Renault 12." Interestingly, *Wheels* voted the Gemini SL sedan their Car of the Year for 1975.

In March 1977 Holden released the TC version of the Gemini. External differences were few but the most obvious was the new grille with its 11 vertical segments and a silver rear garnish panel. Inside the dashboard looked the same but behind it was a locally-sourced Smiths heater/demister unit and the two air vents either end of the dash were gone except in cars fitted with the integrated air conditioning unit.

Holden made a so-called 'Fashion Pack' available in which some interior items were upgraded to include a heated rear window, the package later being extended to include steel-belt radial tyres and a front stabiliser bar; side impact door beams were added to the body's specification to meet safety requirements. A month after the TC's release Holden offered the Gemini 'Sandpiper' which was a limited edition model available in both sedan and coupe bodies. Its specification included gold pin stripes, black grille with a stainless steel top edge, check cloth upholstery and door trims, wood-grain inserts on the dash, radio/cassette player and a four-spoke steering wheel. An A9R suspension package was part of the deal. Sandpipers were easily recognised by the name on the body side of the coupe and on the rear doors of the sedan along with a bird decal.

A year later, in April 1978, Holden released the TD Gemini that

GEMINI

GEMINI

DIESEL

sported the famous Radial Tuned Suspension that was sweeping through Holden at the time. RTS-equipped Geminis came with the option of a five-speed manual gearbox and there was a new Salisbury differential (it was shared with the UC Torana) that used Timken tapered wheel bearings; in April 1979 the rear drum brakes were changed to the same ones as those on the Commodore.

With TD came a new grille that featured three thin horizontal bars and seven thin vertical bars and square headlights either end (round on the base sedan and van), slightly wider wheel rims (now 13 x 5-ins) and a new SL/E edition that had alloy wheels of a similar design to those on the Sunbird SL/E. In addition to the sedan and coupe Holden added the three-door station wagon and panel van to the range and both were immediately successful. Incidentally the rear body work for the wagon and van were taken from the English Vauxhall Chevette / Bedford Chevanne models.

The SL/E was the replacement for the Sandpiper in the new range as it featured much the same interior specification. In early 1979 the SL/E was superseded by the SL/X plus there was the limited edition 'Gypsy' package that was available for the panel vans.

The last edition of the Gemini that meets our criteria was the TE that Holden introduced in October 1979. This was a major change for the model that had now been on the market virtually unchanged for five years – a long time by most manufacturers' standards but not for Isuzu. The passenger compartment remained unchanged but all the panel work front and rear was new. It was now much squarer and in some ways similar to the Commodore which was deliberate. It was no longer in step with Opel in Germany because by now their Kadett featured a front-wheel drive configuration. The grille now comprised nine horizontal bars with the Holden lion badge prominently displayed in the centre and the name Gemini off to the left, and there were square headlights sitting in recessed nacelles with the parking lights squeezed into the outer edge of the light's surround and the indicator light lens was in the new bumpers that had rubber buffers on their facing surface and large protective rubber end caps. At the rear was a new large horizontal taillight unit each side and again there was a substantial bumper with rubber facings and edgings.

Some changes were made to the TE model range with the coupe no longer being available – the range consisted of a base sedan (with round headlights), SL and SL/X sedan plus the wagon and van. With the sedans the Trimatic three-speed automatic was an option as were alloy wheels, integrated air conditioning and a five speed manual gearbox.

Wheels conducted a full road test of a Gemini SL/X in a four-car comparison in its March 1980 issue; it compared the SL/X with the Escort RS2000, Honda Civic and Mitsubishi Lancer hatch. It was $6426 and 50kW for the SL/X versus $6669 and 70kW for the Escort, $6635 and 56kW for the Lancer and $5669 and 45kW for the Civic. All four featured much extra equipment which inflated their prices although having said that all items would be taken for granted in today's soft and pampered world. To nobody's surprise the Escort was the runaway winner on the test track having the largest capacity engine. It ran to a top speed of 165km/h against 160km/h for the Lancer, 156km/h for the Gemini and 153km/h for the Civic; ran the 0–100km/h dash in 11.5 seconds versus 14.3 seconds for the Gemini, 14.6 seconds for the Civic and 15.5 seconds for the Lancer.

As for road dynamics, the *Wheels'* guys wrote of the Gemini: "The Gemini's handling is just impossibly capable. For stability, precision, feedback to the driver, and sheer good manners it runs rings around the others: around most cars on the road, for that matter."

The Gemini story did not end in December 1979 as does our book but went on with the TF being released in March 1982 followed by the TG a year later and then the front-wheel drive Giugiaro-designed RB Gemini that arrived in May 1985 and lasted until early 1987 to be replaced by a Holden-badged version of the Nissan Pulsar.

COMMODORE

Following the Yom Kippur war in the Middle East in 1973 and the ensuing world shortage of fuel GM had been looking to down-size its model range and develop its 'world car' concept. We saw that first here as the Gemini. In the background, Holden's stylists and engineers were working on the WA series of cars to replace the HQ-HZ model range. Size-wise the WA was line ball with the HQ, in other words a large family car in the Australian tradition. However, new winds were blowing through the corridors of power and the folks at Holden were instructed to develop a smaller family car in keeping with the needs of the day.

To expedite the whole design and development process the Australians took the German Opel Rekord with the idea that they would transform it into the next generation Holden car. In simplistic terms what they did was to graft onto the Rekord bodywork a new front section (actually taken from the Opel Senator) that housed the longer and heavier Holden engines and gearboxes; and while the Rekord also featured a MacPherson strut front suspension, the German struts were considerably lighter and smaller than those required for the Holden version. Holden continued with the Rekord live axle and coil spring rear suspension, albeit strengthened and for the first time on a large Holden it featured a rack and pinion steering system.

It was an interesting cross-pollination experience for the Australian and German engineers involved who had great difficulty understanding the need for a far stronger structure than the one they had designed and developed for European conditions. The frailty of the German structure was highlighted by extensive testing north of Port Augusta in the Flinders Ranges where many issues came to light, much to the chagrin of the Germans.

The new Holden, to be christened the VB Commodore, was a smaller and more space efficient package then the HQ-HZ; in fact it was something of an in-betweener because it was smaller than the Kingswood but larger than the Torana. It sat on a wheelbase of 2668mm (105-ins), was 1722mm (67.8-ins) wide and 4705mm (185.2-ins) in overall length – by comparison, the HZ was 4844mm (190.7-ins) long on a wheelbase of 2819mm (111-ins); kerb weight was 1220kgs for the basic Commodore compared with around 1350–1400kgs for a Kingswood. Under the bonnet buyers had the choice of either a 2.85- or 3.3-litre 'red' six-cylinder engine or two V8s, one of 4.2-litres and the other of 5.0-litres. All four engines were heavy, no wonder the Germans were confused because the Rekord in Europe was powered by mostly four-cylinder engines …

Holden released the Commodore to the media in November 1978 and the public two weeks later with considerable hype. After all, it represented a huge gamble ($110 million) on Holden's part to down-size when neither Ford nor Chrysler was going to, although Chrysler was not long for this world so did not really count.

At the press event chief engineer Joe Whitesell offered the comment "This is absolutely the finest car ever produced in Australia." The new Commodore was regarded by the company and the media as Australia's first world-class car and additionally the best car in the world for Australian conditions.

Holden offered the Commodore in three versions: the standard or base

model sedan and wagon powered by the 2.8-litre six, the Commodore SL powered by the 3.3-litte six and the SL/E that had the 4.2-litre V8 as standard. The 5.0-litre V8 was an option across the range. Interior trim levels varied from basic to downright plush. Bucket front seats were standard – no bench seat was ever offered – and there was a bench seat in back with a capacious boot at the back where the spare wheel was stood upright to the side for easy access. The interior offered ample room for mum, dad and three kids or four adults. Despite initial misgivings from some folks in Marketing, this seating arrangement was not a handicap on the showroom floor.

To nobody's real surprise *Wheels* magazine voted the Commodore as the Car of the Year for 1978, the fifteenth winner of the award, and just three years after the Gemini had won the same award. David Bentley, *Wheels*' resident designer – he had worked at BMCA – offered some insightful comments about the Commodore's styling in the March 1979 issue of the magazine when he wrote, "The Commodore's styling is a success because it visually expresses the functional characteristics of the car – the large glass area suggests that it is roomy inside, it has an air of elegance confirming the well appointed interior and it has a good wheel/body relationship indicating good handling qualities."

In a comparison test between the Commodore, Torana, Kingswood, Cortina and Falcon the Commodore came out as the winner by quite a margin. The new Holden was powered by the 3300 six-cylinder engine, the Torana by allegedly the same engine as was the Kingswood while both the Cortina and Falcon were powered by the 4.1-litre six-cylinder engine giving them an advantage in on-road performance. And that's how it worked out with the lighter-smaller Cortina powering away on the 0–110km/h (0–68mph) acceleration run to record a time of 14.8 seconds compared with 16.2 seconds for the Falcon, 16.4 seconds for the Commodore, 17.4 seconds for the Torana and 19.2 seconds for the Kingswood.

As for maximum speed, the Commodore and Cortina tied on 164km/h (102.5mph) with the Falcon close behind at 162km/h (101.2mph), the Torana on 158km/h (98.7mph) and the Kingswood on 156km/h (97.5mph). Not one of the five cars bettered 20mpg on the test …

And so a whole new chapter in Australian car manufacturing began with the Commodore which did prove to be a little on the small size where the buying public was concerned because Ford took over market leadership with the XD Falcon. However, years later the Australian designers and engineers were able to develop their own version of the Commodore where they widened it considerably and re-engineered it completely to build what was quite possibly the best car made anywhere in the GM world.

VB
COMMODORE

CHAPTER 2

FORD

Ford's star was very much on the rise during the Seventies as it continued its push for market leadership with the Falcon range, as well as the Fairlane and LTD models that were derived from the Falcon. Complementing them were the Cortina, Escort and Capri models that were based on Ford UK designs and assembled locally from CKD packs.

FALCON

The decade began with the Falcon three-quarters of the way through its model cycle with the big selling Mustang-bred XT and XW series that were basically revisions of the 1966 XR. Most of the differences were outside where for XW the stylists led by Jack Telnack squared-up the front to make it more aggressive looking; this required new bonnet and front quarter panels, and the taillights were changed from the traditional Falcon round units to squared-off (but slightly vee-shaped) units which again required new boot lid and quarter panels. Inside the basic theme of the dash was kept but altered in minor details. Distinguishing a new XY Falcon from the previous XW required a keen eye because externally the changes amounted to a new split grille and the taillights now had only two lenses – red for tail and brake lights over an amber lens for reverse and indicators.

The big news with the XY Falcons was a revised range of six-cylinder engines. The focal point of the range was the new 250-cid six; with a bore and stroke of 93 x 99mm (3.68 x 3.90-ins) it had a capacity of

4.1-litres or 250-cid, power output was 115kW (155bhp) at 4000rpm and a huge 325Nm (240lbs-ft) of torque at 1600rpm. This thoroughly revised engine was Ford's response to GM-H's 253-cid V8 and Chrysler's 245-cid 'Hemi' six. Accompanying the 250-cid six was a smaller 200-cid unit that developed 97kW (130bhp) at 4000rpm, it being the base engine for the Falcon range. Retained from the XW range was the 302-cid V8 that developed 164kW (220bhp) and the two-barrel 351 that provided

186kW (250bhp) at 4600rpm. The Falcon GT and GT HO were powered by a 4V 351 that developed 224kW (300bhp), this engine being exclusive to the two top models. Later in the year Ford offered an optional 250 2V engine where the single-throat Stromberg carburettor was replaced by a Bendix-Stromberg twin-barrel carburettor that helped the engine develop 127kW (170bhp) at 4000rpm and 332Nm (245lbs-ft) torque.

It is interesting to note that Ford USA announced a 250-cid six at the same time as the Aussies but by this time the development of the six-cylinder engine in Australia had diverged from that in the US, our engine being significantly more robust for our harsher conditions.

As before, Ford offered the Falcon with a bewildering array of options from which the buyer could choose starting with the plain Falcon and progressing through Falcon 500 to Fairmont, to Futura and then to the GT and GT-HO.

FALCON
GT

A full road test of a Falcon 250 2V was published in *Wheels* (September 1971) and revealed some surprises. As they said at the top of the article, "For a 10 per cent increase in power, Ford's 250 2V cuts seconds off the quarter mile times. There is little to approach it on a performance per dollar basis." They followed those words with more, saying "Just occasionally we happen upon a car which is better than it has any right to be. It can be perfectly conventional in specification, rather mundane to look at and, generally, just another car that has to be road tested. Such a vehicle is Ford's Falcon 500 250 2V." The 2V's ride, handling, steering and brakes all came in for praise but it was the car's performance against the clock that impressed, considering the relatively small changes that had been made to the engine. The top speed rose to 170.5km/h (106mph) with in-gear speeds of 67.5km/h (41mph) in first, 96.5km/h (60mph) in second and 135km/h (84mph) in third while the standing quarter mile took 16.9 seconds; acceleration from 0–96km/h (60mph) took 10.7 seconds. However, to put Ford's claims into some perspective, a VH Valiant Ranger sedan fitted with the new 245-cid D series engine and a three-speed manual gearbox ran to 169km/h (105mph) and did the 0–96km/h (60mph) sprint in 10 seconds even.

The apex XY Falcons were the GT and GT-HOs. They were considered to be the world's fastest four-door family sedans in the day which was quite an accolade. Performance figures published at the time, while very impressive, do not account for the brick-like aerodynamics of the car. *Wheels* published a full text of an XY Falcon GT Shaker (June 1971) that featured the 4V version of the famous 351-cid Cleveland V8 that developed 300bhp at 5400rpm and 380 lbs/ft of torque at 3400rpm. Against the clock it registered a maximum speed of 204.8km/h (128mph) at 5200rpm in top gear of the four-speed manual fitted with 76.8km/h

(48mph) in first, 110.4km/h (69mph) in second and 158.4km/h (99mph) in third; 0–96km/h (60mph) took 8.3 seconds, 0–112km/h (70mph) took 10.5 seconds. Pretty damn good for a four-door family sedan that weighed 1530kgs (3360lbs) and had the aerodynamics of a brick. It was just brute force …

On March 1972 Ford announced the XA series Falcons to the media and public, six months after Holden had released the HQ and Chrysler the VH Valiant. In May of 1968 Jack Telnack, Brian Rossi and Allan Jackson had been called to Detroit to begin work on the new car's styling which was completed at the Broadmeadows styling studios by Australian stylists – it was the first all-Australian designed Falcon. Included in the program was the Falcon Hardtop, a revival of a theme first explored by Ford here back in the mid-60s. While the copywriters wanted to describe the XA as 'all new' it was no such thing – it was in reality a new suite over old mechanical components. That mattered not in our relatively unsophisticated market where style very much dominated buyer thinking. And as Bill Tuckey wrote in his Ford history book, *True Blue*, "The XA was a milestone for Ford Australia. It was the design that

FAIRMONT

broke from the tradition of adapting North American designs for the Australian market and created the unique Australian Falcon. It was very much the child of Bill Bourke and Ford's chief of design, Jack Telnack."

As Dr John Wright wrote in his history of the Ford Falcon, "Very early in the project the Americans suggested that an abbreviated version of the new Fairlane/Torino would do the job. By using the centre section of the car in conjunction with a shorter wheelbase and shorter front and rear overhangs, an attractive car of Falcon dimensions could be created." A clay model of this concoction was built but as Brian Rossi related to the author some years later, "It just looked awkward, the lines did not flow at all and we were not happy. So, off our own bat we created the design that eventually became the XA."

The lines of the XA flowed smoothly from a wide-but relatively-narrow grille to the C-pillar region where there was a noticeable Coke bottle hip before the line flowed down to the taillights; substantial chromed steel bumpers were fitted front and rear. Single 7-inch headlights were either side of the grille, three-part taillight units of moulded plastic featured each side at the rear.

Inside was completely new although roominess for up to six people was no better than in the XY. The most striking feature of the interior was the dashboard. For the XA the designers sculpted a broad cockpit-style dash that curved around the driver's environment and had two large round dials set low and deep in the panel with minor dials and warning lights above. In the centre and at either end were adjustable vents for the flow-through ventilation system, something Ford had pioneered on the 1964 Cortina!

Integral with the XA Falcon range was a new Hardtop that would share its doors with the Falcon ute and panel van. Up to the A-pillar the sedan and Hardtop shared sheet metal but from there back the Hardtop was unique. As Rossi later admitted, "There was a fair amount of the Gran Turismo in the rear half of the Hardtop, particularly around the rear wheel arch area." It could be said that the Hardtop had 'big hips!' That was because even at this early stage the Hardtop was destined for glory at Mount Panorama and the rear wheel arches were deliberately flared to accommodate much wider wheel and tyres.

A full road test was published in *Wheels* October 1972 under the headline "Ford's Hardtop ... the Challenger." After all, Ford had been beaten to the punch by both its main rivals, the Holden Monaro having been available since mid-1968 and Chrysler's Charger since mid-1971. The *Wheels* crew really liked the Hardtop's styling even if rearward visibility was badly compromised. And as they wrote, " ... but open the wide doors (they are actually a full 10-inches longer than the sedan doors) and the front compartment is all Falcon." Getting into the rear seat was easy once the trip lever had been activated and the front seats folded forward giving reasonable access and once, ensconced, was reasonably comfortable for two passengers with the caveat that headroom was marginal for average-to-tall people.

As for its road dynamics, unsurprisingly the *Wheels* guys said it drove just like the sedan! Against the clock the Fairmont Hardtop they tested, which ran a 2V 351 V8 developing 260bhp at 4600rpm and three-speed automatic and 2.75 rear axle, ran the 0–96 and 0–112km/h (0–60 and 70mph) runs in 9.2 and 12.5 seconds respectively with 88km/h (55mph) held in first, 146km/h (91mph) in second and 183.4km/h (114mph) flat out; average fuel consumption was 19 litres per 100km (15mpg)! Thirsty camel.

Ford gave buyers three trim levels from which to choose plus a plethora of extras off the options list, starting with the Falcon 500 (same as the sedan) going up to the Fairmont but skipping the Futura and then up to the GT.

Ford, through its 'skunk works' at Lot 6, Mahoney's Road, Campbellfield was well into the preparation of the Phase IV GT-HO Falcons when the so-called 'Supercar scare' hit the newspaper headlines and Ford quietly stopped the program for political reasons and used the parts manufactured to homologate the Phase IV on the assembly line until the already manufactured parts were exhausted.

A facelifted XB arrived in October 1973 that featured a tidier front plastic grille and restyled wrap around taillights as external signs. The best news, however, was hidden in the form of ventilated front disc brakes as standard equipment across the range except for the base models. The GT now had four-wheel discs that had appeared a few months earlier on the LTD and Landaus. Inertia reel seat belts were now fitted for front seat occupants. Sadly the 2V 250 Special six-cylinder engine was discontinued as was the Futura trim option.

In July 1976 the final iteration of this body style appeared, the XC. This was really just more titillation of the original XA styling from an external viewpoint although the rear door profile was changed slightly to remove the so-called 'Coke bottle' hip line – the new doors actually came from the Fairlane! Under the bonnet there had been significant developments where the mainstream six-cylinder engines were concerned. To enable them to pass the new ADR27A emission requirements Ford produced a new cross-flow cylinder head. The Falcon GT had been discontinued but remained in spirit in the form of the 5.8-litre V8 powered GXL. Lesser Falcons continued with round headlights but the Fairmont and GXL scored new rectangular headlight units. Inside was a new dashboard and colour trim to give a lighter mood.

The 302 V8 engine (4.9-litres) gained a four-barrel carburettor which gave a significant performance boost. But the loss of the GT – it was dropped because of the extortionate cost of insurance – was compensated for by buyers ordering the GT Power Pack option.

Ford launched the Hardtop editions of the XC in December 1973 in two versions – Falcon 500 and Fairmont; there was no GXL option interestingly enough. From a marketing point of view, the days of the Hardtop were numbered. Ford had 400 body shells in storage and these were used to create a future classic in much the same way as Holden created the Monaro LE. In Ford's case it was called the Cobra and came to showrooms in August 1978. The Cobra was definitely NOT a Falcon GT according to Ford's PR folks but in every way but its name that is what it was.

The decade was closed out with the release in March 1979 of the XD series Falcons at the Melbourne Motor Show. Unlike Holden, Ford decided to stay with the so-called 'standard-sized' Australian family car format rather than down-size. The Australian engineers did consider adopting the European Granada and modifying it to suit local conditions (the Granada and the Opel Commodore were serious rivals in Europe) but eventually the decision was made to rebody the existing mechanical components with a body style that was influenced – but not copied – from Europe. Where the XA-through-XC was flowing curves in its styling the XD was the opposite in that it had a distinct edginess to its exterior beginning with a sloping back grille with square headlights (apparently to improve the car's aerodynamics) with large black plastic energy absorbing bumpers through to a squared-off rear with broad fluted lens taillights. Glass area in comparison with the XA was significantly increased giving the XD passengers a bright and airy ride but it also meant that integrated air conditioning was a must for our hot summers.

Mechanically not a lot changed from the XC although the V8s now had an electronic ignition system; there were minor revisions to the suspension (still old fashioned cart springs at the rear) and the power assisted steering now had just 2.6 turns lock-to-lock.

FORD
FAIRLANE

FAIRLANE

During the time of the ZC Fairlane (1969–70), both GM-Holden and Chrysler belatedly weighed-in with their competition: the Brougham and VIP by Chrysler respectively. The Brougham was little more than the existing Holden Premier with an extended tail – it looked what it was, an after-thought. It looked awkward stylistically and is remembered with embarrassment by Holden people today while the VIP is an irrelevance to all but a handful of diehard Chrysler enthusiasts.

In November 1970 Ford launched the fourth, and last, of the first generation Fairlanes. Like ZA-to-ZB, the ZC-to-ZD upgrade was largely a spot the differences challenge for future car spotters. At the front was a new egg-crate style grille moulded from plastic for the first time on a local Ford and at the rear was a full-width dress panel across the trunk lid while the new wheel dress trims were courtesy of Lincoln Continental, the chrome wheel arch trims now went full body length and there was again new badging. Unseen was added sound deadening material that greatly improved the car's noise, vibration and harshness (NVH) qualities when compared with the ZA, ZB and ZC.

Another change, or upgrade really, came under the bonnet. For ZD the capacity of the six-cylinder engine that was standard in the Custom was increased from 221- to 250-cubic inches. Its cylinder dimensions were now 93.47 x 99.31 mm, for a capacity of 4.1-litres (3.68 by 3.91 inches), power was up from 100kW (135bhp) to 115kW (155bhp) at 4000rpm and torque was now 325Nm (240lbs-ft) at 1600rpm. Described in Ford's literature at the time as 'all new,' the 250-cid six was an impressive upgrade of the existing engine with a deeper and stronger cast iron block, new seven-bearing crankshaft with eight counter-weights, tri-metal conrod bearings, 'auto-thermic' alloy pistons, larger capacity oil pump for improved engine lubrication, larger water pump and radiator and, interestingly, it retained the same 100mm cylinder bore centres as the original 144-cid six from 1960! Ford was really getting value for money from its investment in engine tooling!

This engine change brought Ford into line with Chrysler and their new so-called 'Hemi' 245 six-cylinder engine and Holden's new 253-cubic inch V8. What neither could yet match was Ford's big 351 V8, however.

Wheels magazine carried out a two-car comparison test between the ZD Fairlane Custom fitted with the new 250-cid six, three-speed manual gearbox and drum brakes and the Fairlane 500 with the 302 V8, three-speed T-bar automatic and many other luxury extras. Of the Custom they wrote: "It has slightly less understeer, less dead feeling in the steering, it is more controllable in the wet, dirt and other tricky situations but lacks the absolute smoothness of the V8." It proved to be virtually as quick as the V8 over more than 1000 miles of testing and was much more economical.

They were critical of the poor output from the air conditioning system and the lack of a steering column-mounted headlight flasher/dipper – it still had the tried-and-true old floor dipswitch.

As good as the ZD Fairlane was, and it was very good in so many ways, according to several critics Father Time was catching up with it.

A major body change arrived with the release of the XA Falcon that brought with it the ZF Fairlane in March 1972. XA Falcon and ZF Fairlane were joined at the hip as both shared a great many components, the ZF in effect being an extended XA as far as the under-structure was concerned.

The ZF was a physically big motor car, and in the opinion of many looked little more like a bloated four-headlight Falcon! Gone was that individuality of style that quite clearly previously separated Falcon from Fairlane. Not with ZF. Sure it was a little wider at 1905mm (75-ins) versus 1879mm (74-ins) for the Falcon, sitting on a wheelbase of 2946mm (116-ins) compared with 2819mm (111-ins), stood 1372mm (54-ins) high against 1346mm (53-ins) and weighed 1761kgs (3875lbs) in 500 guise against 1482kgs (3260lbs) for a Falcon 500 GS with a V8 engine. The 80-litre (17.5 gallon) fuel tank was shared with Falcon.

Whereas previously styling was visually different from the Falcon this new generation mimicked Falcon – no doubt the money-men at Ford had a lot to do with that. Up front was a broad W-shaped nose to the bonnet with four horizontal headlights placed within a slatted plastic grille that had a prominent centre section, the grille being outlined at the top by a chromed strip across the leading edge of the bonnet and below by the chromed bumper that looks to be exactly the same as that on an XA Falcon. On the slight prow of the bonnet, above the Fairlane badge in the grille was the name F-O-R-D spelled out in separate letters. The XA Falcon had the same four letters spread across the bonnet's edge … And either side of the front of the Fairlane were Falcon parking/indicator light units.

The front fender line rose up over the wheel arches and dipped slightly along the window line before rising again by the C-pillar and dropping to the rear, the effect being that of the ubiquitous Coke bottle style that was so popular at the time. At the back was a broad-but-narrow section housing the taillight assembly with a chromed highlight strip across the top and a chromed bumper below that was not shared with the Falcon sedans; in the centre of the lighting unit the name F-O-R-D was spelled out in discreet letters. The wheel arches and sill panels were picked out by chromed strips and the wheel trims were Lincolnesque in style.

In Ford's eyes the ZF looked dramatically large and stylish emphasising its dominance of all that it surveyed; it also looked expensive.

From a technical pint of view there was no adventurism on Ford's part whatsoever – ZF simply was a body change over existing mechanical components. As Ford's engineers said at the time, "If it ain't broke don't fix it." That meant that the Falcon upper-and-lower wishbone front suspension with big coil springs, telescopic dampers and a thick anti-roll bar continued as did the live rear axle with semi-elliptic leaf springs. Braking was by 285.7mm (11.25-ins) diameter ventilated and turbo-cooled front disc rotors and the rear drums were 254mm (10.0-ins) in diameter, the system's pedal pressure being reduced by a vacuum booster. Standard wheels and tyres on the Fairlane were 14-ins shod with ER70 H14 radial tyres although a range of other wheels and tyres was available either from Ford or the accessory industry.

Inside the Fairlane was more Fairmont than actual Fairlane. The dashboard moulding appeared to be the same with its curved cockpit feel for the driver, but where the Falcon instruments were round for the Fairlane the 120mph speedometer was fan-shaped with small fuel and temperature dials to the left and right, warning lights below. An excellent flow-through ventilation system was part of the ZF equipment with an optional air conditioning system designed to be integrated. By the standards of the day the Fairlane was reasonably well equipped but

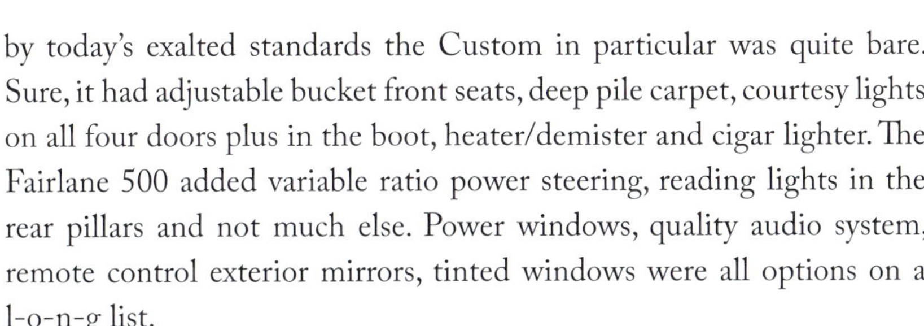

by today's exalted standards the Custom in particular was quite bare. Sure, it had adjustable bucket front seats, deep pile carpet, courtesy lights on all four doors plus in the boot, heater/demister and cigar lighter. The Fairlane 500 added variable ratio power steering, reading lights in the rear pillars and not much else. Power windows, quality audio system, remote control exterior mirrors, tinted windows were all options on a l-o-n-g list.

The high-backed front bucket seats with adjustable backs *looked* like Fairmont seats and were undoubtedly comfortable although several road tests commented on poor lumbar support. In the back was stretching room for three although two were far more comfortable. Sound deadening was everywhere so travel in the Fairlane was always a hushed affair.

Fairlane came in two guises – Custom and Fairlane 500, as before – which meant that the 4.1-litre OHV six-cylinder engine was standard with buyers being able to order either the 302-cid or 351-cid V8 as an option. Initially Custom buyers could order a manual gearbox but during 1973 that option was deleted from the range. Power outputs for the three engines were 115kW (155bhp) at 4600rpm for the six, 180kW (240bhp) at 5000rpm for the 302 and 194kW (260bhp) at 4600rpm for the 351 V8.

Wheels road test June 1972 achieved a top speed of 176km/h (110mph) out of their 500 fitted with the 351 V8, ran the 0–80, 96 and 112km/h (0–50, 60 and 70mph) runs in 7.5, 9.4 and 12.7 seconds respectively – damn quick for nearly two-tonnes of car! Fuel consumption worked out at 20 litres per 100km (14mpg). Apart from the styling issue they enjoyed the Fairlane. Bill Tuckey wrote, "The big aces the Fairlane has going are for it are steering, silence, ride and handling. It really is a quiet car. Even at 144km/h (90mph) not much wind noise is apparent." He liked the accuracy and responsiveness of the Bishop steering system and described the handling as "really quite good." "You can punt the Fairlane across country at 128–144km/h (80–90mph) and it goes where you put

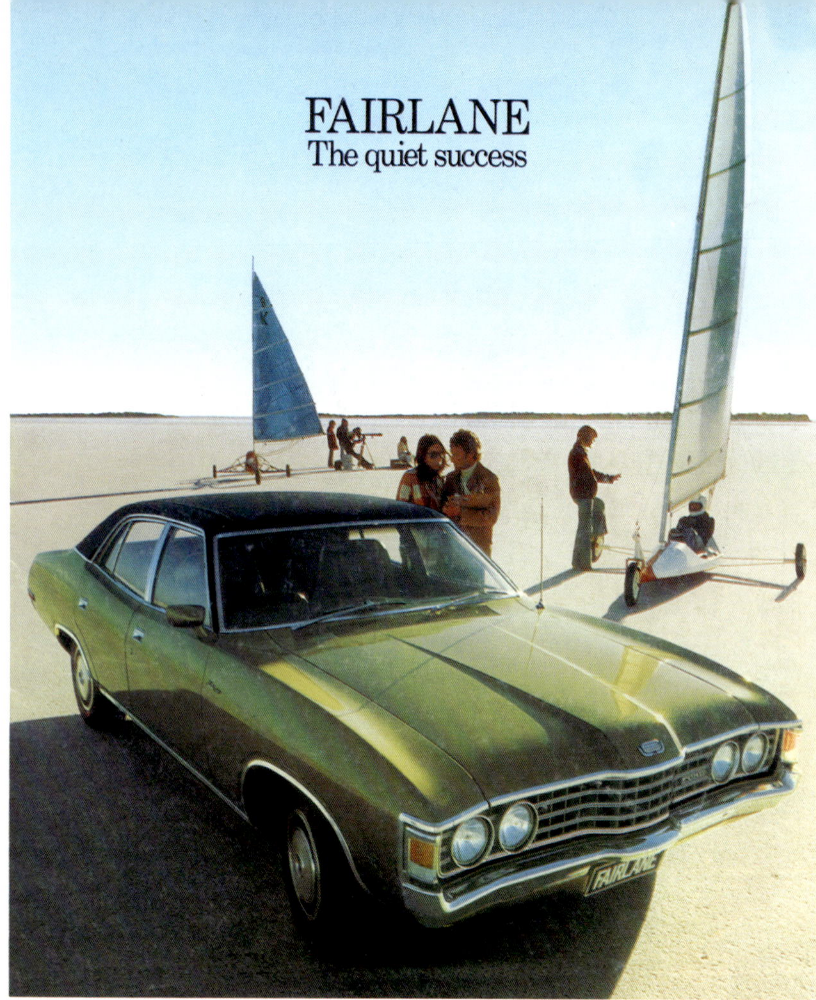

it without drama," he wrote.

Ford released the mildly updated ZG Fairlane in November 1973, most of the changes being cosmetic like the new bold egg-crate grille texture, revised taillight lenses and garnish panel. Inside the most notable new feature was the multi-function column stalk – yes, really-- that incorporated the headlight hi-lo beam facility and the horn.

In July 1975 Ford released its 50th Anniversary models to celebrate half a century of building Ford vehicles in Australia. 500 were built, 250 of them were Fairlanes and the other 250 were LTDs.

The last range using this body, the ZH, arrived in May 1976 and was a much-changed automobile in an effort by Ford to counter the perceived shortcomings of the previous Fairlane that was considered to be too close to the Falcon in styling. The 2946mm (116-ins) wheelbase was retained but overall length now stretched out to 5181mm (204-ins) and kerb weight rose to 1951kgs (3640lbs) for the Fairlane 500 and 117kgs (258lbs) more for the top of the range Marquis (pronounced mar-kee) that was aimed squarely at Holden's Caprice.

Every exterior body panel with the exception of the front doors has been changed; the styling was now big, bold and brassy in many ways and yet there was a degree of conservatism there because most Fairlane buyers apparently were aged over 50. Inside was a new dashboard with a strip speedometer and fake wood trim and in the Marquis the front seats came from the US Thunderbird and according to the guys from *Wheels*

magazine were not as comfortable as the locally designed seats in the less expensive Fairlane 500! Also, the 500's steering wheel was from the Falcon parts bin while that in the Marquis was unique to the model and had a thick-but-soft rim and wide spoke.

The standard power unit for the ZH was Ford's renowned 4.9-litre (302-cid) V8 pumping out 119kW (159bhp) at 4400rpm – the 5.8-litre (351-cid) was optional – and despite the bulk, could propel the big Ford down the road at up to 172km/h (107mph) and sprint from 0–110km/h (0–68mph) in 13.3 seconds. Mind you, the price you paid was a fuel consumption anywhere between 13mpg and 20mpg.

In May 1979 the completely restyled ZJ appeared on Ford showroom floors around the country. The ZJ was based on the new XD Falcon and was styled with the intention that it would look more American than European but in that I do not think the stylists succeeded. It sat on a 2946mm (116-ins) wheelbase and looked for all the world like an elongated Falcon with a third window in each C-pillar. Not long into the life of the ZJ Ford dropped the V8 engine from production, a move that created quite a deal of controversy in the media and the industry. Power for the ZJ then came from the 4.1-litre six-cylinder engine, just like you could order in your Falcon!

LTD

Late in the reign of the ZF, in August 1973, Ford released the LTD sedan and Landau luxury two-door coupe, the sedan carried the designation P5 and the coupe was the P4; both were Bill Bourke's babies. David Ford (no relation) was Ford's Product Planning manager at the time and he tried very hard to dissuade Bourke from building the Landau in particular – "Market research did not support Bourke's views," he told the author – but as with most issues Bourke had his way.

Of Australia's Big Three, only Ford went the long-long wheelbase route above their already successful Fairlane. GM-H stayed with their Statesman-De Ville and Chrysler with their Chrysler by Chrysler. The LTD's wheelbase was stretched out to 3073mm (121-ins) although the Landau retained the Falcon Hardtop's 2819mm (111-ins) wheelbase. Apart from the size of the LTD sedan the most distinguishing feature of both models was their concealed headlights, just like on a Lincoln in the States and in fact the mechanism was sourced from the Mercury Cougar. When the lights were turned on by the driver a vacuum-operated lever system retracted a section of the grille at either side to reveal the quad lights. The P4 Landau and P5 LTD are the only Australian-made cars to have had this feature. Standard equipment on the LTD and Landau included the 5.8-litre (351-cid) V8 engine, automatic gearbox, integrated air conditioning, electric windows and mirrors and just about everything else that could be crammed in. And both came with garish fake spoke wheel trims that showed a complete lack of taste. Early P5s had an ancient floor button dipper switch for hi-lo beam and the single function indicator stalk on the column, and the 'squeeze the rim' horn system taken from the Falcon GT; the LTD also featured that oh-so American idiocy, the foot-operated 'hand brake.'

Inside Ford lavished great efforts on providing occupants with the best they could come up with by way of very comfortable seating, almost perfect climate control and silence. The dashboard used the same padded moulding as the Fairlane but had different instrumentation – in the LTD the driver was faced with a big round speedometer to the right of the cluster, four smaller round dials to the left covering fuel, temperature, volts and oil pressure and a large clock on the far left, all in a faux wood surround.

Modern Motor published a full test of the LTD in its September 1973 issue and headed the test, "Ford's Fabulous Flyer" with the sub-heading "It reeks of luxury, it's under $8000, and it's all-Australian. Ford's new LTD is a high-performance tourer disguised as a luxury limousine." The LTD was compared with the Jaguar XJ6 4.2 and Mercedes-Benz 280E for equipment such as air conditioning with rear ducting – optional on the Jag, not available on the Merc – push button radio (optional), power steering which was an option on the Merc(!), vinyl roof (optional on both), and so it went on. Ford conveniently avoided any comparison with the technical features of the LTD and the two other cars ...

The reality was that a Jaguar or Mercedes-Benz buyer was highly unlikely to shop an LTD despite a $3000-to-$3500 lower price – no, most LTD sales would have come from Fairlane owners stepping up.

And as Wayne Cantell wrote in the test, "To drive it is to pick the message right away – performance!" He went on to say, "The car has a charisma all of its own. Rocketing down a wide straight highway, sweeping through high speed curves or through twisty wet mountain roads, the LTD is beautiful." "And while the performance is great, so are the brakes. The four-wheel discs – fitted for the first time as standard on an Australian produced car – pull the car up in a straight line every time."

With 216kW (290bhp) and 515Nm (380lbs-ft) of torque at the driver's disposal, the 1795kgs (3950lbs) LTD topped out at a remarkable 196.3km/h (122mph) and ran the 0–80 and –96km/h dashes (0–50 and 60mph) in 7.0 and 9.8 seconds respectively; the downside was a fuel consumption rate of 21-litres per 100km (13.5mpg)!

P5 gave way to P6 LTD in September 1976 that was readily identifiable by its mini-Rolls Royce style upright grille; there was no Landau with the P6 as sales did not warrant the expense of producing it. David Ford was vindicated! It was a rather clever update of the LTD as the new front clip not only had the quasi Rolls-Royce grille but the four headlights were now exposed in a new panel that simply bolted on to the front of the original structure. The two outer headlights were 7-inch halogens and the two inner lights were 5.75-inch in size, also halogen which was a pretty big deal in Australia in 1976. At the rear were new taillight units, much smaller than previously and situated either side of the license plate. And those garish wheel trims of the P5 gave way to more sober trims with the LTD insignia in the centre.

As well as the significant exterior changes, there was also a significant change in the interior. Gone was the original cockpit-style dashboard to be replaced by one that featured two equal symmetrical flat areas, one in front of the driver and the other in front of the front seat passenger,

both covered in plastic 'wood.' Where the P5 had lovely clear round dials, the P6 had a less grand-looking and harder to read horizontal speedometer with the minor gauges and switches (lights and wipers) to the left and right of the steering column, with the heater/demister/air conditioning slides below that. At either end were rectangular air vents and in the dash centre were two more rectangular air vents with radio and tape deck below. In the eyes of many Ford aficionados it was regarded as retrograde. New, too, was the inclusion of a multi-function steering column lever – with P6 came turn indicators, headlight dip and flasher all in the one control! This does not sound like much but it was almost a palace revolution as most of the rest of the world's automobile manufacturers had long gone to such convenience.

Mechanically little was different between P5 and P6 and so it retained its storming performance.

In June 1979 Ford released the FC LTD which has been regarded by Ford enthusiasts as the beginning of the end for the LTD. The FC was built on the 2946mm (116-ins) wheelbase of the ZJ Fairlane to which it was related but gradually any differences disappeared including the V8 engine option to be replaced by the 4.1-litre six-cylinder engine.

Both the Fairlane 500 and LTD versions looked for all the world like stretched Falcons with a different grille and taillights plus the third side window incorporated in the C-pillar. To differentiate the Fairlane from the LTD you needed to be a real car spotter. The grille texture was unique to the LTD and consisted of a large number of thin vertical bars set within a chromed frame alongside wide rectangular headlights, smoked glass lens for the wide rear light units plus a fluted panel in the sixth window.

The LTD was very luxuriously equipped as befitted its place in the motoring scene in Australia. Standard equipment included the 5.8-litre V8 engine (until it was phased out), four-wheel disc brakes, larger diameter vacuum brake booster, power steering, electronic ignition, alloy wheels shod with 205/70 Michelin XVS steel radial tyres, dual chromed exhaust pipes and so the extensive list went on and on …

CORTINA

The Mark II Cortina continued until August 1971 when it was replaced by the Mark III, otherwise known as the TC Cortina. The TC was as far away from the original concept of what the Cortina was to make one question the continued use of the same name. Compared with the Mark I, the Mark III was a revolution. However, market research in the UK convinced Ford to keep the Cortina name, so Ford here followed.

What became the TC Cortina in Australia had a quite convoluted upbringing. The badge TC stood for Taunus-Cortina, competing mid-sized Fords from Germany and England. Ford UK had the lead role at a time when Ford was integrating its German and English operations and many experienced people defected to the newly formed British Leyland. To fill the gaps Ford brought many American over and that was a bit like oil on water – the Poms and the Yanks did not gel as a team. Through all of this Ford UK was playing catch-up with Vauxhall and Opel where styling was concerned. The end result was the panel fit on the body was variable to say the least …

Ford UK had embraced the Coke bottle school of styling and at the same time made the car look bigger than before and, indeed, what it really was. At the front was a broad stamped aluminium grille with seven thin bars and a dominant chromed surround, a bold horizontal bar across the centre with the a circular badge denoting what trim level the car was, the company's name being spelt out in separate letters on the leading edge of the bonnet. Flanking the grille were single 7-inch headlight each side, the indicator lenses being small triangles at the lower edge of the front fender; parking light function was incorporated into the headlights. Below the grille was a minimalist (and useless) chromed bumper.

At the rear the bootlid came all the way down to the minimalist (and useless) bumper and at either side were the taillight units that curved around the corner so they were visible from the side. The tail and brake functions were in the red plastic lens (top and bottom) with the indicator (amber) and reversing lights (white) in the centre of the light unit. It was all quite neat and functional without being overstated.

Inside was a large plastic moulding for the dashboard that was divided into two parts – a section that swept up, across and downwards in front of the driver and a matching section in front of the passenger. Three round instrument dials were in front of the driver, one for speed (centre), on the right for fuel, temperature and warning lights while a clock or a tachometer could be fitted to the other. Squeezed above the instrument section directly in front of the driver was the flow-through ventilation outlet which was adjustable for direction – it was about 4-inches wide by less than 1-inch high. In front of the passenger was the large drop-down glove box again with the air vent squeezed into the moulding above it. Controls for the heater/demister and/or air conditioning (when fitted) were in the centre along with space for a radio.

The front passengers sat on tombstone bucket seats with the gearshift (manual and automatic) on the floor with the pull-up handbrake. Those in the back sat on a bench seat, upholstery being reasonable quality vinyl on most models.

Underneath the Mark III (nee TC) was quite different from any Cortina that had gone before. Ford UK it seems was ridding itself of the MacPherson strut front suspension, something it led the world with from 1950. This time there were pressed steel upper-and-lower wishbones with coil springs, telescopic dampers and a stabiliser bar attached to a separate sub-frame; at the rear there was still a live axle but it was now suspended by coil springs and telescopic dampers with trailing links and two lateral control bars on top of the axle housing. Braking was by 9.6-ins discs up front and 9-ins drums at the rear with dual circuits and a vacuum boost. Gearboxes were either a Ford manufactured all-synchromesh four-speed manual or a Borg Warner Type 35 three-speed automatic. And for the first time on a compact Ford, rack and pinion steering was a standard fitting.

Physically the Mark III was bigger than the old Mark II but only fractionally, although it was wider by a significant 101.6mm (4-ins). The wheelbase was 2578mm (101.5-ins), overall length was 4267mm (168-ins), width 1702mm (67-ins), height was 1321mm (52-ins) and the wheel tracks were 1422mm (56-ins) front and rear, the widest in its class. Kerb weight was 989kgs (2176lbs) for the 1600 version, another 30kgs (66lbs) for the two-litre.

At first two four-cylinder engines were offered – the 1600cc Cross-Flow from the Mark II and the rather hoary Pinto 2-litre SOHC unit. Both units had a cast iron cylinder block and head with a five main bearing crank each, pushrod operated overhead valves in the 1600 – 80.77 x 77.5mm for 1598cc – while in the Pinto unit the single overhead camshaft was driven by a toothed rubber belt. Its cylinder dimensions were 90.42 x 76.7mm for 1998cc – and on a 9.2:1 compression and using a single Autolite two-barrel carburettor it developed 83.5kW (112bhp) at 6000rpm, and 165Nm (122lbs-ft) of torque at 3500rpm. Compared with the latest SOHC engines from the various Japanese manufacturers the new Ford unit lacked refinement, smoothness and to some extent power. The 1600 developed 58kW (78bhp) at 5700rpm and 127Nm (94lbs-ft) of torque at 2600rpm using a single barrel carburettor; it was discontinued in June 1973.

Wheels tested a 2-litre XL GS in its November 1971 issue and opened with "If it wasn't for the low price tag and Ford badges you'd swear the Cortina 2000 was another of those very pleasant, but expensive, middle-class European sports sedans. The size is right and so is the performance, accommodation and styling." Not a bad start to a road test of a car that was very important to Ford's future in Australia.

Performance was strong, the *Wheels* guys achieving a top speed of 175.2km/h (109.5mph) and dashed off the 0–80 and –96km/h (0–50 and 60mph) runs in 7.8 and 10.3 seconds respectively with in-gear maxima of 51km/h (32mph) in first, 94km/h (59mph) in second and 137km/h (86mph) in third, overall fuel economy was in the 11.8–10 litres per 100km (24–28mpg) range which was pretty good for a sedan weighing in at 1025kgs (2260lbs).

Wheels tested a base 1600L in it February 1972 issue and wrote, "The 1600L is a well-balanced, good looking and pleasant light sedan, but paying the extra $85 for the bigger engine gets you performance that is scintillating rather than mundane, big car smoothness rather than strain plus wider wheels and power-assisted discs. It's hard to justify NOT paying the higher price." The 1600 achieved a top speed of 90mph and

a 0–80km/h time of 13.5 seconds while returning 11 litres per 100km (26mpg). You can see why the recommendation was to go for the 2000 model.

With Holden raking in sales with its six-cylinder compact Torana it was obvious to all that Ford would follow, it was just a matter of how and when. The Mark II body was unsuitable but the TC had the right ingredients for the company to enter this new segment albeit nearly four years after Holden had created it!

The recipe was relatively simple: take the TC body, strengthen the front underbody and bulkhead and then squeeze either one of the Falcon's six-cylinder engines in the available space. It must be said that the Falcon 200- and 250-cid engines fitted but there was precious little working room around them. In September 1972 Ford released the six-cylinder versions of the TC to some acclaim from the media. They were fairly easily recognised because they had dual 5-ins headlights each side of the same grille and they had a unique bonnet pressing with a hump to clear the engine and on the fender sides were badges denoting either the 200 or 250 six-cylinder engine. It was marketed in two trim levels – L and XL with the XLE following with the release of the six-cylinder versions – to be replaced later by the Ghia.

To accommodate the physically large and heavy six-cylinder engines Ford had to strengthen the Cortina's body structure, particularly at the front where the side rails were reinforced and there was a tubular cross-member under the gearbox plus the bulkhead and transmission tunnel were reshaped, enlarged in size and made from thicker steel. For manufacturing economies the same stronger body was used for both four- and six-cylinder Cortinas. Other engineering changes included a cross-flow radiator for the Six versus a down-flow radiator in the Four and it was mounted three-inches further forward, the four-speed manual gearbox was straight from the Falcon GT, the brake master cylinder was a Falcon part, the steering ball studs were forged instead of case hardened, the engine sump on the Sixes was different to clear the front cross-member, spring rates were slightly different to account for the 50kgs (110lbs) greater weight of the Sixes. Many sundry, minor items were sourced from the Falcon parts bin to keep costs down.

FORD
CORTINA

Apart from the style of the body and the two four-cylinder engines the local Cortina was uniquely Australian.

Wheels published a great report on two Cortina Sixes in the December 1972 issue. One was powered by the 200-engine driving through a three-speed manual gearbox and the other had the 250-engine and four-speed manual gearbox. The team loved the size, accommodation, quietness and the whole concept and stated quite clearly that Ford's solution to the compact six-cylinder market was far superior to the Torana from Holden.

As for performance, both cars gave a good account of themselves. The 200 Cortina ran to 171km/h (107mph), the 250 to 182km/h (114mph), the slight difference being due to the 2.92 rear axle ratio in the 200 and a higher 2.76:1 in the 250. 0–80 and –96km/h (0–50 and 60mph) times were 8.7 and 11.7 seconds for the 200, 7.9 and 11.0 seconds for the 250 so they were pretty quick by the standards of the day. They were inclined to be thirsty, though … which means the 55-litre (12-gallon) tank limited how far you drove before having to fill up again.

Despite the gloss there were some fundamental underlying issues that no amount of warranty work could fix. Whilst the new front suspension looked good on paper its wheel travel was very limited allowing the front end to bottom out on relatively minor road irregularities and the geometry of the front end was such that if the wheels hit two different surfaces simultaneously the steering wheel could be wrenched from the driver's hands. And particularly when the six-cylinder engine was fitted, the front cross member and pressed steel wishbones were barely adequate. Water and dust entry were also a problem created by ill-fitting doors and boot lid.

The TC was followed by the TD in December 1974 and was little more than a running change that included a new plastic grille now with square headlights either end, revised dashboard and instruments, new exhaust system, improved seating and an articulated wiper arm for the driver's side arm.

Modern Motor published an intriguing three-car comparison test in its July 1975 issue between a TD Cortina 2000, Torana 1900 and Centura 2000. Ford would not have been pleased with the outcome as the Centura romped away with the chocolates in virtually every aspect of the comparison. The Cortina did win plaudits for its superb four-speed manual gearbox and its slick gearshift and its control layout for the driver was deemed best of the three.

A more dramatic change came with the TE announced July 1977. Stung by media criticisms – justified – Ford set to and thoroughly reworked the whole package. This time the British designers and engineers had very little input into the TE. Styling, for example, was carried out under the supervision of Uwe Bahnsen in Cologne, Germany, and this style was adopted by the UK production people as a part of the unification of the two European branches of the Ford business. The TE was still recognisably a Cortina (or a Taunus) but it no longer featured the kick-up over the rear wheels to give that Coke bottle effect that was so popular a few years previously. This time the body hip line was virtually straight. The 'face' of the TE was all about rectangles – the grille was a simple plastic rectangle lying on its side with a single Ford badge in the centre flanked either side by rectangular headlights and squeezed in at the extremities were the amber indicator lenses. A strong character line half way down the door skins gave rigidity to the panels as well as providing a styling element. At the rear were taillights of a very similar design to its predecessor. Inside were better seats with integral head restraints and a reworked dashboard with three large round dials in front of the driver, heater/demister/air conditioning controls in the centre plus a slot for a radio/audio system.

In the August 1977 issue of *Wheels* magazine, the team published an article headed "A Cortina The Engineers Like." A rather telling headline. They told the story of how, out of the $16 million allocated to the TE program, a massive $5 million was spent on the suspension development alone. Intriguingly, the suspension *looked* the same as before but in its geometry it was quite different. To improve the durability of the front end Ford straightened the body longitudinal members and welded the cross member to them rather than use rubber bushes and the brake reaction struts were relocated behind the suspension whereas in the TC and TD they were mounted forward of the suspension. At the rear Ford opted for variable rate coil springs with longer travel than before.

Compared with the TD, the TE was 212mm longer and 88mm wider with side door intrusion beams, more sound proofing and a rear cross member which made it 30kgs heavier. The sound deadening might have made the car's interior slightly quieter in which to ride but it did nothing to stop the enormous amount of heat soak that entered the cabin on hot days from the exhaust system that ran along the central tunnel. The luggage compartment floor, too, could get very warm from radiated heat from the large muffler under the floor. On a hot day the air conditioning system would really struggle to cool the car interior so great was the heat soak. And the Cortina still had an appetite for tyres and front disc pads due to the weight over the front wheels.

The final iteration of this theme came with the TF announced in October 1980. Many critics believed the TF was what the TC should have been from the beginning. Here was a car worthy of its position and for Ford to promote in the marketplace. Why had it taken so long? It was better made as a TE and TF than the original TC and TD but Ford could not disguise the fact that this was a car designed around a four-cylinder engine and in its home territory if buyers wanted more power and more performance Ford could fit a 2.5- or 3.0-litre V6 engine that was both lighter and more compact than the huge Falcon six-cylinder engines the local engineers were working with.

ESCORT

The Escort was a rather belated replacement for the popular 105E Anglia. I say belated because there was a gap of several years between the demise of the Anglia and the arrival of the Escort here in Australia although this was not the case in England. Not that Ford dealers were concerned because they were busy selling Cortinas, Falcons and Fairlanes.

Although released in the UK in February 1968, the Escort did not arrive in Australia until two years later where it was committed to the 85 per cent local content plan with assembly taking place at the company's re-equipped Homebush plant in Sydney.

The Escort came after the Mark II Cortina in the scheme of events at Ford's Dagenham styling studios but none of the neatness of that design seemed to washed off onto it. Its styling could not have been more basic if they had tried – it was totally nondescript to the point where it made some of the bland offerings from Japan Inc seem interesting! At the front was a dog's bone-like stamped aluminium horizontal grille with four slats and single square headlights each end, rectangular orange indicator lens between the lights and the flimsy chromed bumper. At the back was another flimsy bumper with small rectangular (white) reversing lights above it and then small taillight units above that in a plain rear valance panel. In between were curved panels with cut-outs for windows and doors as required and a faint character line along each side that stylistically 'joined' the headlights to the taillights.

In the UK the range was vast offering buyers the choice of a 2-door or 4-door body or 3-door wagon and panel van multiplied by the choice of 1100 or 1300 engines and a special DOHC unit for the Escort Twin Cam. For Australia the wagon was unavailable but we saw the rest of the range with either standard or Super interior trim. This put it right in the middle of the field competing with the Datsun 1200, Toyota Corolla, Mazda 1300, Mitsubishi Galant, Morris 1500 and the ubiquitous VW Beetle. The Standard was just that, a bare car with little by way of equipment at an economy price of $1770; the Super (by far the biggest seller and priced from $1920) had a heater/demister with fan, floor carpets, mock wood finish on the dash, cigarette lighter and chrome wheel trims. The GT at $2350 not only had more power but better contoured seats, floor console around the gearshift, two-speed wipers, torque rod on the rear axle and full instrumentation – speedo, tacho, fuel, oil pressure, volts and temperature – in a wider instrument binnacle. In the upper-centre of the dash were two large round adjustable air vents for cabin ventilation.

Physically the Escort was bigger than the Anglia but smaller than the Cortina so it dovetailed in nicely in the UK, but was the smallest offering by Ford here. It sat on a 2400mm (94.5-ins) wheelbase, was 4045mm (156-ins) overall by 1570mm (62-ins) wide and 1486mm (58-ins) tall and weighed 767kgs (1690lbs) in 2-door saloon form. Base models were powered by the 1098cc (80.98 x 53.3mm bore and stroke) cross-flow OHV Kent engine developing 30kW (40bhp) while the 1298cc (80.98 x 62.99mm) cross-flow OHV engine developed 36kW (48bhp) and the 1300GT developed 47kW (63bhp) using a higher compression ratio and a Weber twin-throat carburettor; both the 1300 engines now had a five-bearing crankshaft and a 'bowl in piston' combustion chamber, the actual cylinder head facing being completely flat. The cylinder block and head were cast in iron and pushrods operated the valves via rockers. At the top of the range (from late 1970, at $3000) was the Escort Twin Cam that featured a 1558cc (82.55 x 72.75mm) double overhead camshaft four-cylinder engine that had originally been developed by Lotus for the Elan sports car and the Cortina-Lotus sedan. Power for this limited-edition model was 115bhp at 6000rpm which gave it staggering acceleration for such a family car for the day. *Wheels*, for example, tested an example and recorded times of 8.5 and 11.5 seconds for the 0–96 and 112/km/h (0–60 and 70mph) sprints with in-gear maxima of 61km/h, 93km/h, 136km/h and 168km/h (38mph, 58mph, 85mph and 105mph) all at the 6500rpm limit. However, as the report said, the fit and finish left much to be desired and in conclusion opined that it would make an excellent rally car!

Power for all versions went to the rear wheels via a slick four-speed all synchromesh gearbox with a snappy floor gearshift. A first for Ford was the use of a rack and pinion steering system!

Selling against the Holden Torana, BMC Mini and 1500 plus a horde of Japanese cars the Escort managed to carve out a sizeable niche for itself mainly through Ford's marketing muscle rather than any intrinsic excellence in the product. Quality issues blighted the car throughout its five-year life cycle because the body engineers in the UK did not work to the same engineering standards (it was *always* a cost issue at Ford) as their Japanese rivals in particular – nothing fitted quite as well with the Escort as with any of the Japanese cars. And nor could it compete with the Japanese when it came to interior fittings – even in Super trim it was comparatively bare when compared with a Mazda 1300, Toyota Corolla or Mitsubishi Galant, for example. Inside the plainness continued with a dash panel that was inoffensive to view, having a raised binnacle directly in front of the drive that housed two large round Smiths dials, speedometer on the left, combination meter on the right with two round, adjustable air vents in the centre and heater/demister in the middle of the facing panel; if a radio was ordered it was fitted below the dash between the steering column and the door! Unreachable and amazing! Front seat passengers sat on bucket seats, those in back sat on a flat bench and the floor was covered with plastic-rubber mats unless otherwise specified.

However, in its time it was a fierce competitor for sales and was as conventional in its design as the various Japanese models, that is, front engine-rear wheel drive, independent front suspension by MacPherson struts and coil springs, live rear axle held up by semi-elliptic leaf springs, and disc/drum braking system. It was a formula well known to Ford people.

A minor realignment of fittings came along in November 1971 when the Twin Cam was discontinued, the GT was uprated to the 1600cc engine from the Cortina GT plus a radio and a clock were standard fittings. All models now had high back front seats and on the XL the front seats reclined.

Wheels magazine, (July 1970) for example, carried out a full comparison test between the Escort 1300, Mazda 1300, Corolla and Datsun 1200 generally rated the Escort last of the quartet in some aspects – performance, accommodation, finish and equipment, the Escort lacking a glove box, four-way hazard flashers, no reversing lights, single-speed wipers, no headlight flasher for example – but they rated it highly in driving, gearshift, handling and luggage capacity. Performance-wise, it was the slowest of the four by quite some margin, taking 13.1 seconds for the 0–80km/h (0–50mph) dash versus a Corolla's 10.1 seconds.

Perhaps that would explain its comparatively poor results in its class at the annual Bathurst race, Class A being dominated by the Datsuns and Mazdas.

In March 1975 Ford announced the second-generation Escort in

RS 2000

Australia. While recognisably an Escort, it was a much cleaner and attractive design inside and out and was largely the work of the German design centre led by Uwe Bahnsen. Essentially, however, it was really a new suit of clothes over virtually the same mechanical components.

What was very noticeable was the much better fit and alignment of the doors, bonnet and boot lid plus the better-quality materials in the interior. The Escort II was, in fact, a far better product. It needed to be if Ford was going to be competitive in the local (indeed, the world) small car market.

Initially power was provided by carry-over 48kW (65bhp) 1300 for the L and XL versions with the 63kW (83bhp) 1600 OHV cross-flow engine reserved for the Ghia. Again, 2- and 4-door bodies were available along with the superb 4-speed manual and 3-speed automatic gearboxes. Prices ranged from $3430 through to $4420. Ford had learned from the Japanese insofar as the Escort came as standard with radial tyres, radio, halogen headlights, rear window demister as well as a good heater/demister with fan boost. Inside were better seats and a far more attractive and ergonomic dashboard that followed the Mark I in style with a wide binnacle in front of the driver with the large speedo to the right and the large combination dial to the left with various warning lights in between. In many ways it reminded me of the binnacle fitted to the large BMW sedans …

Wheels pitched the Escort II against the Holden Gemini, Mazda Capella and Mitsubishi Galant in its February 1976 issue and the resulting article was not good for Ford. The problem was under the bonnet where Ford continued with the 1300cc Kent engine in a car that was slightly bigger and heavier than before where the other three contenders all had 1600cc SOHC engines. So, while the Escort might have had competitive equipment levels, good road dynamics, excellent steering and brakes, against the stop watch it was s-l-o-w! For example, its 0–100km/h (0–62mph) sprint took 27.5 seconds versus 16.1 seconds for the Gemini, 18.3 seconds for the Galant and 19.6 seconds for the Capella. Top speed was 142km/h (88mph) for the Escort and 150km/h (93mph) for the Capella and 152km/h (94mph) for the other two.

To improve the car's competitiveness against particularly its Japanese rivals Ford substituted the 1599cc cross-flow OHV engine in place of the 1298cc unit in late 1976. This move was also predicated by the first of the local emission requirements, ADR27A, but despite claims from Ford the Escort's performance continued to be below par; only its consumption of fuel increased.

Inevitably during 1977 Ford offered the Escort with a slightly detuned version of the 2-litre SOHC 'Pinto' engine it was using in the Cortina. In Escort tune it produced 70kW (94bhp) for the manual and 64kW (85bhp) for use with automatics. Interestingly, the Australian 2-litre engine was certified by Ford in Sweden because their emission standards mirrored ours. Model nomenclature was changed at this time to L and GL (replaced XL) with the top model again (or still) being the Ghia.

In a further marketing effort to attract younger buyers in 1979 Ford Australia created their own take on the RS2000. It featured a four-headlight grille with a sloping nose and body stripes and under the bonnet was a much-uprated version of the SOHC 2-litre engine. Using a twin-choke Weber carburettor, 9.2:1 compression and a less restricted exhaust system owners now had 82kW (110bhp) to play with. Performance was class-leading now at 177.6km/h (111mph) top speed with the standing 400 metres taking 16.8 seconds.

The RS2000 did achieve the odd class win at Bathurst so while it might not have had a stellar race circuit career both the Mark I and Mark II Escorts were a huge success in rallies winning many championships around the world as well as here in Australia.

Market forces were by now catching up with the Escort in Australia and elsewhere in the world. In Europe Ford developed a completely new model with transverse engines, front-wheel drive and a fully independent suspension system but it was for Europe only although a much-modified version was sold in the US, however.

In Australia, Ford had developed a relationship with the Mazda Motor Corporation in Hiroshima, Japan, and in 1980 began manufacturing and selling a mildly modified version of Mazda's popular 323 known locally as the Ford Laser as a hatch and the Meteor as the sedan. However, that is a story for another time and place.

HER ONLY MISTAKE
HER ONLY MISTAKE
HER ONLY MISTAKE
ESCORT

CAPRI

With the huge success of the Mustang in America it was no surprise to any industry observer that Ford Europe would follow the same path by developing a long hood-short deck stylish coupe off the Cortina platform. And so it happened with the release of the Ford Capri at the Brussels Motor Show in January 1969 to enormous acclaim. As their advertising by-line said, "This is the Car You Promised Yourself."

Initially the project was called Colt within Ford (like in mustang …) but Mitsubishi owned the world-wide rights to that name so Ford once again went to Italy for the name Capri. Because the roads in the UK (and much of Europe) are considerably narrower than in the USA, the Capri was significantly smaller than the Mustang but that did not hamper its success.

For the time in the UK, the Capri was quite a stunning-looking car. No competitor had anything comparable which in a way helped its success. The styling was rather plain in many ways with its long bonnet carrying the name F-O-R-D up front and sloping down to a very plain and narrow grille with seven horizontal chromed bars and a small square headlight each end, the indicators and park lights being incorporated into their outer edges. The fender line swept back to a very short rear end with the almost flat rear window sunk between small sail panels each side. A slightly recessed rear panel was picked out by a chromed piece, the taillights being taken from the sister Escort to save money. In front of the rear wheel arch each side were fake air vents to give the car some character while sweeping forward from behind the rear wheel arch was a broad character line to give the body panels some rigidity. Overall, it was a neat and interesting package for its time.

Despite it sleek two-door body style the Capri was a genuine four-seater albeit with a much-reduced luggage capacity.

Under the long (for England) bonnet were several engine options for UK buyers, from 1300 and 1600 OHV Kent engines to the lusty 3-litre V6 Essex engine. Here in Australia we had but three choices – from Capri 1600, Capri 1600GT and Capri V6 GT. For all three, the engine/gearbox assembly came out from the UK already built-up, the bodies came out as CKD kits for assembly in the Homebush factory in Sydney. Local content was in the region of 60 per cent and consisted mainly of glass, interior trim items, carpet, tyres and paint.

In developing the Capri, the UK engineers raided their corporate parts bin quite successfully. With minor modifications the front suspension was Cortina Mk II, as was the rear axle although the semi-elliptic leaf spring suspension was Capri-only, the rack and pinion steering was from the Escort and the four-cylinder engines were in production for the Escort and Cortina and the V6 engine and gearbox come from the Zephyr/Zodiac range.

As mentioned, the Capri was based on the existing Cortina Mk II underbody with minor alterations to suit the new application. The wheelbase was 2560mm (100.8-ins) with the overall length being 4267mm (168-ins), body width 1646mm (64.8-ins), height 1288mm (50.7-ins), kerb weight was 1077kgs (2370lbs) for the V6 GT, slightly less for the four-cylinder versions Inside there was seating for four, reclining and fold-forward buckets in front, bench in the rear, carpets on the floor, armrests on both doors and a reasonable heater/demister with fan boost.

A broad dashboard faced the driver with a full set of Smiths dials in front – large speedometer on the left, matching tachometer on the right with four smaller dials for fuel, temperature, oil pressure and amps ranged two each side, one above the other. To the left, in the centre, were the slides for the heater/demister and some warning lights, switches for ignition, wipers and lights behind the steering wheel. The column stalk on the right handled indicators-flash-main beam-and horn. Neat.

The two four-cylinder Capris were released first, in May 1969 with the sporty one badged as the GT and powered by the revised 1599cc OHV cross-flow Kent engine. *Wheels* published a comparison test between the Capri GT and a Torana GTR in its February 1970 issue and found the GT to be a bit of a surprise package seeing as how it had only 1599cc under the bonnet. They timed it at 99mph flat chat versus 105mph for the Torana, got a 0–80km/h (0–50mph) time of 8.6 seconds versus 7.5 seconds but found that it was just as quick point-to-point because of its superior balance and lighter weight.

In February 1970 Ford realigned the range by renaming the plain Capri as the Deluxe and the GT became the XL – it was a badging exercise only. The GT badge was now applied to the new V6 version, the Capri V6 GT. Externally the only clues were the Rostyle wheels shod with 175 x 13 radial tyres, a black body stripe running parallel to the character line and a blacked-out bonnet with a slight bulge to clear the air cleaner plus the 3000 V6 badge on each fender. A real wolf in sheep's clothing. And indeed, it proved to be. *Modern Motor* tested one (May 1970) and came away mightily impressed with its storming performance but disappointed by the poor finish and attention to details during the assembly process, something that seemed to afflict Ford cars at the time.

Against the clock the V6 ran to 179.2km/h (112mph), sprinted from 0–96 and 112km/h (0–60 and 70mph) in 10.1 and 13.9 seconds respectively and ran the quarter mile in 17.2 seconds; in-gear maxima were 54km/h (34mph), 85km/h (53mph) and 136km/h (85mph). By comparison, *Wheels* recorded a maximum speed of 183km/h (114mph) at 5600rpm with 63km/h, 90km/h and 141km/h (39, 56 and 88mph) at 6000rpm; they also recorded fractionally quicker acceleration times. Both testers commented on the poor choice of ratios for first and second gears.

With the extremely compact V6 engine positioned up against the bulkhead weight distribution was very little changed from the 1600 but some of the service ancillaries were hard to get at; the big benefit was in handling, the *MM* tester writing, "The V6 is an impressively responsive car, and initially at least gives the driver the impression of a track-bred racer." He described its road behaviour as well-balanced with neutral steering, with excellent brakes. Against the Torana GTR, he opined, the Capri V6 would do very well.

As events unfolded, Ford Australia rather quickly lost interest in the Capri and discontinued assembly of it in April 1973.

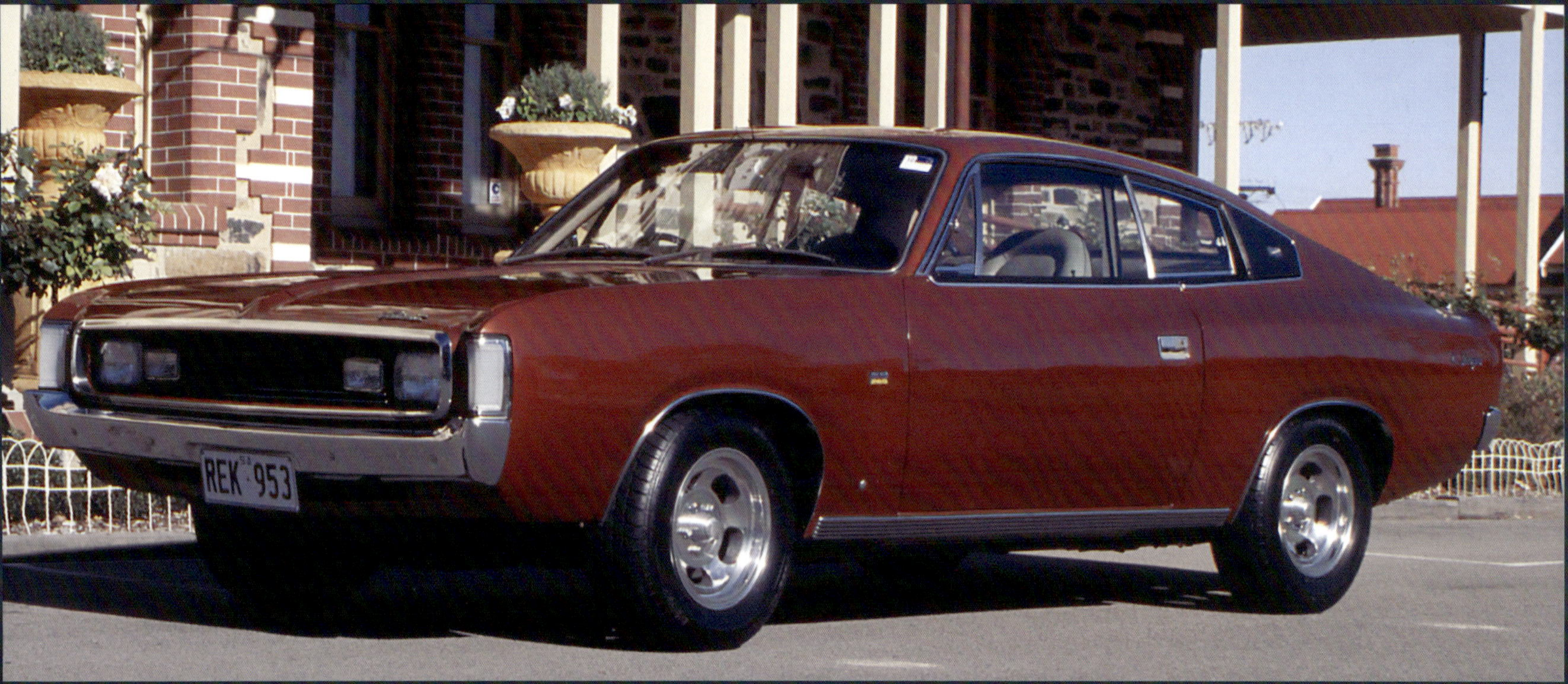
REK 953

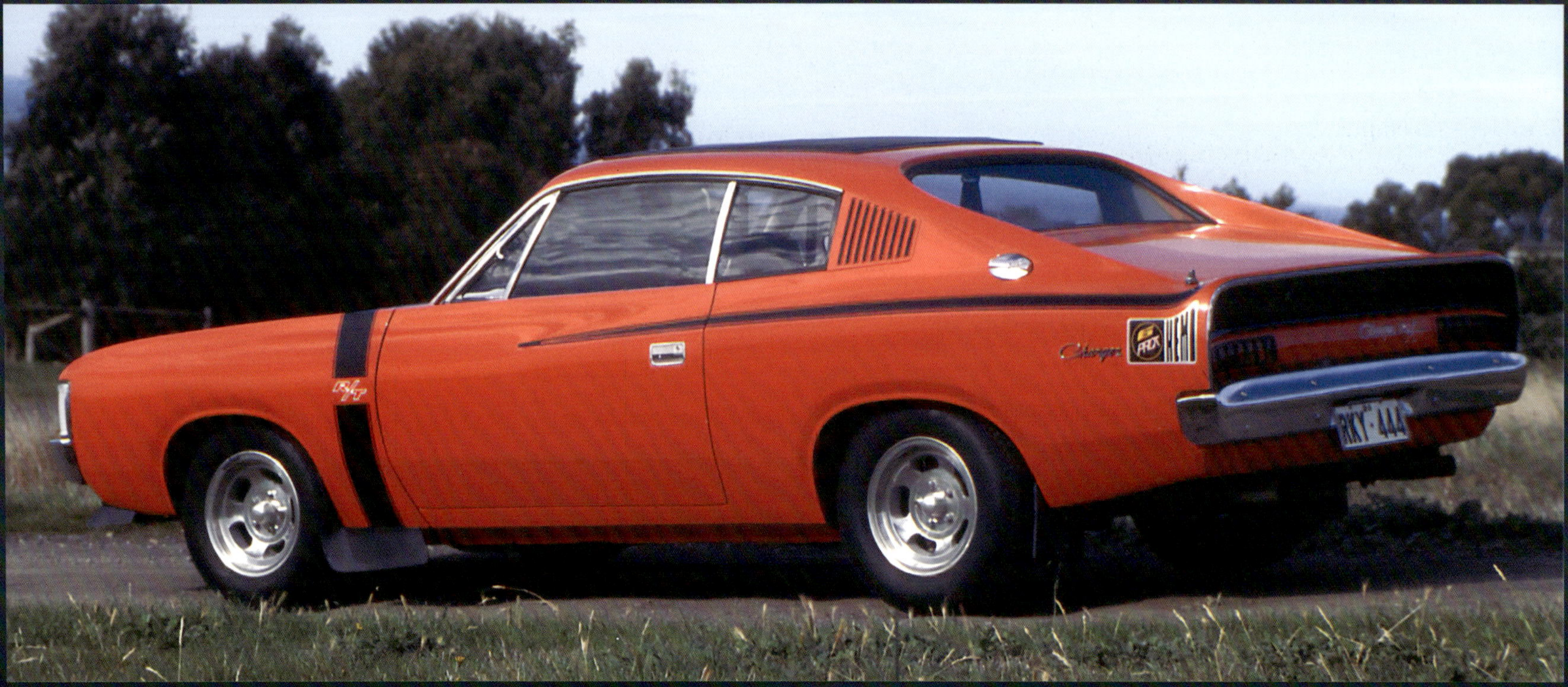
Charger
HEMI
RKY 444

CHAPTER 3

CHRYSLER

Chrysler began the Seventies with some confidence and deservedly so. The company had recently opened its new engine manufacturing facility at Lonsdale, south of Adelaide, and the reception from the media where the new upright OHV six-cylinder D engine was concerned was extremely positive. Having Stirling Moss as the front man for their advertising campaign did them no harm either – remember him drawing diagrams in the sand on a beach? And the slogan, "Valiant, the Right Cars for All the Right Reasons."

In March the company released the VG series Valiants comprising sedans, wagons, utility and hardtop plus the long wheelbase VIP by Chrysler – it definitely was NOT a Valiant in the eyes of the marketing people! The major difference between the preceding VF series and VG was under the bonnet. Gone was the much admired RG slant six and in its place was the new D engine, known as the Hemi but in truth it was no such thing. What it was, was a well-designed upright six-cylinder engine with hydraulic tappets and the valves splayed at just 14 degrees included angle *along* the centreline of the engine to improve the combustion chamber shape. The D engine was manufactured in the state-of-the-art Lonsdale factory using thin-wall casting techniques that made it around 20kgs (42lbs) lighter than the previous engine. It also had a seven main bearing cast iron crankshaft supported by large bearings with a harmonic balancer on the front of the shaft to ensure smoothness of operation.

Interestingly, Chrysler had opted to locally manufacture a completely new six-cylinder engine (rather than the old RG) to comply with the Federal Government's Plan A requirements where GM-Holden went the V8 route. Ford remained faithful to their development and evolution of the original Falcon six-cylinder engine along with small-scale manufacturing of its V8s to satisfy local demand.

Externally the VG was identified by the rectangular headlights in the new grille and square(ish) taillights that curved around the corner of the rear quarter panels. The grille pattern comprised fine horizontal bars – 10 of them – with a bold surround, and the difficult-to-see parking/indicator lights on the upper forward slope of the front fender were retained despite misgivings from the New South Wales Department of Transport at the time.

Initially Chrysler offered the new D engine in one capacity only – 245-cid achieved from a cylinder bore of 96mm by stroke of 93mm for a capacity of 4014cc. Running a high 9.5 compression ratio and using a single-barrel Carter carburettor made under license by Email in Sydney, the engine developed 123kW (165bhp) at 4400rpm and 318Nm (235lbs-ft) of torque at 1800rpm. There were two engine options, both for the sporting Pacer sedan. The first, the E31, had a twin-throat Carter carburettor that added 15kW (20bhp) and 7Nm (5lbs-ft) of torque while the second was the E34 option that had a different camshaft, a Carter four-barrel carburettor and dual exhaust system and developed 157kW (211bhp) at 4500rpm and 321Nm (237lbs-ft) of torque at 2500rpm. A further option offered in the range (but not for the Pacer) was the respected small block V8 at 318-cid capacity that offered 171kW (230bhp) at 4400rpm and 461Nm (340lbs-ft) of torque at 2400rpm.

Naturally the Valiant was rear-wheel drive, the engine's power going through either an all-synchromesh three-speed manual gearbox with a column gearshift lever – only the Pacer versions had the floor shift – or a three-speed automatic with a column selector for certain models, floor selector for higher-spec models like the Regal and VIP. At the rear was an industry-standard locally made (by Borg Warner) live axle suspended by long semi-elliptic leaf springs. Up front were wishbones and Chrysler's famous torsion bars. The standard braking system offered was by four-wheel cast iron drums of only 228mm (9-ins) diameter with 157.9 square inches of lining area. An option that most people took was for the 279mm (11-inch) ventilated disc front brakes.

The VG series Valiants had a comparatively short production life – it has been suggested that VG was an interim model to buy Chrysler time while it readied the VH for production, its release being in June 1971. VH was a completely new body over the existing mechanical components. It was a bigger car styled primarily by Bob Hubbach with support from local stylist Brian Smyth who spent time at Highland Park in Detroit working on it. Our Valiant was something of a crossbreed in US terms because it was larger than a normal Chrysler B-bodied car and yet smaller than a C-bodied, a little like a B-and-a-half! It rode a 2819mm (111-ins) wheelbase (same as Holden and Ford now) and stretched 4894mm (192.7–ins) overall by 1885mm (74.2–ins) wide and 1407mm (55.4–ins) high making it line ball in length with the P76 and 127mm (5-ins) longer than the Kingswood and Falcon; the other three were an inch narrower and practically the same height. As for kerb weight, the Valiant Ranger (the base model and therefore the lightest) weighed in at 1418kgs (3120lbs), the Falcon 500 at 1409kgs (3100lbs), Kingswood at 1340kgs (2950lbs) and the P76 at just 1282kgs (2820lbs) regardless of whether it had the six or V8 engine under the bonnet. In one fell swoop the Valiant had gone from lean and clean to a porker!

VH was characterised by what can only be described as bulky-looking styling that was intended to make it *look* large – typically American thinking at the time – and was influenced by the corporate 'fuselage' styling that ran rampant through Chrysler's Detroit studios at the time. To US executives it undoubtedly succeeded in doing what it did to US tastes but Australian buyers, and the media, were less than impressed. Compared with the squareish design of the VG with its large areas of glass, and hence superb visibility, VH was the exact opposite – you sat low on poorly designed seats with the window area very much reduced and the belt line was so high some drivers (physically short ones!) could hardly see over the dash!

As before, VH was available in a wide variety of models and options

– as a Ranger (new name) sedan in various levels of specification from basic Valiant with the new D engine in either 215-cid, 245-cid or 265-cid and three-speed manual gearbox with column shift, drum brakes all round, bench seats and little else – it was a real poverty pack like the Belmont from Holden and plain Falcon from Ford, with prices starting from $2895. Then came the Valiant Ranger XL from $3420 that had more features but it really was a matter of ticking boxes on the order form for either of the three six-cylinder engine options, 318-cid V8, manual or automatic gearbox, drum or disc front brakes and so on; next up the line was the Valiant Regal that had large round dials in front of the driver set in a wood-grained panel, an electric clock, heater/demister (air conditioning was optional), bucket front seats with high backs incorporating head restraints, centre console, centre armrest in the back, brocade upholstery, floor carpets, padded fully upholstered door panels with a carpet kick panel at the bottom and power assisted front disc brakes were standard. Prices for the Regal started at $3685 with the 245-cid engine through to $4125 for the V8 wagon. Above the Regal was the Regal 770 that had a sporting overtone and was distinguished from lesser Valiants by quartz halogen driving lights inset into the grille alongside the square headlights, bumper over-riders at the rear but not at the front(!), sports steel wheels 6.5J x 14 with 185SR 14 radial tyres, front anti-roll bar while inside the upholstery was special to the 770 and the automatic selector was in the centre floor console regardless of whether the high performance 265-cid engine or the 318-cid V8 was ordered. Pricing for the 265 models was from $3885 and for the V8 from $4015.

New with VH were wider wheel rims – 5.5J x 14 on six-cylinder models and 6.5J x 14 on Regal 770 (V8) and Pacer sedan plus the hand brake was placed to the right of the driver between the seat and the sill. The extended family of six-cylinder engines offered buyers more choice, the 215-cid unit (89 x 93mm, 3522cc) developing 104kW (140bhp) at 4400rpm and 271Nm (200lbs-ft) of torque at 1800rpm on an 8.0:1 compression and using a tiny single barrel downdraft Carter-type carburettor. The 245-cid unit remained unchanged from VG and the new 265-cid unit (99 x 93mm, 4345cc) developed 151kW (203bhp) at 4800rpm and 362Nm (262lbs-ft) of torque at 2000rpm on a 9.5:1 compression and with a two-barrel downdraft carburettor. The 318-cid V8 continued with 171kW (230bhp) and 461Nm (340lbs-ft). Intriguingly, to the casual eye it would seem that the differences between the six-cylinder engines was only their bore diameter but looks can deceive – during the casting process the bore cores were repositioned so that there were cooling passages around each cylinder and a consistent wall thickness was retained.

An integral part of the VH family at the release was the Pacer sports sedan which was visually distinguished by the black decals along each side and over the boot lid as well as three red bars in the grille and vented sports wheels, and inside was a neat instrument pack that included matching round speedometer and tachometer flanked by fuel, temperature and volts gauges with front tombstone bucket seats standard along with a floor gearshift lever. Chrysler described it as "one of the most strikingly beautiful cars of the sporting type anywhere." To reinforce that hype the Pacer had its own version of the 265-cid engine that developed 162kW (218bhp) at 4800rpm and 370Nm (273lbs-ft) of torque at 3000rpm, the three-speed manual gearbox had its own ratios, a heavy duty clutch, front anti-roll bar, 185SR 14 tyres and a Sure Grip differential with pre-loaded friction cones and a ratio of 3.23:1. Pacers sold for a very reasonable $3235 which made them exciting value for money.

The October 1971 issue of *Wheels* carried a three-car comparison test of the Holden Kingswood versus the Ford Falcon versus the Chrysler Valiant. It was 202 manual against a 250 manual and a 245 manual respectively; 100kW (135bhp) versus 115kW (155bhp) versus 123kW (165bhp); new HQ body versus old XY Falcon body versus the new VH body Valiant so it was not entirely apples versus apples.

Body styling was a contentious issue, the *Wheels'* guys liking the HQ over the VH which they opined was styled 'to look big' which it did successfully although at the expense of visibility compared with the HQ and, indeed, the VG Valiant. Ergonomically the HQ was the winner, its circular instruments and better placement of the various controls being superior to the strip speedometer in the Valiant although the VH gained extra points for the most comprehensive minor instruments. Considering their physical size, available space was poor, both the HQ and VH having their spare wheels on the boot floor taking up valuable luggage space, interior accommodation being line ball between them. The 245 engine made the Valiant the performance king of this group, running to 164.8km/h (103mph) flat out and taking 10.0 seconds exactly to sprint from 0–96km/h (0–60mph) where the HQ ran to only 145.6km/h (91mph) and took 13.4 seconds to 96km/h (60mph), this despite the Valiant running a 2.92 rear axle ratio against 3.55 in the Holden.

Released in September 1971 was the Valiant utility and two months later came the VH Valiant two-door hardtop. This used the exterior panels from the Chrysler by Chrysler hardtop but with normal Valiant front sheet metal.

The VJ Valiant series arrived in May 1973 and was really the most basic of model upgrades. Styling was unchanged although there was a new eight segment grille with single 7-ins round Lucas headlights and new horizontal taillight units. Equipment levels were raised with VJ and the options list was pruned somewhat to keep expensive inventory levels at the factory down – standard equipment now included electronic ignition, front disc brakes, door reflectors, lockable glove box, retractable seat belts, better rust proofing of the body and a floor gearshift.

VJ morphed into the VK in October 1975 and again exterior sheet metal changes were not to be found. Only the grille and taillights were 'new.' Inside, the only significant new feature was the ex-Galant combination function control stalk on the steering column that operated the windscreen wipers and washers, indicators and hi-lo beam.

And then in November 1976 Chrysler announced the CL Valiant which was, in the original plan, supposed to have been a completely new body design over the existing mechanical components but because of

The Esses			**Slow Corner**			**Fast Corner**		
Fastest Run	**Average**		**Fastest Run**	**Average**	**Fastest Run**	**Average**		
Valiant	86.7km/h	85.7km/h	Holden	61.9km/h	60.3km/h	Valiant	85.7km/h	84.5km/h
Holden	85.7km/h	83.5km/h	Valiant	61.3km/h	60.5km/h	Holden	84.7km/h	82.9km/h
Falcon	82.8km/h	81.5km/h	Falcon	60.0km/h	58.8km/h	Falcon	80.9km/h	79.5km/h

the company's financial straits that never happened. What was presented was the same ex-VH/VJ/VK bodyshell with revised sheet metal front and rear. At the front was a large rectangular-shaped grille flanked by dual headlights each side (just like on the R and S) while at the rear the bootline was raised and the lid flowed down to new taillights either end of a garnish panel. The Ranger name was discontinued now with the base model being simply called the Valiant, then came the Chrysler Regal (note, not Valiant Regal) and finally the Regal SE that replaced the Chrysler by Chrysler.

Interiors were carried over from VK but with some subtle differences. The Valiant retained the horizontal ex-Ranger dashboard and instruments while the Regal had the large circular dials with a clock, the Regal SE could be ordered with luxurious buttoned-leather upholstery as an option.

Transmission options remained as before but by far the majority of cars were built with an automatic gearbox; the 215-cid and 360-cid engines were discontinued at this time. The two sixes (245- and 265-cid) now featured Electronic Lean Burn (ELB) emissions technology – it was already on the 318 V8 – which was a far more elegant solution to the emissions issue than provided by Ford or Holden.

In 1978 Chrysler released the limited-edition Regal Le Baron, the name coming from luxury US Chryslers; it was only available in Silver and came with either a red or blue interior, the 265-cid engine was standard with the 318 V8 as an option. Only 400 were built. Also in 1978 Chrysler introduced their radial tuned suspension package that required far less modifications than Holden had to do to achieve their aims when they introduced their version. As *Modern Motor* said in a comparison test published in the July 1978 issue, "The Valiant offered a far better ride than the Holden as well as more precise handling." The comparative testing of the new suspension set ups was carried out at the Oran Park circuit in Sydney, sadly demolished some years ago for housing developments. It makes for interesting reading (see table above).

Well-known and respected racing river from the time, Sue Ransom, drove all three cars and wrote these comments about the Valiant: "Of the three cars tested, the Valiant gave me the biggest surprise because – on the track at least – it seemed to come up trumps. And I must say I wasn't expecting that to be the case!

"True, on the open road and in city traffic, it is still 'tankish' – somewhat big and heavy due in part to the very heavy steering and also the high dash and steering wheel coupled with the low seat.. But on the test track it was easy to predict and place and was No. 2 to the Falcon as far as driver comfort was concerned." Sue further added that she really liked the brakes and found the 4.3-litre engine the smoothest of the three.

Finally, in November 1978, Chrysler released the CM series that was virtually unchanged and today needs an experienced Valiant spotter to notice the differences. In an effort to spice up showroom traffic Chrysler announced the GLX version (option A16) that featured the CL Charger grille and dashboard, special cloth upholstery, black door frames and Cheviot hot wire magnesium alloy wheels. The 265 engine was standard mated to a four-speed manual gearbox with an automatic as an option plus the 318 V8 was available as well.

The CM was the last of the Mohicans as far as Chrysler and the Valiant was concerned. Production in small numbers took place until August 1980 when David Brown was asked to drive the last one off the Tonsley Park line. That car exists in private ownership to this day.

CHARGER

Of all the muscle cars in Australia's recent motoring history the Chrysler Valiant Charger was the most unlikely. Sure, it has achieved iconic status in the last few years but it was always the dark horse.

Why was this so? A large part of the answer has to do with its parentage – it was a Chrysler product and in Australia the company was a distant third in the rankings behind GM-Holden and Ford who dominated the market, especially during the 70s. Another part of the answer has to do with the fact that the Charger was *never* planned as a part of the vast VH program that was signed off by Chrysler in Detroit. And thirdly, it was powered in its R/T versions by a *six*-cylinder engine where the Holdens and Fords all had V8s.

For any other car and company this would have been three strikes and you're out!

When managing director David Brown returned from Detroit in mid-1968 with $22 million for the signed-off VH program the only sporting Valiant in it was the Pacer sedan; the only coupe in it was the vast CH Chrysler by Chrysler hardtop which was hardly sporting. After the development program had begun Brown and key colleagues Roy Rainsford and Walt McPherson discussed adding a further model without advising Detroit. This was a momentous event, one unheard of in corporate circles at the time. Brown okayed skimming a paltry $2 million off other parts of the program and authorised the designing of a sporting coupe that would have significant youth appeal.

Brian Smyth along with his small team of stylists and modellers began the process that would lead to the Charger (initially still called Pacer) in late 1969, well after work on the overall VH program had started. Later they received assistance from Bob Hubbach, Peter Perry and two modellers from the corporation's international styling studios in Highland Park who came to Tonsley Park. This small team finalised the styling of what became the Charger by mid-1970. The wheelbase of the floorpan was reduced from 2819mm (111-ins) to 2667mm (105-ins) and the rear overhang was shortened, all sheet metal forward of the A-pillar being common to the other VH models. A new roof was required that had a smallish rear window of flat glass recessed in behind two sail planes that stretched to the ducktail spoiler at the rear where taillights that were different from the other VH models were fitted; the doors incidentally were donated by the Chrysler by Chrysler hardtop.

On August 6, 1971 the Chrysler Valiant Charger was launched upon an unsuspecting public with one of the most disarmingly simple advertising campaigns ever devised – it revolved around the two-word phrase, “Hey Charger!” I can still picture that gorgeous leggy blonde lady in the Charger in the TV ad gazing at the camera with her fingers raised in the Churchillian ‘V’ sign; it quickly captured the imagination of the youth market and was soon taking up to half of all Valiants built each day – amazing. The Charger became something Chrysler desperately needed – an instant commercial success!

Charger was available with any of the fittings and options that applied to the VH range. This meant that the cheapest car carrying the Valiant badge in 1971 was in fact the base Charger at $2795. It was not a particularly inspiring car, what with its 215-cid D engine, three-speed manual gearbox with column shift and drum brakes all round. Equipment-wise inside it was rather bare – vinyl floor mats, vinyl upholstered bucket tombstone front seats that tilted forwards for access to the back seat, and little else. From there you graduated to the Charger XL spec which gave you wheel arch mouldings, wheel dress trims, white-wall tyres, disc front brakes, remote control exterior rear view mirror, floor carpets and reclining bucket seats plus the option of three different capacity six-cylinder engines and the 318-cid V8, three-speed manual gearbox with either column or floor change, three-speed automatic (a Borg Warner Type 35 labelled as a Torqueflite) with either column or floor selector, drum or disc front brakes with prices starting at $3195. And the top model was the Charger 770 that was in effect a two-door Regal and its prices began at $3625.

The press loved the car and wrote glowingly of it and passed over some of the more obvious glitches because they loved the concept and they loved its style. The combination they seemed to like most was the Regal version with the 265-cid engine mated to the automatic gearbox with power assisted disc front brakes and power steering. It was quick – less than 10 seconds to 96km/h (60mph), 160km/h (100 mph) maximum – and handled well given the suspension’s limited capabilities and was an excellent long distance cruising coupe. Writing in *Modern Motor*, October 1971, editor Rob Luck said, “Chrysler’s new Valiant Charger is

a remarkable and quite exciting new product offering almost exceptional value-for-money on the Australian market." Tim Britten at *Motor Manual* wrote, "With a bold out-flanking move Chrysler has swept its new Charger onto the market as the surprise release of the year."

Chrysler surprised everybody when in August 1971 they summoned members of the media to Oran Park race track in Sydney where they were introduced to the Chrysler Valiant Charger R/T. This was the beginning of a revolution at Chrysler that sadly would last for less than two years. Known as the E38 (its engine option code) the R/T was NOT what the media or anybody else was expecting from Chrysler. From the outside it was easily recognised by the bumble bee stripes over the rear accompanied by huge 'HEMI 265' decals, three red bars in the grille, a quartz halogen driving light sited alongside each headlight, wide sports style wheels fitted with 185 x 14 radial tyres and a sports fuel filler cap. Inside were tombstone bucket seats, a floor shifter and the same sports instrument pack that had appeared in the VH Pacer sedan.

But it was what was under the bonnet that knocked everybody out. There was the biggest six the company made – the 265-cid unit – resplendent with a finned alloy rocker cover and a brace of *three* Weber 45 DCOE carburettors. It literally was a sight for sore eyes and stuck it up Holden and Ford with their rather humdrum offerings. Available in two versions – E37 and E38 – the big six developed 185kW (248bhp) at 4800rpm, 415Nm (306lbs-ft) of torque at 3400rpm in E37 guise, 208kW (280bhp) at 5000rpm and 420Nm (310lbs-ft) or torque at 3700rpm in E38 form.

Power went to the rear wheels through a twin-plate clutch and an all-synchromesh *three*-speed manual gearbox with no reverse lock-out for the floor shifter; the non-assisted steering had a faster 16.0:1 ratio and either of two rear axle ratios were available – 3.23 or 3.5. 7-ins ROH magnesium alloy wheels were standard.

Road tests showed the engine to have been remarkably tractable in town, trolling along at 56km/h (35mph) in top gear without temperament. However, once outside the confines of the city and the accelerator was flattened the Charger R/T E38 became quite a different machine. From 2500rpm through to the redline at 6000rpm the engine produced an exhilarating surge of sheer power although it was loud – a combination of the rorty exhaust, intake noise and the overhead gear thrash.

Despite the handicap of the three-speed gearbox an E38 would run a standing quarter mile in 14.8 seconds, fractionally slower than a Falcon GT HO, and it would accelerate from 0–96km/h (0–60mph) in 6.3 seconds, 0–160km/h (0–100mph) in 16.5 seconds and run to around 208km/h (130mph) with 88km/h (55mph) available in first gear and 152km/h (95mph) in second. Handling was a revelation compared with the Pacer sedans and especially the humdrum Valiant sedans, the result of many hours honing the suspension settings out at the Mallala race track with Leo Geoghegan driving the prototypes.

An E38 was probably the performance bargain of a lifetime with its showroom floor price starting at $3975.

In the January 1972 edition of *Wheels* magazine came a most unexpected announcement – their Car of the Year was none other than the VH Chrysler Charger! This was the second time Chrysler had won the prestigious award, the first time being in 1967 for the VE Valiant. In summary they wrote, "It is Chrysler's second COTY and one of the most deserving in the history of the award.

"Charger has won the award because of its great versatility, its pricing, its styling and practicality – and the very real engineering advances which have been made in road behaviour. Quite simply, it is a very good car indeed."

In the accompanying road test article the journalists drove a variety of Chargers and published the results for a Charger XL and 770 – 265-cid six-cylinder engine versus a 318-cid V8, 151kW (203bhp) vs 171kW (230bhp), 355Nm (262lbs-ft) of torque vs 461Nm (340lbs-ft)., both were fitted with a three-speed automatic gearbox. At the top end, the XL ran to 182km/h (114mph) and the 770 to 184km/h (115mph) while the 0–80, 96 and 112km/h (0–50, 60 and 70mph) acceleration times were 7.0 (6.8), 9.2 (9.1) and 12.4 (12.3) seconds so again there was negligible difference – it really boiled down to whether the buyer wanted a six or V8 engine given that there was not a huge price differential at $3520 for the XL and $4035 for the 770.

Mind you, the 770 interior was a far nicer place to be whether commuting or cruising. The dashboard had the Regal's large round dials including a tachometer set in a faux wood surround, better quality carpeting and upholstery and so on – it just *felt* a better place to be! The XL, for example, had the VH sedan horizontal speedometer and minor dials that looked cheap …

In conclusion they wrote, "Charger represents a new era of engineering and marketing sophistication from Tonsley Park. With its entire '71 range, Chrysler returns to the time when its cars were different and just a little more exclusive than Holdens and Falcons. With the Charger Chrysler has achieved its aims of building a car for everyone and capturing the youth market at the same time."

Still with VH for the moment, in mid-72 the E38 was uprated to E49, the changes bringing to market a car that has gone on to hero status in this country. Externally an E49 can be recognised by the number 4 in the vertical stripe on the front fenders. All E49s came with the A84 Track Pack option. Where the E38 had 208kW (280bhp) available, through some tuning and camshaft modifications – Chrysler worked with Wade Camshafts in Melbourne on this – the E49 engine produced 225kW (302bhp) at 5400rpm and 434Nm (320lbs-ft) of torque at 4100rpm. It also featured a baffled sump, tuned length exhaust headers, shot-peened crankshaft and connecting rods, special valve springs and a twin-plate clutch.

Wheels published one of their more meritorious road tests in the November 1972 issue of the magazine, titled "The Supercars that got away." It was a full road test comparison between the E49 six-cylinder coupe and the 340 V8-engined E55 coupe. The Charger 770SE 340 E55 to give it its full and clumsy name, had been released at the Sydney Motor Show the previous month and put an end to speculation about a Bathurst special. The 340-cid V8 was a purpose developed small block engine Chrysler US had developed for racing and a small number – believed to be between 320 and 330 units – were brought in and assembled at Lonsdale in early 1970 but never used for their originally intended purpose.

In the 770SE it was mated to the imported A727 Torqueflite automatic gearbox – the Borg Warner 35 would never take the torque

– and so the model was regarded as and marketed by Chrysler as a high speed luxury touring coupe. The E49 tested was running a 3.5:1 rear axle ratio which made the in-gear maxima 64, 97.6, 136km/h (40, 61, 85mph) with a maximum speed of 179.2km/h (112mph) at 5500rpm; if the regular 3.23 rear axle ratio had been fitted the speeds would have been marginally higher with its top speed closer to the 205km/h (128mph) achieved by the E38. Nevertheless, the E49 proved to be the fastest accelerating car made in Australia with 0–96km/h (0–60mph) taking just 6.1 seconds and 0–160km/h (0–100mph) taking 14.1 seconds, the standing quarter mile took 14.4 seconds and the fuel consumption worked out at 21 litres per 100km (13.8mpg) for the test. Still, if you're having that much fun who cares?

By comparison the E55 ran to 192km/h (120mph) as its top speed with 0–96 and 160km/h (0–60 and 100mph) times of 7.2 and 21.2 seconds each, ran the quarter mile in 15.5 seconds and returned 22 litres per 100km (12.9mpg). The retail prices were $4300 for the E49 – an even bigger bargain than the E38 – and the E55 cost $4850. Which to buy? Well, they summed up that dilemma by writing, "It depends on what you want. The E49 is a fire breathing Ferrari-style car while the E55 is more in the Mustang breed of fine looks combined with performance and the ease and comfort of automatic transmission, and even air conditioning, if you so desire.

"Both are fine in traffic, although for crowded city areas there is no beating the automatic." In the end the journalists elected not to pick a winner!

In parallel with the Valiant sedans and wagons, in May 1973 Chrysler announced the VJ series Chargers. Rationalisation was the name of the game at this time with more equipment as standard – front disc brakes, door reflectors, lockable glovebox and retractable seat belts – and a shorter options list. Changes were confined to a new moulded plastic grille with vertical accent bars and 7-ins Lucas round headlights and horizontal taillights. The full range of six engines was on offer initially, later reduced to four as the R/T six-pack engine and the 340-cid V8 were discontinued. The end of the Charger R/T coincided with Chrysler's withdrawal from racing and the 770 (no longer wearing the 'SE' badge) when the last of a small stock of 340 V8s was exhausted. A discreet '340 4BBL' badge on the front fender was the only clue. Gone, too, was the Pacer sedan.

Charger 770s featured the 7-ins wide alloy wheels that were a part of the earlier E38 and E49 R/T's in the VH series. With VJ Chrysler introduced Electronic Lean Burn technology to its V8 engine range which greatly improved starting and gave longer service life to the spark plugs. There was also a change in carburettor with the 340 engine, from an AVS unit to a Carter Thermoquad but exactly when this took place is not known. The main difference between the carburettors was in air flow – from 625cfm for the AVS to 800cfm for the Thermoquad.

Mystery also surrounds the 340's cylinder heads because again during the VJ's time they were changed from having inlet valves of 55.8mm (2.20-ins) diameter to 47.7mm (1.88-ins) and again when this happened has never been accurately documented.

In late 1974 Chrysler added engine option E57 to the VJ Charger program, this being the huge 360-cid V8 from the Chrysler by Chrysler series. A limited edition Charger Sportsman was released in August 1974, all 500 being Vintage Red and white in colour with cloth trim and were powered by the 265-cid engine mated to a four-speed manual gearbox.

The VK Charger arrived in October 1975 and with it further rationalisation, there being just two versions now – Charger XL and 770 – and three engine offerings – 245- and 265-cid six-cylinders, 318-vid

V8 – along with three gearbox options as before. With VK there were no longer any references to the Valiant name, it was now a Chrysler Charger. There was new badging, new grille treatment of the same moulded grille texture, revised taillight design with the most significant addition being the combination wiper/washer/indicator/beam change integrated into the single column stalk taken from the Galant parts bin.

With the arrival of ADR 27A in July 1, 1976 Chrysler deleted the 215-cid six and 360-cid V8 engines from its range. In the same month the company released the Charger White Knight Special that was limited to 200 units, half painted Arctic White, the other 100 units Amarante Red. They were only available with the 265 engine but with either a manual or automatic gearbox. It was a marketing special featuring cosmetic changes inside and out.

The last Charger arrived in October 1976, the CL, and was offered only in 770 format. The CL was distinguishable by the new front sheet metal that had a prominent grille with honeycomb texture and a chromed surround with red edging, quad headlights and wide-but-narrow parker/indicator lights underneath. The name CHRYSLER was spelled out in separate letters on the leading edge of the front panel.

Chrysler's advanced Electronic Lean Burn system (ELB) became available on the 245- and 265-cid six-cylinder engine with CL. And the options list was again pruned and limited to such things as tinted graduated laminated windscreen, air conditioning, audio system, sports stripes, 7-ins alloy wheels, choice of engine and gearbox and a towing package. Chrysler initiated an industry first with CL by offering buyers a 12 month/unlimited kilometres warranty such was their confidence in their cars.

A cosmetic optioned Charger Drifter was offered late in the CL's career to help shift stocks of inventory prior to the close of production of the model on August 16, 1978. A glorious chapter in Chrysler's Australian history was closed at that time – no successor was apparently contemplated apart from a hatchback version that the American managers vetoed unceremoniously!

Homologation for the Charger had been achieved and as a warm-up for the 1971 Bathurst Chrysler entered one in the Toby Lee race at the tight Oran Park circuit; the diminutive Doug Chivas won outright when he out-braked Colin Bond at the last corner. Two weeks later no fewer than 11 Chargers were on the starting line at Bathurst – three works cars and eight private entries. In the race the cars used more fuel and tyres than planned but nevertheless the cars took second place in Class D (Geoghegan/Brown) and sixth outright.

The following year Chrysler felt that they had a real chance for outright victory with the more powerful E49 that also came with the new Borg Warner 4-speed gearbox but despite being in contention all day the remarkable Chivas finished third having driven the whole race.

Although the media were harsh in their criticism of Chrysler for not winning and the car was labelled a 'loser' by some the fact was that the only race it never won was at Bathurst – the Charger was a winner on every other race circuit in Australia and was virtually unbeatable in New Zealand in the hands of Leo Leonard and Jimmy Little.

Despite all else the Charger was a huge sales success for Chrysler, at one stage nearly half of all VH Valiants coming off the Tonsley Park line were Chargers!

CHRYSLER BY CHRYSLER

Although the VIP by Chrysler had not been the success that David Brown and his team hoped it would be, when it came time to negotiate with Highland Park for the finances needed to fund the design, development and production of the next (VH) range it was taken as read that a luxury model to compete with the Ford Fairlane and Holden Statesman would be part of the range. What was unexpected was the Chrysler by Chrysler Hardtop, a somewhat awkward looking coupe built on the sedan's long wheelbase. Maybe that is why the name 'coupe' was never applied; the word of course being French for short.

With the Australian VH program under discussion early in 1967, David Brown along with Sales Director Bob Perkins, Manufacturing Director Roy Rainsford and Chief Engineer Walt McPherson wanted to blanket the entire popular family car and luxury car segments of the market in sedan, wagon, coupe, utility and long wheelbase forms. The company knew that its competitors would be releasing long wheelbase upmarket versions of their forthcoming HQ (Holden) and XA (Ford) programs that would emerge onto the Australian market beginning in 1971, the same year that Chrysler planned to release its VH series. If Chrysler wanted to be competitive, it simply had to have a long wheelbase luxury sedan as part of the new range.

Negotiations with the money people at Highland Park late in 1967 saw Brown and his colleagues return home with only $22 million to spend on what was to be the most expansive and ambitious range of Chrysler products the Australian subsidiary had ever produced. As it eventuated, that amount was really nowhere near enough and in a way contributed to the company's slow downfall in Australia.

Styling for the complete VH program was carried out in the corporation's international studios under the direction of Colin Neale, with Bill Dayton, Bob Hubbach and Hal Pilkey involved with considerable input from Chrysler Australia's chief stylist, Brian Smyth, and modeller Bill Chinnick. During the latter part of 1968 and into 1969 the small group worked up several proposals in 1:1 scale for management to view, all styles being reminiscent of designs being proposed for the 1971 US season Plymouth and Dodge bodies.

Designed as an extension to the VH program, the new luxury Chrysler was coded CH. As the style evolved, Brown made it clear that he wanted far more model differentiation than that which existed between Valiant and VIP. One of the themes developed as part of this process, stretched wheelbase apart, was the Dodge-style front with its distinctive loop bumper that enveloped the grille and four headlights. Brown saw it on a

Dodge mockup when viewing proposals in the company of Colin Neale, so legend has it, fell in love with it and simply had to have it. What was not realised then was the considerable extra cost involved in tooling the front sheet metal and the special grille to accommodate the loop bumper. Brown was, apparently, horrified but still wanted the feature anyway!

At the rear, a horizontal theme was developed for the tail light units consisting of two lenses, the outer being tail and stop lights and the inner lens for indicators and reversing lights, the taillight units sweeping around the corner of the rear quarter panel to include a side reflector that had the crown insignia badge of the Chrysler on it. A plain, brushed aluminium appliqué panel visually joined the lighting units. Above the right hand lighting unit, on the boot lid, was the 'Chrysler' name in script.

To further differentiate the CH Chrysler from the VH Valiant the designers included a smaller rear windscreen achieved by welding a 'plug' into the normal window opening, a chrome strip that began at the leading edge of each front fender and ran along the upper ridge and around the body at waist level, and a hand painted coach-line that was applied along each side, low down that rose up over the wheel arches.

Chrysler knew that the CH had to have a lengthened wheelbase and so the VH floorpan was stretched a further 101.6mm, to 2921mm (4" to 115") for the CH sedan and hardtop while both body styles stretched to 4994mm (196.6") overall. Most of the body panels were common with the VH with the exception of new rear doors, bonnet, boot lid and front and rear quarter panels. Kerb weight was higher because of the extra sheet metal and luxury interior fittings, a six-cylinder Chrysler by Chrysler sedan weighing in at 1528kgs (3370lbs) and if the 360-cid V8 engine was ordered the weight rose by 90kgs (200lbs).

Chassis components remained common with VH having longitudinal alloy steel torsion bars and wishbones up front and 4-leaf semi-elliptic springs at the rear suspending a live axle. An increased diameter anti-sway stabiliser bar was added at the front to minimise front-end kneel and roll when cornering while at the rear the U-bolt clamps were isolated from the axle by rubber pads to reduce noise transference.

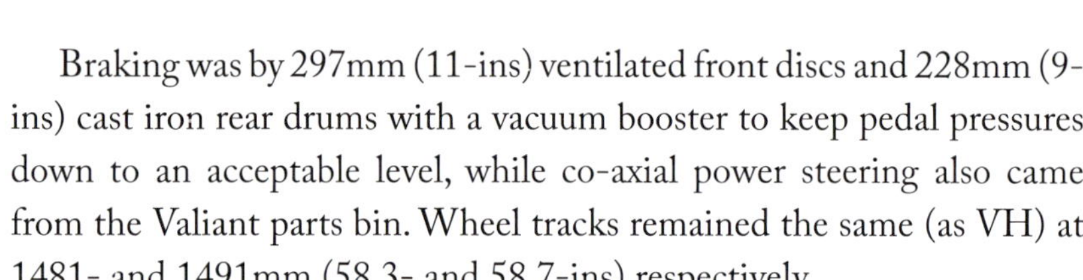

Braking was by 297mm (11-ins) ventilated front discs and 228mm (9-ins) cast iron rear drums with a vacuum booster to keep pedal pressures down to an acceptable level, while co-axial power steering also came from the Valiant parts bin. Wheel tracks remained the same (as VH) at 1481- and 1491mm (58.3- and 58.7-ins) respectively.

Under the bonnet was the 360-cubic inch (5.9-litres) V8 imported from Canada. With a bore and stroke of 101.6 x 90.9mm (4.00-ins by 3.58-ins) it was rated at a lazy 188kW (255bhp) at 4400rpm and 486Nm (360lbs/ft) of torque at 2400rpm. It was a $200 extra option in both the sedan and hardtop. The standard engine for both body styles was the 265-cid (4.3-litres) 'Hemi' six-cylinder that produced 149kW (203bhp) at 4800rpm and 354Nm (262lbs/ft) of torque at 2000rpm. If the 'Hemi' engine was ordered, the transmission was the Borg Warner-built Type 35 three-speed and the marvellous A727 unit if the buyer wanted the 360 V8.

It was in the interior where Chrysler really wanted their luxury-liner to be a standout from the competition. The company loaded it up to the gunwales with equipment in an effort to attract buyers to *their* luxury limousine. By the standards of 1971 the equipment list was impressively complete. It included tinted electric windows, 13-transistor Searchtune push button radio with a power antenna (the influence of the Japanese!), a light over the ignition switch with a 30-second delay on it, enough interior lights to light up the most presumptuous boudoir – they could be found in the glove box, ash receiver (not ashtray, please note), reading lamps in the C-pillar, on each door and in the boot – plus a superb heater/demister, driver's side remote control exterior rear view mirror and a prismatic day/night interior rear view mirror, electric windows and electric powered front seats; chrome wheel arch mouldings; and a formal padded roof in either Paisley patterned brown vinyl, leather grained black or parchment. Buyers of the two-door Hardtop got the vinyl roof as standard.

Available options included AirTemp air conditioning (yes, really!) that was ordered by around 90 per cent of buyers and choice of E70HR black sidewall tyres or F78 x14 tyres with white sidewalls; the air conditioning added around 45kgs (100lbs) to the car's weight.

Standard seating was a US-style divided front bench with individually adjustable squabs and twin centre armrests, the upholstery being expensive-looking woven nylon brocade material in what Chrysler described as 'an Interlaken pattern.' The rear seat was a conventional bench with a fold-down centre armrest. On the floor was specially moulded loop pile carpet, including the luggage compartment and over the spare wheel.

To achieve the level of silence deemed necessary for any luxury car, Chrysler placed soundproofing pads everywhere. The dashboard utilised the VH Valiant upper moulding but the instrument cluster, comprising speedometer, clock, fuel, temperature and ammeter, was set in a Carpathian elm surrounding. To distinguish the Chrysler instruments from the Regal version of the Valiant, the Chrysler's dials were squared off in shape, not circular.

To further separate the Chrysler from its lesser siblings it had uniquely styled full dress trims on the wheels and the tyres featured a narrow white wall.

Production began in late October for a release in November (1971), some four months after GM had released their completely new Statesman series but five months before the appearance of the market leading ZF Fairlane.

Naming the car had created some controversy within the company. Marketing wanted a name that spoke of quality and performance, a name that required no explanation. Several staffers wanted to retain the VIP badge but as that car had not been a sales success they quickly lost the argument. Names like Le Baron, Saratoga, New Yorker and Imperial were tossed around the boardroom, names that in the US stood for exactly what the Australians were seeking, but they were names that had little relevance (or meaning) locally.

It was Managing Director David Brown who proffered the name Chrysler by Chrysler, his logic being that the name Chrysler was recognised in the Australian community as one that evoked visions of excellent engineering, strength, reliability and longevity as well as luxury. And so it was that the CH series was badged Chrysler by Chrysler.

The aim of their marketing and advertising activities was to convince the public that the Chrysler by Chrysler was *not a Valiant* – that it was a luxury limousine built by Chrysler.

Full road tests did not appear in the national magazines until early 1972. *Wheels,* in its March '72 issue, had this to say: "The Chrysler is the company's first all-out attempt at gate crashing the Fairlane and Statesman market. It succeeds the not-so-popular VIP, but relates far more intelligently to its intended market." The magazine's report went on to say, "Whether or not the Chrysler looks different enough is debatable. Certainly it looks like a big car, but then so does the Valiant. It's a case of the Chrysler being 'more big' than the Valiant."

What the *Wheels* people were impressed with was the Chrysler's storming performance. Weighing in at a hefty 1668kgs (3670lbs) and running on 7.35 x 14 Goodyear cross-ply tyres it sprinted from rest-to-96km/h (60mph) in 8.8 seconds, to 128km/h (80mph) in 14.6 seconds and to the magic 160km/h (100mph) in 28.1 seconds. The standing quarter took 17.1 seconds and maximum speed was recorded as 184km/h (115mph).

Their comment on the Chrysler's performance was interesting: "The Chrysler comes with the genuine, fully imported Torqueflite automatic transmission rather than the locally produced unit which goes under the same name and is fitted to the six-cylinder Valiants. It is beautifully smooth and free of temperament and confirms the impression that

America builds fine, indeed the world's best, engine/transmission combinations."

As tested, the Chrysler by Chrysler retailed for $5095. The test car came equipped with the optional AirTemp air conditioning and a padded vinyl roof. Base price off the showroom floor for the 265-equipped Sedan was $4895 with the Hardtop priced identically.

Modern Motor in their June 1972 issue ran an article titled "BIG 3's BIG 3" in which they conducted a comprehensive comparison between the Chrysler 360, Ford Fairlane with 351-cid V8 and Holden Statesman with the 308-cid V8. They did not actually pick a winner in their summary but the writers clearly favoured the Statesman. They used various categories to compare the three protagonists; for example, under Style and Design they said, "… but in the Fairlane and Chrysler we couldn't help feeling visibility took a poor second place to styling, and the low seating position in both cars emphasized the styling (and visibility) deficiencies." The testers clearly preferred the Chrysler 360-cid V8 and the smoothness of the A727 Torqueflite gearbox although it came second for responsiveness. In the Ride and Handling section, they said, "For this class of car ride is more important than handling. To this end, the ideal car should be extremely comfortable, a complete pushover to drive and as quiet as possible.

"Of the three, the Chrysler comes closest to fulfilling these requirements."

Having said that, the Statesman came first in the category followed by the Chrysler and Fairlane. While all three were good on smooth surfaced roads, the unsophisticated suspension with the leaf spring live axle on the Chrysler (and Ford) displayed many shortcomings on rough-surfaced roads and the steering lacked precision, relegating it to second place. The Fairlane was judged as the most Comfortable, the Chrysler rating second while in both the Equipment & Fittings and Lighting segments the Chrysler was the clear leader. Luggage carrying capability rated the Chrysler last because of the ill-conceived placement of the spare wheel on the trunk floor.

MM's performance results are interesting when compared with those of rival *Wheels*. Either the *Wheels* car was tweaked (not unheard of), or their driver was more aggressive but the *MM* figures were much inferior. They achieved a 0–96km/h (0–60mph) time of 9.3 seconds [Fairlane 10.1, Statesman 11.2 seconds], 0–128km/h (0–80mph) in 18.0seconds [Fairlane 17.9, Statesman 19.9 seconds] and a standing quarter time of 17.6 seconds [Fairlane 17.9, Statesman 18.1 seconds]. Maximum speeds were 172.8km/h (108mph) for the Chrysler, 177.6km/h (111mph) for the Fairlane and 176km/h (110mph) for the Statesman. Not one of the three could have been considered frugal in their use of fuel. The smallest engined car, the Statesman, led the field with a 16.5 litres per 100km (17mpg) overall figure followed by the Chrysler on 18.8 litres per 100km (15mpg) and the Ford on 20.5 litres per 100km (14mpg). Despite having a 90-litre (19.5 Imperial gallon) tank, the Chrysler's maximum range was only 467km (292 miles) [Fairlane 392km (245 miles), Statesman 448km (280 miles)], which in reality was insufficient for a country as large and sparsely populated as Australia.

Despite the marketing line that the Chrysler by Chrysler was a separate marque in the minds of the factory folks, the buying public it would seem were less than convinced. As with the VH Valiant, public response to the new models was underwhelming to say the least. It is true that from the front and rear the Chrysler was different but in profile it was pure Valiant and in a nutshell, that is where many of its problems lay.

When discussing the Chrysler by Chrysler most historians have written the story as if there was only one model, the Sedan. But an integral part of the range from the very beginning was the two-door Hardtop. Quite why is another question, but it would seem that automobiles of that genre were extremely popular in the USA at the time as 'personal coupes' and so it was presumed by the management at Chrysler International that what was good for the USA was even better for Australia.

Its styling was based on the CH that resulted in it having an ungainly stretched appearance that looked out of proportion – it lacked aesthetic appeal from the buyer's perspective and they responded by ignoring it. Goodness knows what it cost Chrysler to manufacture the tooling for its unique outer panels but it would seem doubtful that the company would have seen a return on its investment. The Hardtop's only claim to fame is the fact that its doors and associated hardware were donated to the Charger.

With little fanfare the CH series was replaced by the CJ on the production line in March 1973, in the showroom a month later. The differences were so slight that only an eagle-eyed Chrysler aficionado would spot them: the chromed wheel arch mouldings that were previously an option became a standard fitting, the vinyl roof mouldings were lowered in an attempt to visually reduce the car's height, and the hand-painted coach-line was deleted.

What was missing from the lineup, surprise, was the Hardtop. Sales had totalled a mere 474 units which made manufacturing it uneconomical.

Sales of the Sedan actually increased in 1973, the total being 2714 units made up of 333 CH and 2381 of the CJ series. Prices rose slightly to $4925 for the 'Hemi' powered Sedan and $5125 for the V8. In September 1975 the CJ gave way to the CK but there were no discernible differences between the two! Chrysler marketing people simply changed the model nomenclature in line with the Valiants. What did change, however, was the price which climbed dramatically with rampant inflation and spiralling wage rises to $8784 for the V8 Sedan.

Officially the Chrysler by Chrysler was laid to rest in August 1976 when it was announced that it was to be withdrawn from production and replaced by the Regal SE edition of the regular Valiant series. However, dealers continued to place orders for the sedan and through the remainder of 1976, all of 1977 and until December 1978 by which time a further 1421 were quietly manufactured. Remarkable.

Marketing of the Chrysler by Chrysler during its time was low-key to the point of virtual obscurity. Apart from the usual initial splurge of advertising, mostly in the print media, there were virtually no follow up themes and advertisements to keep the car in the conscious mind of potential buyers. As it was, conquest sales from rivals Ford and Holden were few while European luxury car buyers rarely gave any of the Big Three a thought. What sales the Chrysler generated were almost without exception sales taken from the Valiant Regal off the same showroom floor.

Today there is considerable interest in these large luxury saloons and hardtops within Chrysler-interest clubs and the Hardtop has seen the growth of an enthusiast club specifically for owners and collectors of this most unusual and, now, rare automobile.

CENTURA

The Centura was Chrysler in its 'me too' frame of mind. Having set the benchmark in 1962 with the R and S Series Valiants, within three or four years the company had thrown away that leadership and was meekly following in the wheel tracks of Holden and Ford. Centura was a continuation of that thinking – Holden had their Torana six-cylinder range and Ford had their six-cylinder Cortina so Chrysler had to have *something*!

No suitable offerings were available from Detroit so they had to look elsewhere and from France there was the Chrysler 180, the first car from the European branch of the family to carry the Chrysler name instead of Simca. During its design and development it had been both a Humber Sceptre to replace the Hawk and a Simca 929 to replace the aged 1501 series. Its reception from the media in Europe was lukewarm at best even though it had many admirable features.

1 HOUR
PARKING
9AM-5:30PM
MON TO FRI
SAT 9AM-NOON
ANTIQUES
UPHOLSTERY
RESTORATIONS
CENTURA
Centura

Chrysler Australia desperately wanted a mid-range car to fit between the Valiant and Galant and the 180 was ideal in their opinion. It was, in reality, exactly the right package for local needs, far better than the Valiant if truth be known and potentially a better car than either of its rivals. Plans to incorporate the 180 into the local assembly operations were floated in 1972 when engineers and stylists were despatched to Paris to collaborate with the French to modify it to our requirements, most notably to lengthen the front to accommodate the long (and heavy) six-cylinder D engine. The French, of course, shrugged their Gallic shoulders and walked away! However, the Centura as it was to be badged in Australia had a traumatic start to life down under following union bans after the French decided to carry out atomic testing in the Pacific region. A planned 1973 release was delayed until March 1975.

The 180 sat on a wheelbase of 2667mm (105-ins), was 4585mm (180.5-ins) long by 1727mm (68-ins) wide by 1430mm (56.3-ins) tall and like the Torana and Cortina could be purchased with either a four-cylinder engine or a six. The four-cylinder engine was assembled from French components and was a modern unit featuring a cast iron cylinder block, forged five bearing crankshaft, a chain-driven SOHC and a cross-flow alloy cylinder head. Its dimensions were 91.7 x 75mm for a capacity of 1981cc, power output was 89kW (120bhp) at 5700rpm and torque was 175Nm (129lbs-ft) at 3500rpm using a Solex twin-throat carburettor and a 9.45:1 compression ratio. It really was quite a sophisticated engine and relegated both the asthmatic Torana four and rough and crude Cortina four to the bottom of the pile where they belonged. It was also a most un-Chrysler-like engine!

As an option, and to qualify for tariff reductions and comply with local content requirements, Chrysler offered buyers the option of the 215- and 245-cid versions of their locally manufactured D engine. It developed 104kW (140bhp) at 4400rpm and 271Nm (200lbs-ft) of torque at 1800rpm in 215-cid form, 123kW (165bhp) at 4400rpm and 318Nm (235lbs-ft) at 1800rpm in 245-cid form; their weights were around 70kgs (150lbs) more than the French engine, all that extra weight being over the front wheels.

For a Chrysler product the Centura's chassis was a revelation. Wedded as they were with the Valiant to torsion bars up front and semi-elliptic leaf springs at the rear, having a MacPherson strut coil spring front suspension allied to a live axle with links and coil springs at the rear was a breath of fresh air. Add in disc front brakes (not an option) and rack and pinion steering (stupidly not power assisted) and it was something to experience. There were minor detail differences between the fours and sixes insofar as both the sixes had rear stabiliser bars, the rear axle ratio for the 2.0-litre engine was 3.727:1 while the 215 used a 3.23 ratio and the 245 used an even higher 2.92:1 ratio, the 2.0-litre's front disc rotors were 248mm (9.8-ins) diameter where the six-cylinder cars had 279mm (11.0-ins) rotors, solid in each case, and the 2.0-litre had a single circuit master cylinder where the two sixes had a dual line master cylinder with vacuum boosting and a load sensing proportioning valve in the rear circuit. The transmissions were different, too, with the 2.0-litre versions using a French-made all-synchromesh four-speed manual or three-speed automatic while the sixes used either a three- or four-speed all-synchromesh manual made by Borg Warner who also provided the three-speed automatic.

The KB series Centura was available in either XL or GL trim, the XL being the poverty-pack special that manufacturers seemed to think they had to offer while the GL was better equipped by having carpets, centre console, illuminated heater/demister controls, a tachometer, clock, low fuel warning light, rubber over-riders on the rear bumper (but not the front!) and face-level ventilation. A four-cylinder GL retailed for $4466 but many buyers opted for the laminated windscreen at $68 and the heated rear window at $58.

A full road test of the Centura 2000 was published in *Wheels*, August 1975 and from Chrysler's point of view they could not have been more pleased. In their opening *Wheels* wrote, "The Centura 2000 is car enough to make waves on both the four- and six-cylinder markets." This was followed up with, "The Centura four also goes to show that a well-designed medium size model can offer a genuinely realistic alternative to six-cylinder and larger models in space, comfort and performance while having tangible advantages in handling and economy."

The test crew also loved the engine, writing "The engine's a ripper

– amply strong, adequately quiet and smoother than most in its class. A match for any of the Japanese, the French-built 2000 makes the Cortina's engine seem dated and the Torana's positively industrial." The competence of the suspension, the powerful brakes and accurate steering made driving enjoyable with the only real let down being the illogical arrangement of the instruments on the dashboard and the perhaps dated exterior styling – it was four years old by the time it arrived in Australia.

As for its performance, the Centura 2000 would dash to 80km/h (50mph), 100km/h (62mph) and 110km/h (68mph) in 8.5, 12.9 and 13.4 seconds respectively with in-gear maxima of 60kmh (37.5mph) in first at 65000rpm, 90kmh (56mph) in second, 132km/h (82.5mph) in third and 165km/h (103mph) in top gear at 6000rpm. In a comparison test in *Modern Motor* (July 1975) between the Centura 2000 XL, the Ford Cortina TD XL and the Holden Torana 1900SL the Chrysler product romped away as the winner in almost every aspect of the test. It was slightly more expensive at $3740 but it was bigger, roomier and far better performing so in the eyes of the *MM* test crew it was the one to buy

A Centura 245 XL had been tested in June 1975 by *Wheels* and the performance differences were marginal – the four took 13.4 seconds to accelerate from 0–110kmh while the six took 12.4 seconds – and was thirstier and heavier to drive into the bargain and more expensive to buy.

Chrysler released the mildly updated KC Centura in June 1977. Differences were minor – you had to be a Centura anorak to spot the changes – but by now the car's gauges were sourced locally from VDO in Melbourne, they were now sensibly arranged in the dash, the steering wheel and column came from the Valiant parts bin and buyers no longer had a choice of engine – it was the 245-cid D engine or nothing.

The Centura was a much maligned family car at the time, probably because of a few assembly gremlins and possibly because Chrysler put no effort into marketing it. In so many ways it was a better car for the average family man than the Valiant which might have motivated Chrysler's disinterest. Today they are few and far between, specially the four-cylinder versions. In so many ways the Centura was a missed opportunity by Chrysler. It would have been so easy for the company to

offer buyers a far wider range of models and equipment that could have paralleled the Valiant. Entry level models would have been powered by the excellent ex-Simca SOHC 2-litre engine, mid-range models by the 245-cid D engine and the top-of-the-range model by the 318-cid V8 which we now know slotted straight into the car's engine bay. Hindsight is wonderful, isn't it?

HILLMAN

Production of the Hillman Hunter at Port Melbourne spilled over into the 70s although if truth be told Chrysler Australia had little interest in the car. The HE series was released in October 1970 and was little more than a cosmetic touch-up. From the outside the biggest change was for twin rectangular lights each side at the rear to go with a mildly modified grille texture. Three sedan models were listed – plain Arrow sedan, luxury Royal 660 sedan and the sporting Hustler – plus the Safari wagon that was only available in a plain Jane version.

Only the Hustler was of any interest as it had replaced the GT to get around the greed of the insurance companies. Both the Hustler and Royal 660 shared the 70kW (94bhp) ex-Rapier engine; the differences were inside where the Royal 660 had the former GT's polished burr walnut dashboard and full set of round Smiths instrumentation while the Hustler was Pacer-like insofar as it had the Arrow's poverty interior. On the outside the Hustler was adorned with large blackout panels on the bonnet, broad black decals along each side, black door window frames and the wheels were minus their hubcaps.

Wheels road tested a Royal 660 (September 1971) and found it to be something of a curate's egg. Where it was good – seating, interior comfort, performance and braking for example – it was very, very good but where it was bad – ride and handling on rough road surfaces in particular – it was dreadful. As they said, "The suspension reveals an alarming inability to cope with bumps, corrugations and gravel. The ride becomes very uncomfortable, jarring passengers and inducing rattles." Engine noise above 4000rpm was, they said, deafening such was its coarseness but nevertheless they coaxed 150km/h (94mph) out of the Royal (at 5400rpm) and times of 8.3 and 11.3 seconds for the 0–80 and 96km/h (0–50 and 60mph) sprints with fuel consumption in the 11.5–9.8 litres per 100km (25–28mpg) range. At $2698 it was considered to be reasonable value for money although they concluded the article by saying, "Under the tinsel it just doesn't compare with the high level of mechanical sophistication being offered by other small cars."

Chrysler persevered with the Hunter until late 1972 when the decision was made to close the Port Melbourne factory. By March 1973 the factory had been shuttered and the Hillman name disappeared from the Australian market after a career spanning more than half a century.

GALANT

Mitsubishi entered the compact family car market with serious intent when it announced the Colt Galant at the 1969 Tokyo Motor Show. It was a clean sheet design – Mitsubishi's third in five years! – and took the challenge to Toyota, Datsun and Mazda in particular. The Galant was larger than the Toyota Corolla, Datsun 1200 and Mazda 1200 but smaller (slightly) than the Corona, 1600 and Capella and yet offered superior performance. In many ways it was a clever strategy.

Chrysler began assembling the Mitsubishi Galant at its Port Melbourne plant in 1971. The Chrysler Corporation owned 15 per cent of Mitsubishi Motors' stock and it seemed logical to a struggling Chrysler Australia to make use of that connection. Initially only the four-door Galant sedan was assembled with local content amounting to little more than paint, some trim items, glass, tyres and labour. What was immediately noticeable to the Chrysler engineers was the ease with which the Galant went together – no more rubber mallets bashing doors and other panels to make them fit as was common on the Hillmans! Several months after the sedan came the Galant station wagon.

The Galant was a much more modern design and in tune with products from Toyota and Nissan who were growing their market share rapidly as sales of English and European cars diminished locally. Styling was described as 'wedge-shaped' by Mitsubishi but that was stretching the imagination somewhat. Its styling was neat and bang up-to-date with its main rivals; features included a slight hip rise by the C-pillar,

Galant

square headlights up front in a two-section grille comprising vertical plastic bars and wide multi-lens rectangular taillight units with thin chromed blades for bumpers front and rear.

Inside were front bucket seats (no headrests) and a rear bench, all upholstered in black dimpled plastic over a urethane foam base, the front seats including a reclining mechanism. The dash was an impressive design comprising a moulded foam padded surround that was designed in such a way that left- and right-hand conversions were simple. A section directly in front of the driver contained the rectangular instrument cluster – fan-shaped speedometer flanked by temperature and fuel gauges plus warning lights – while a similar section in front of the passenger housed the glove box. Between them were the heater/demister slides and push-button radio. At either end were large circular rotatable air vents for the flow-through system. As was typical for the time, the steering wheel was large in diameter with a thin rim and slightly vee-shaped spokes that doubled as the horn. Like Mazdas of the time, the Galant had a multi-purpose column stalk for indicators, hi-lo beam and wipers/washers.

The Galant rode on a wheelbase of 2420mm (95.3-ins), overall length was 4064mm (160-ins), width 1559mm (61.4-ins) and height was 1384mm (54.5-ins). And kerb weight was 830kgs (1820lbs) for the 1300 Deluxe or 840kgs (1841lbs) for the 1500 Deluxe. Up front were MacPherson struts with coil springs and a forged lateral rod with a drag link for longitudinal location and compliance while at the rear was a conventional live axle with semi-elliptic leaf springs; braking was by four-wheel drums with 95 square inches of lining area, and the steering was of the recirculating ball type, wheels were 4 x 13 shod with 6.15 x 13 cross ply tyres with narrow band whitewalls. All very conventional, conservative perhaps but it worked well and proved to be reliable for owners.

Under the bonnet the Galant offered buyers the choice of two engines – the 4G30 of 1289cc capacity (73 x 77mm) or the 4G31 of 1499cc capacity (74.5 x 86mm). Both were in-line four-cylinder units featuring a cast iron block and aluminium alloy cross-flow cylinder head with a single chain-driven overhead camshaft, a five-bearing crankshaft and camshaft, and semi-spherical combustion chambers. Both carried the marketing name of Saturn.

The 1300 version developed 65kW (87bhp) at 6300rpm and 108Nm (79.5lbs-ft) of torque at 4000rpm while the 1500 developed 71kW

(95bhp) at 6300rpm and 129Nm (95.5lbs-ft) of torque at 4000rpm with the assistance of a 9.0:1 compression ratio and a dual-barrel downdraft carburettor. This power went to the rear wheels through a new four-speed all-synchromesh manual gearbox with (for Australia) a sporty floor shift, the rear axle ratio being 4.222 for the 1300 and 3.889 for the 1500.

In the February 1971 issue of *Wheels* magazine there was a four car comparison between the (imported) Galant Deluxe 1300 at $2305, Datsun 1600 at $2309, Mazda Capella at $2339 and the Toyota Corona SE at $2414. Apart from the Galant, two of the other three cars were powered by 1.6-litre SOHC engines with the Corona being the odd one out with an all-cast iron OHV engine. It was 65kW (87bhp) versus 61kW (82bhp) for the Corona, 72kW (96bhp) for the Datsun and 77kW (104bhp) for the Mazda. Even though the Corona was the most expensive on test it had by far the oldest specification – decade-old engine, wishbone-and-coil spring front suspension, leaf spring rear suspension and drum brakes all round. From a size and weight perspective all four cars were remarkably similar albeit in the case of the Galant it was fractionally smaller and lighter.

Having the smallest capacity engine was no hindrance to the Galant on the test strip – it ran to a 152km/h (95mph) maximum with a 0–80km/h (0–50mph) acceleration time of 8.0seconds which was the quickest believe it or not. Only the Capella was faster overall at 156.8km/h (98mph) but was slower to 80km/h (50mph) at 8.9 seconds.

Local assembly of the GA began in August 1971 at the Port Melbourne factory with local content initially at around 35 per cent; the car was badged Chrysler Valiant Galant. Prices were keen, starting at $2229 for the 1300 rising to $2345 for the 1300 Deluxe and $2509 for the 1500 Deluxe.

Modern Motor published an interesting group test in its September 1972 issue when it compared the Galant 1500 Deluxe with the Toyota Corona 1600, Holden Torana 1600, Ford Cortina 1600, Morris Marina 1750 and the Datsun 1600. All six were remarkably similar in size – from 4064mm (160-ins, Galant) to 4267mm (168-ins, Cortina) – and price with less than $100 covering them. Each was powered by a four-cylinder in-line watercooled engine that varied in capacity from the 1499cc of

the Galant to 1748cc of the Marina; power outputs ranged from 58kW (78bhp, Cortina and Marina) to 60kW (80bhp, Torana), 67kW (90bhp, Corona), 71kW (95bhp, Galant) and 72kW (96bhp) for the Datsun. All were front engine-rear drive sedans but that was the only similarity, none of the group displayed any really advanced technology in their steering, brakes or suspension although the Datsun did feature an independent rear suspension.

Out on the test track against the clock the Galant was third quickest on 12.8 seconds for the 0–96km/h (0–60mph) sprint and ran to 145.6km/h (91mph) for its maximum speed compared with 145km/h (90mph) for the Cortina, 145.6km/h (91mph) for the Marina, 147.2km/h (92mph) for the Corona and 148.8km/h (93mph) for the Datsun and Torana.

In its assessments, broken into various categories, the Galant had the best engine; was rated fourth for its gearbox – ratios were too short; last for its ride – too hard and bouncy; first for handling; second for

manoeuvrability; third for braking ability; fifth for interior comfort; fifth for finish; fourth for equipment; third for safety and last for luggage carrying capacity.

So similar were they in every way that the testers backed away from giving an overall winner!

At the end of 1972 Chrysler decided to close the Port Melbourne plant which meant that production of the Galant was transferred to Tonsley Park. At around the same time, November 1972, Chrysler released the GB Galant that was virtually indistinguishable from the GA apart from the adoption of four round headlights, two each side of a grille with a new texture. Under the bonnet were two new versions of the SOHC engine – a 1439cc unit (73 x 86mm) that developed 68kW (92bhp) at 6300 and 122Nm (90lbs-ft) at 4000rpm, and a 1597cc unit (76.9 x 86mm) that developed 74.5kW (100bhp) at 6300rpm and 137Nm (101lbs-ft) at 4000rpm.

In July 1974 the GC Galant sedan and wagon were released, this time with considerably altered exterior styling. In fact, only the front door skins were carry-over. The new style was more curvaceous, more bulbous in response to the needs of crash safety requirements in the USA. It was 140mm (5.5-ins) longer in the nose and was now 4204mm (165.5-ins) in overall length, and weighed around 70kgs (150lbs) more. It had a new grille that was uncannily like that on the VK Valiant and now had two round 7-ins headlights, one each side. The 1.4-litre engine was discontinued making the 1.6-litre unit the only one available although buyers now had the option of a manual or automatic gearbox.

Inside there was really no more room than before but there was a new dashboard that had round instruments in place of the former rectangular unit. . Prices, however, had risen significantly – the 70s was a very inflationary decade – to $3195 for the base Galant, $3445 for the popular GL manual sedan, $3420 and $3670 for the base and GL manual wagons.

A little more than a year later, April 1976, Chrysler released the GD Galant that featured a return to a four-headlight front with a new grille, slightly different taillights and side indicator lights. Significantly, the car was now badged as the Chrysler Galant, the Valiant name being dispensed with; the GD was a top-seller for the company so maybe somebody in Marketing realised that the Valiant name was hindering sales! You needed to be a real car spotter to pick the differences between the GC and GD, headlights apart. As with the GC, a sports pack that included a tachometer, sports road wheels and cloth seat inserts was available. The last Galant GD was made in September 1977.

Galant GL

Galant XL

SIGMA

After several lean years – interest in the Valiant was low and largely unrewarding financially – Chrysler announced in October 1977 what became a marketing sensation in the form of the thoroughly rejuvenated Chrysler Sigma that replaced the Galant on the Tonsley Park assembly lines. The exterior styling was certainly contemporary with nice proportions and smooth curves; it was far sleeker in style than the Toyota Corona and Ford Cortina and much less ornate than the Nissan 200B, for example, while the interior allowed room for four adult passengers in reasonable comfort. Physically the new Sigma was right on the money for the market, having a wheelbase of 2517mm (99.1-ins) and an overall length of 4333mm (170.6-ins); width was 1668mm (65.7-ins) and height 1360mm (53.6-ins); wheel tracks were 1350mm (53.0-ins) and 1340mm (52.7-ins) front and rear. Kerb weight was between 975kgs (2145lbs) and 1075kgs (2365lbs) depending on equipment, making it class average.

With the Sigma Chrysler unwittingly hit the big time, again. Suddenly dealers were being inundated with buyers and the Tonsley Park assembly line was running full bore. It was one of those rare Japanese cars that was more than simply the sum of its parts. In fact, compared with the likes of the Toyota Corona, Datsun 180B, Mazda 626, Ford Cortina and Holden Torana and Gemini it did not seem to offer anything special. No doubt buyer's interest was piqued by the fabulous TV advertising campaign that kicked off with a Sigma crashing through a huge sheet of plate glass. Talk about grabbing viewer's attention! In its own way that was as clever a campaign as the *Hey Charger* one earlier in the decade.

In concept the Sigma was a carbon copy of the Galant but was a major step forward in many technical areas and it wore a style that was a major upgrade that put the ultra conservative Toyota and Datsun designs in the shade. The Sigma introduced Australian motorists to the wonders of the 'Balance Shaft' Astron engine family that would gradually replace the D six-cylinder engine at Lonsdale and the rear suspension was a far more modern four-link system with coil springs replacing the centuries-old semi-elliptic leaf spring arrangement.

At the beginning of the Sigma era it was largely a CKD program with the major components coming in from Japan and items such as upholstery, carpets, tyres and a host of other parts being sourced locally. "In the early days the local content was around 60 per cent," commented Ian Webber, "but as Valiant production waned we gradually increased the locally-made componentry."

The dashboard was a pleasant design with a broad binnacle that curved slightly around in front of the driver containing the dials – the two main ones were the speedometer (on the right) and tachometer (on

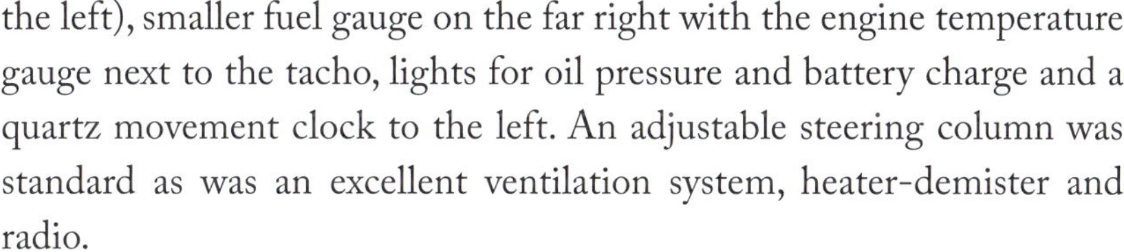

the left), smaller fuel gauge on the far right with the engine temperature gauge next to the tacho, lights for oil pressure and battery charge and a quartz movement clock to the left. An adjustable steering column was standard as was an excellent ventilation system, heater-demister and radio.

To cover as much of the market as possible the marketing and product planning people at Chrysler decided to offer the Sigma in three versions: the base L model that retained the 1.6-litre Saturn engine and 4-speed manual gearbox from the previous Galant series; the GL that was the mid-range model and expected to be the biggest seller that could be ordered with either a 1.85- or 2.0-litre Astron engine mated to either a 4- or 5-speed manual gearbox sourced from Mitsubishi or 3-speed Borg Warner automatic transmission; and at the top of the range was the luxury SE that was a mini-Regal in its equipment levels and could only be had with the 2.0-litre engine initially connected to the 3-speed automatic gearbox or the 5-speed manual. Pricing was keen, the base model retailing from $5180 for the manual version, the 1.85 GL 4-speed manual sedan selling from $5570, $6020 with the automatic option; if you choose the 2.0 GL the prices rise to $5826 (5-speed manual) or $250 more for the sports pack. The top model, the SE, retailed for $6280 for the 5-speed manual version and $6545 for the more popular automatic.

The Sigma SE was by far the most luxurious four-cylinder car on the market in 1977, its list of standard features including brushed velour upholstery with leather edgings as an option, deep pile carpets, reclining seats, rear centre armrest, adjustable lumbar support, multi-adjustable front seats, overhead console, rear reading lights and metallic paint. For those who wanted something sporting, there was the option of the Sports Pack (only available on the GL) which consisted of black body stripes and door window frames, quartz halogen high beam headlights, sports steering wheel, sports instruments including a tachometer and steel belt radial tyres

The Sigma's Astron engine was another new family of engines and also featured the concept of balance shafts that had originally been patented by the prolific English engineer Dr Fred Lanchester in 1904 but had remained idle for most of the 20th century. Mitsubishi engineers developed their version using two contra-rotating shafts in the engine's cylinder block that looked a little like camshafts but had eccentric weights integrated into their casting, weights that had been carefully calculated to generate an imbalance that was exactly equal-to-and-opposite from the out-of-balance forces generated by the reciprocating masses of the crankshaft. These contra-rotating shafts were chain-driven from the crankshaft using an additional sprocket to that which was used to drive the (also) chain-driven single overhead camshaft. The cylinder block of the Astron engine was an iron casting initially imported from Japan but

from late 1979 poured and machined at the company's Lonsdale facility that at the time was also still making the six-cylinder D245 and D265 engine. The aluminium alloy cylinder head castings were also poured and machined at Lonsdale.

In a full road test headed "Chrysler Strikes Paydirt" *Wheels* said, "Chrysler is convinced it has the right car in the right place at the right time, and on the face of it even cynical, Chrysler-bashing old *Wheels* has to agree." The magazine's testers were particularly impressed with its quietness that no doubt was helped by the balance shaft engine, the moulded roof lining and double-skinned dash panel that Ian Webber called "one of its finer points of design." As for its dynamics, they wrote, "The car's grip in corners is high and its balance is very good. It will understeer when flung into a bend very fast, but it feels stable and safe at all times." Against the clock the 2.0-litre manual SE returned a maximum speed of 161km/h (100.6mph), ran 0–110km/h (68mph) in 15.8 seconds and used petrol at the rate of 11.6 litres/100km or 24.2mpg.

At the end of the day they said, "There can be no doubt that Chrysler

Australia is on a good thing with the Sigma. It is interesting, well-priced and available in model levels which suit Australians."

Almost a year after the Sigma sedan's release Chrysler introduced the Mitsubishi-designed and locally-tooled Sigma station wagon with a lift-up single piece rear door. In every respect it paralleled the saloon in its mechanical and equipment offerings except there was no SE version.

Development continued and in January 1980, after some serious discussions between product planning and marketing, the Sigma became available with the largest capacity Astron engine made, the big 2.6-litre version, and it was offered in GL and SE editions. Critics might have argued that a four-cylinder this big was ridiculous, better to go for a medium-sized six because of Noise Vibration Harshness (NVH) issues but they were proved wrong with the Astron and its twin contra-rotating balance shafts. Despite the size of each cylinder and the length of the stroke it was remarkably smooth for what was the world's largest capacity production four-cylinder engine at the time.

In May 1980 Chrysler released the next Sigma model, the GH series. The styling remained basically unchanged but there was a new grille with four rectangular quartz halogen headlights up front and larger taillight units at the rear, black plastic bumpers 'joined' by a thick side protection mouldings, 14-ins wheels, new badge scripting and wheel dress trims. Unseen improvements to the suspension included a thicker front sway bar and a rear stabiliser bar was added while the suspension's coil springs were changed to new variable rate units with recalibrated dampers and the rear axle ratio was raised on cars with the 2.0-litre engine to 3.23 for automatics and 3.70 for manuals. Inside the general layout of the dashboard was carried over but the instruments now had square faces. With the arrival of the GH series the 1.85-litre engine option was discontinued making the 2.0- and 2.6-litre engine capacities as the only options for buyers. The L version faded from the scene and the GL became the so-called base model followed by the GLX and then the SE. The arrival of the GH Sigma also saw the fitting of Borg Warner-made 4- and 5-speed manual gearboxes.

Interestingly, the GH series saw the release of the limited edition 'Peter Wherrett' Sigma of which only 1000 were made at $9985 each and the Sigma Turbo that was priced at $13,750 and of which only 500 were made.

A solitary GJ Sigma Turbo 2.6 was built in Experimental and it was apparently an even better car to drive but unfortunately it had no production future because the company had experienced some difficulty in selling the original, many being 'sold' to employees through the in-house car leasing scheme.

Sigma gave way to the award-winning Magna in 1985 but that is a subject for another day.

Kimberley
RUL·969

CHAPTER 4

LEYLAND AUSTRALIA

Leyland Australia, or the British Motor Corporation of Australia (BMCA) as the company was still known here until 1972, was not in a position of strength as it entered the Seventies. The main reason for this situation was the lack of profitability in the Issigonis-designed front-wheel drive cars but also the company had been squeezed out of the mainstream market (mainly by the various Japanese manufacturers) and into a niche where it was difficult to achieve volume sales. BMC UK had never properly costed any of their vast model range and so had no *real* idea what a car owed them when it reached the end of the production line and was about to be trucked off to a dealer! Amazing but sadly true. BMCA had inherited this *laissez-faire* system, knew it was wrong, and had implemented a costing system for some of their own models, the Major Elite and Freeway-24/80 for example.

Through the Sixties BMCA had been transformed into a company that had a seemingly logical range of small cars and a dealer network that had been severely rationalised. At the bottom of the range was the Mini in various guises plus the Moke, then the 1500 sedan and Nomad hatchback that had evolved out of the long-lived and best-selling Morris 1100 and finally the 1800 Mark II that sat at the top as the biggest and most expensive model. Curiously, BMCA never offered a Wolseley version of the 1800 as a luxury model like they so successfully did with the 24/80 derived from the Freeway. From a manufacturing point of view each range was unique insofar as there was virtually no sharing of components between them making economies of scale of production impossible to achieve which meant that manufacturing costs were significantly higher than at GM-H and Ford, for example.

As the new decade began BMCA released their new six-cylinder twins, the Austin Tasman and Kimberley, sometimes referred to as the X6 range. These new models were released in November 1970 to great acclaim and positive reviews from the media. What nobody realised, or probably even cared about, at the time was the importance of these cars historically – *they were the world's first six-cylinder transverse-engined front-wheel drive volume-produced family sedans.* Today everybody's doing it but it was a significance sadly missed at the time.

To say that the Tasman/Kimberley were merely a reskinned 1800 would be simplifying things a little but that would be essentially accurate. The complete underbody was retained as was the roof panel and the four door skins but the four fenders (quarter panels), bonnet and boot lid were new. This brought new grilles – two round headlights and a plain plastic slat grille for the Tasman, four square headlights (another world first for a volume-produced car?) and a more ornate plastic grille for the Kimberley – and new horizontal taillight units.

Compared with an 1800 the X6 twins were a fraction larger; wheelbase was 2743mm (108-ins) compared with 2692mm (106-ins), overall length was increased to 4432mm (174.5-ins) (plus 254mm/10-ins), width was 1689mm (66.5-ins, same) and height was 1448mm (57-ins, up from 1435mm, 56.5-ins) while kerb weight was 1170kgs (2572lbs) for a manual Tasman compared with 1145kgs (2520lbs) for a manual 1800.

It was under the bonnet where the most significant change had been made. Gone was the ancient-but-worthy OHV B series four-cylinder engine and in its place was a new SOHC in-line E series six-cylinder engine (76.2 x 81.28mm, 2227cc) featuring a cast iron block and head that were cast at Birmid in Geelong, single SU carburettor on the Tasman and dual SUs for the Kimberley and a radiator repositioned at the front of the engine bay with a thermo-electric fan to keep temperatures under control. Both engines ran an 8.6:1 compression and developed 76kW (102bhp) at 5500rpm in the Tasman, 86kW (115bhp) at 5500rpm in the Kimberley with torque outputs being 157Nm and 170Nm (116 and 118 lbs-ft) respectively. It was a repeat of the same exercise that BMCA went through in 1962 when they developed the Freeway's six-cylinder engine out of the B series four only this time the Tasman/Kimberley engine was a six-cylinder version of the E series SOHC four and was machined on the same line. The gearboxes, four-speed manual and three-speed automatic, were carried over from the 1800 but had a new (larger) adapter plate to cater for the longer engine and used a cable shift mechanism. The engine/gearbox ensemble fitted in as if it was intended from the beginning!

Carried over, too, was the fabulous Hydrolastic fully independent suspension system, the non-assisted rack and pinion steering and the power assisted split circuit disc/drum braking system, the solid front rotors being 267mm (10.5-ins) in diameter with 228mm (9-ins) diameter cast iron drums at the rear. Power steering was never offered as a factory option which was a marketing (and engineering) mistake by BMC.

As a pair of cars designed and intended to compete with the Holden Belmont/Kingswood, Falcon/Falcon 500, and Valiant Ranger/XL the BMCA twins were incredibly sophisticated. Not one of the Big Three products could match them for roominess inside the cabin, useable luggage space, smoothness and quietness on a long drive, straight line stability in inclement weather or general road dynamics. Having only one engine and that being a mere 2.2-litres capacity the BMCA cars were always at a disadvantage in straight-line acceleration because the other three all had bigger capacity sixes or even V8s as an option. In retrospect BMCA made a marketing mistake in pitching the X6 cars up against the Holden-Ford-Chrysler products but that is now a lesson learned from history.

Wheels carried out a four-car comparison in its June 1972 issue between a Holden Kingswood 202 manual, Ford Falcon 500 200 manual, Chrysler Valiant Ranger 245 manual and an Austin Tasman manual sedan in a test they called "The Battle of the Basics!" It really was a case of three clones battling it out with the individualist, the Tasman. As they observed, despite the Tasman being almost a foot shorter than the other three, roominess inside was comparable. They said, "Of the four this is easily the best car in which to ride in the back. There is more leg and knee room and the seat itself is superior with enough space for three adults." As for the dynamics of the Tasman they opined that it had many positive features but there were drawbacks to being different. For example, the fully independent suspension certainly gave a better ride and fine roadholding but it was spoiled by the cheap cross-ply tyres that did not allow the car to take advantage of its superiority.

Against the clock the Tasman was not disgraced like many critics believed it might have been. It ran to a top speed of 150km/h (94mph) compared with 146km/h (91mph) for the Holden, 150km/h (94mph) for the Falcon and 164.8km/h (103mph) for the Valiant; 0–96km/h (0–60mph) took 13.1 seconds versus 13.4 seconds for the Holden, 12.4 for the Falcon and 10.0 seconds for the Valiant; all four were in the 14–11.4 litres per 100km (20–25mpg) range for economy. As a cruising car on a long journey the smoothness and quietness of the Tasman made it a far better choice. As for pricing, the Tasman cost $2830 against the Falcon at $2965, Holden at $3000 and Valiant at $3055 so quite clearly it was good value.

A Mark II version of the X6 twins arrived in April 1972 and it was

changed only in the tiniest of details because the company was well advanced on a completely new and totally Australian model so there were not the resources to do much at all. The Mark II can be discerned by the new badge in the centre of the grille, rubber insert on the rear bumper (but not the front!), chrome side mouldings, carpet on the floor, head restraints on the front seats, reversing lights and a 'Mark II' badge on the lower right side of the boot lid. In addition, the Kimberley had a black-painted rear centre panel between the taillights, re-shaped reclining front bucket seats and the single SU engine was standard on both models although the previous twin SU engine was available as an option for a time but discontinued when stock was all used up.

Wheels tested a Mark II (March 1973) and generally liked it being impressed with the fit and finish of the interior but saying the dashboard was "an ill-matched assortment of rounds, rectangles and squares." Its performance was satisfactory and again they remarked on how much better the car rode and handled when fitted with radial tyres. As for outright performance, its figures were very similar to those obtained earlier from the Tasman. Production of both cars stopped in December 1972 but several thousand units were stocked in holding areas in and around the factory with dealers still able to source stock even after the release of the Leyland P76.

MORRIS/LEYLAND MARINA

BMCA management was keen to get away from the totally front-wheel drive situation that they had found themselves in under orders from Longbridge. To better compete in the Australian market they really needed cars that were simpler to engineer, less expensive to manufacture and would make use of existing high volume components made locally. Plans existed for BMCA to design and manufacture locally two models – Model A which would be a competitor to the Torana and Cortina, and Model B that would compete with the Holden Kingswood, Ford Falcon and Chrysler Valiant. Longbridge convinced the Australians to take their latest and greatest model, the Marina, because it would allow them to concentrate their resources solely on Model B.

While that seemed like a good idea the problem for the Australians was that the Marina was a very poorly engineered car that amazingly was based in many ways on the Morris Minor! British Leyland's management found the new model cupboard absolutely bare apart from the awful Austin Maxi and with the Pom's fondness and nostalgia for the Minor (still in production in the UK, amazingly) it seemed logical that the Marina utilise as much of that car as possible. The connection was particularly obvious in the suspension which was simply not up to modern standards of ride and handling – it might have been top of the tree in 1948 but times and expectations had well and truly moved on.

Roy Haynes, an ex-Ford UK stylist recruited to show the BL people how to design a modern car, was responsible for the exterior styling of the Marina which, given the short lead time – work began in late-1968 for a mid-1971 release in the UK – and lack of resources available to him and his team, came out rather well in a nondescript kind of way. The Marina was no stunner in the looks department, it was nice-but-inoffensive to the majority of buyers and that was important. It sat on a 2438mm (96-ins) wheelbase and stretched 4216mm (166-ins) overall for the sedan, 4140mm (163-ins) for the coupe, was 1600mm (63-ins) wide and 1397mm (55-ins) high with wheel tracks of 1333- and 1330mm (52.5- and 52.4-ins) front and rear respectively; kerb weight was a light 905kgs (1990lbs) for the coupe and only 923kgs (2030lbs) for the sedan. Although described by Leyland as a 'Coupe' the two-door was in reality a two-door sedan with a coupe-like fastback styling because the body engineers were forced by BLMC management to use the sedan's front doors. So stupid but typical.

Within those dimensions the stylists and engineers managed to create quite a roomy interior for four adult passengers and there was a decent-sized boot at the back. Front passengers sat on bucket seats with separate adjustable headrests and there was a wide bench in the back. A plain dashboard faced the passengers with a binnacle in front of the driver – two round dials for the Deluxe (speedo and combination) and a three dial unit for the Super that added a clock. Equipment levels varied depending on the version selected. The base model was badged as the Deluxe just to confuse people and that was *really* basic even down to not connecting the eyeball vents for the ventilation system. By far the most popular version was the Super which featured floor carpets, rear armrests, a clock, front parcel tray, cigarette lighter, wood-grained instrument and switch surround, face level eyeball flow-through ventilation and aluminium scuff plates. And then there was the TC that had reclining front bucket seats, opening rear quarter vents, wood-grained three-spoke steering wheel, a tachometer in place of the clock and the gearshift lever was enclosed in a console. On the steering column were two stalks – on the right was indicators and hi-lo beam while on the left was the wipe/washer functions; these set a new standard ergonomically in the small-

to-medium car class, specially for British cars.

Under the bonnet Leyland offered three engines – a 1500 and two 1750s – that were the new E Series engine that replaced the old B Series in Australia. All three engines shared a cylinder bore of 76.2mm with the 1500 engine having a crank stroke of 81.28mm for an actual capacity of 1485cc; the 1750 engine had a stroke of 95.76mm for a capacity of 1748cc. With a single SU carburettor and an 8.6:1 compression the 1500 developed 46kW (62bhp) at 5500rpm and 104Nm (77lbs-ft) of torque at 2500rpm, the lower-spec 1750 developed 58kW (78bhp) at 4800rpm and 134Nm (99lbs-ft) of torque at 3000rpm with the same carburettor and compression while the higher performance TC version of the 1750 used a 9.0:1 compression and twin SU carburettors to develop 67kW (90bhp) at 5200rpm and 141Nm (104lbs-ft) at 3400rpm. Compared with rival Japanese makes these engine outputs were not at all competitive with the possible exception of the TC version; also these new Leyland engines were heavier than their rivals and even though they had a single chain-driven overhead camshaft the cylinder head was not a cross-flow design. Back in the UK the Marina was offered with either the 1275cc A series engine or 1798cc B series engine but local management decided not to upgrade those old-design engines and re-equipped the Unit Factory at Zetland with new machine tooling for the E series engines which was a smart move.

Power went to the live rear axle through either a four-speed manual gearbox or, if you ordered the 1750 engine, a three-speed Borg Warner Type 35 automatic. The front suspension was a copy of the torsion bar and wishbone system developed by Alex Issigonis for the 1948 Morris Minor while at the rear were simple semi-elliptic leaf springs albeit with a single anti-tramp rod – the Marina's suspension had none of the sophistication of the 1100 or 1800 but from an engineering and production cost point of view it was what Leyland needed to compete in the market. Steering was by a non-assisted rack and pinion setup and the brakes were a split-circuit disc/drum system with a remote vacuum booster on the Super (it was optional on the Deluxe), the front rotors being 252mm (9.8-ins) in diameter and solid while the rear drums were small 203mm (8-ins) diameter.

Leyland Australia released the Marina on April 7, 1972 as a Morris with much hullabaloo in the media and to the advertising by-line "Change Your Ideas" which undoubtedly was a silent plea by them for Australian motorists to forget all they knew from experiences with the front-wheel drive models and to give Leyland (nee BMCA) a second chance. After all, the Marina replaced the dreadful Morris 1500 on showroom floors around Australia whereas in the UK it replaced the ancient Morris Minor and decade-old Farina cars! Can you believe that?

Priced from $2350 for the two-door Deluxe coupe, $2450 for the Deluxe sedan, $2490 for the Super coupe and $2590 for the Super sedan and a further $260 for the automatic gearbox the Marina was going head-to-head with the Toyota Corona 1600 (from $2549), Datsun 1600 (from $2484), Mazda Capella 1600 (from $2634), Chrysler Galant 1500 (from $2509), Ford Cortina 1600 (from $2590) and VW Type 3 1600 whose price began at $2628. It really was a most competitive and congested segment of the market with all the major players being front-engined and rear-wheel drive; front-wheel drive had yet to penetrate the market in any major way but it was clearly on the way despite buyers' experience with BMC products.

Wheels carried out a detailed first impression drive and published it in the May 1972 issue and were positive which must have given Leyland some heart. The interior especially was praised with comments like "Inside both models set a very high standard of finish and comfort with excellent seats, both front and rear, and both create a warm feeling which has been lacking in some past BL cars." As for the dynamic qualities the word that kept appearing in any road test text was 'understeer.' The Marina could be set up on the throttle but it always seemed to want to drift wide on a corner and woe betide the driver if there were bumps in that corner because the poorly suspended rear end would want to skitter all over the place; there were also issues with spongy brakes and with windscreen wipers lifting off the screen at 104–112km/h (65–70mph) rendering them useless. What owners would subsequently experience with the Marina were many little niggles to do with the engine not maintaining tune between services to door leaks, door window winders breaking and other annoyances that rarely occurred with the Japanese cars. Leyland Australia management were well aware of this but typically Longbridge was not listening!

Modern Motor's road test, May 1972, was headed "Success with Simplicity." In it they discussed the pros and cons of the Marina and its competitors which, with the exception of the Renault 12 and VW 1600, were all conventionally engineered cars with engine capacities of around 1600ccs. Its conformity, in contrast to its predecessor (the dreadful Morris 1500), would be a huge sales plus they opined. Despite conservative looks they said, "The whole thing works. The cockpit is roomy, comfortable, well laid out and modern." They were not very complimentary where the suspension was concerned saying, "It bottoms-out easily on rough surfaces and transfers a good bit of shock and noise to the passenger compartment." When driving on dirt roads they said it was noisy and harsh but not uncomfortable – the excellent seats masked much of it – and on smooth surfaces it was "up with the best." Against the clock in a 1750 Super automatic sedan they achieved a top speed of 150km/h (94mph), 0–80 and 96km/h (0–50 and 60mph) times of 12.6 and 19.9 seconds and a fuel consumption of 12.5 litres per 100km (22.6mpg) for the test. Despite some reservations about the fit and finish of some items they predicted a big future for the Marina.

From early 1973 armed with a renewed marketing strategy the car was renamed the Leyland Marina and had new hubcaps to mark the event, the new caps having the circular Leyland spinner with an L in the centre. Towards the end of the same year, in November, Leyland released the Mark II version of the car along with the Marina 262 Six. It was Leyland's riposte to Ford and Holden who were doing rather well in the market place with their six-cylinder Cortina and Torana models.

The Marina Six was a hybrid model made only in Australia. It comprised the 2.62-litre SOHC in-line six-cylinder engine from the P76 program dropped into the Marina engine bay with as few modifications as possible; only the fitting of a small sub-frame was different from the four-cylinder version. Curiously the six-cylinder Marina came with a *three*-speed Borg Warner-sourced manual gearbox – interestingly, the P76 had a four-speed manual available – as standard with the Borg Warner Type 35 three-speed automatic as an option. According to ex-Leyland engineers the reason for the three-speed manual was its smaller size that fitted the Marina floorpan whereas the four-speed was apparently too big …

The engine was an extension of the previous program whereby the 2.2-litre six found under the bonnet of the X6 range was two cylinders added onto the 1485cc four, the new 2.6-litre six was an extension of the 1748cc four. Its cylinder dimensions, therefore, were 76.2 x 95.76mm for a capacity of 2622cc; with a 9.0 compression and a single HS6 SU carburettor the engine developed 90kW (121bhp) at 4500rpm and 224Nm (165lbs-ft) of torque at 2000rpm. With the sedan weighing a tad over 955kgs (2100lbs) it had a very favourable power-weight ratio (compared with the Cortina and Torana) to counter any perceived deficit from using a smaller capacity engine.

A number of changes – none of them significant – came with the Six and were automatically a part of the Four's specification. These included a new grille that was unique to the Aussie Marina comprising fifty seven vertical bars (I counted them!) flanked by Lucas 7-ins single headlights, chromed plastic strip across the top and the rectangular Leyland badge in the centre; a deeper front apron under the blade bumper needed to accommodate the Six's larger radiator that was positioned slightly further forward in the engine bay, a slight increase in spring and damper rates for the Six to cater for the added weight of around 32kgs (70lbs), better suspension bushes and an anti-roll bar was standard on the Six as were 5.5 x 13 wheels. Unique to the Six was the use of a thermo-electric cooling fan in place of the engine-driven windmill on the Four, a change necessary because of the length of the six-cylinder engine. And where the Marina Four had a single track rod on the rear suspension, the Marina Six had one each side. As an aside here, Pedders (the national suspension experts) developed an upgrade for the front suspension where Monroe-Wylie telescopic dampers were adapted to fit and replace the dreadful lever arm units and together with a sway bar transformed the handling of a Marina. Quite why the factory never went down this path is another one of life's mysteries.

Wheels conducted a comparison test between a Marina 175/4 and 262/6 in its June 1974 issue and criticised the unacceptably high noise levels, the dangerous windscreen wipers, the understeer, the lack of feel in the steering and the nose-diving under brakes. At the end of the day they preferred the Six because its dual personality appealed to them and added, "It's a smoother car, with a lot of power which can be used either for reasonably fast open road work, or for pottering sedately around town without using all that much more fuel than the four. Its downfall is its indifferent handling." As for performance, the Six automatic ran out to a top speed of 156.8km/h (98mph) (compared with 131km/h, 82mph) and it ran from 0–80, 96 and 112km/h (0–50, 60 and 70mph) in 8.5, 11.4 and 15.3 seconds respectively, quite a bit quicker than the Four; and fuel economy showed the Six to average 12.4 litres per 100km (23mpg) against the Four's 10 litres per 100km (28mpg).

As an option Leyland offered the Rallye Pack on the Coupe only and this comprised a power output of 100kW (135bhp) brought about by a second HS6 SU carburettor, 6-ins cast alloy rims, firmer suspension, black-out sills and a body stripe all for $250. I wonder how many were built and sold?

At the release of these Mark II editions of the Marina the retail prices of the Six were $2870 for the Deluxe manual Coupe, $3390 for the Super manual Coupe, $3000 for the Deluxe manual sedan, $3190 for the Super manual sedan and an extra $270 for the automatic.

Production of the Marina ceased in November 1974 after David Abell came out from England under orders from Lord Stokes to close the Leyland Zetland operations. Survivors are few and far between which is a (sad) indication of what the classic car people think of them.

As a postscript to the Marina tale is the fact that Leyland Australia's engineers were working on what was known internally as the P82 which would have replaced it in 1975. One running prototype had been built in the Engineering workshops that featured MacPherson strut coil spring front suspension, live rear axle with coil springs and links with power coming from a 3.3-litre OHV V6 engine derived from the P76 V8 unit. That one prototype, a four-door sedan, was shipped back to Longbridge when the closure took place and has never been seen or heard about since – it was most likely broken up under orders from Stokes.

LEYLAND P76

Many of the senior engineers at BMCA and then Leyland Australia (LA) had been recruited from GM-H where they had been deeply involved in the genesis of the 48/215 and FJ Holdens. To nobody's surprise they continually badgered UK management for permission to develop a six-cylinder car exclusively for local sale. Longbridge continually denied them their wish and kept telling them to sell the four-cylinder offerings they had – after all, they were selling by the hundreds of thousands in the UK so they must be what buyers wanted!

The first stirrings surfaced in 1962 with the release of the Austin Freeway and Wolseley 24/80 but as good as they were, they were seen as merely uprated four-cylinder Pommie cars, not true-blue Aussies. So it was back to the drawing board. Studies were carried out during the early 60s for a two-model program with a high commonality of components – Model A and Model B. Model A eventually became the Morris Marina by default and Model B became the Leyland P76.

It really was quite an ambitious program for the small outpost of

the giant British Motor Corporation which up until then had many years' experience in adapting UK designs for local conditions but had no real practical experience in the design and development processes of a complete car. In early 1968 when it was still BMCA and just prior to the formation of British Leyland in the UK, the Australians pitched their proposal to management who OK'd it and allocated around $21 million for it. Later, they had to re-pitch their proposal to the new British Leyland management and made it by the skin of their teeth!

A number of decisions had to be made and quickly. For example, what engines would be used, what gearboxes, suspension components and, critically, who would style the new car. The Australian engineers actually concepted a family of all-alloy engines that included an in-line OHV four-cylinder, in-line six, V8 and a V12 but these studies led nowhere through a lack of resources. With Model A and Model B it was planned to use as many components that were already in high volume production in Australia. Many old-timer engineers at the company were disgusted with this approach – they called it 'Catalogue Engineering!' However, management was adamant that for the company to return to profitability it had to go this route and move away from the costly Issigonis-engineered front-wheel drive cars from which the company had made a loss for the previous decade!

In the event the Australians were licensed to use the ex-Buick alloy V8 engine for which Rover (by now part of British Leyland) had purchased the manufacturing rights. That solved one engine problem and opened another – what about a price-leader six-cylinder engine? Having had experience at developing the 2.2-litre SOHC six out of the 1.5-litre E Series four, it was relatively simple to build a 2.6-litre six out of the 1.75-litre four. It was smaller in capacity than they wanted but

that was all that was available in the short term. And the 3.5-litre V8 Rover engine lacked the torque they needed for local driving conditions and so a 4.4-litre version was developed locally. The six developed 90kW (121bhp) at 4500rpm and 224Nm (165lbs-ft) of torque at 2000rpm while the V8 developed 143kW (192bhp) at 4250rpm and 386Nm (285lbs-ft) at 2500rpm.

As for the gearboxes, Borg Warner supplied the Type 35 three-speed automatic and two manuals – a three-speed with column shift and a four-speed with a floor shifter – plus the rear axle assembly. Armstrong York were contracted to supply the MacPherson struts, Bishop Engineering supplied the rack and pinion steering and PBR supplied the braking system.

Initial studies had the P76 being slightly smaller physically than the Kingswood/Falcon/Valiant triumvirate but a visit by the new management team from BLMC forced the locals to extend the wheelbase to 2819mm (111-ins) and overall length to 4877mm (192-ins) so that it matched them inch-for-inch. Body width was 1905mm (75-ins) and height was 1372mm (54-ins) while the kerb weight of the P76 was 1282kgs (2820lbs), some 114–135kgs (250–300lbs) *lighter* than its rivals because of the alloy V8 engine. In fact, because the 6-cylinder engine and V8 weighed within 2kgs (4lbs) of each other the P76's body structure did not need to be as heavy in its construction as its rivals whose bodies had to be able to cope with biggest and heaviest cast iron V8 engines that were available.

Styling was a contentious issue. BMCA canvassed four potential studios – Longbridge in the UK, Karmann in Germany, Ital Design and Giovanni Michclotti, both in Italy. Their reasoning was to be able to use the stylist in their planned advertising campaign. In the event the genesis of the P76's design came from within their own studio at Zetland in the form of Romand Rodbergh, the company's in-house stylist. His sketches and 1:10 scale models were taken to Michelotti who "tidied them up a little" as body engineer Graham Hardy commented and viola! There was the P76. And curiously, neither Rodbergh nor Michelotti were a part of the subsequent advertising campaign.

Hand-built prototypes were made, the first of them looking like an HT Holden, and they were extensively tested in the Charleville area of Queensland where some faults were uncovered. The next batch of prototypes were built at Abingdon in the UK under the supervision of two Australian engineers – they were there to make sure the Poms built them the way the Aussies wanted them, *not* the Pommie way!

Durability and reliability proved to be up to standard and so progress towards full production continued. The Zetland factory was totally re-equipped with new body presses to press the panels as single items – BMC generally made large panels in parts and welded them together! – while the machine shop was equipped with new automatic transfer machines for the V8 engine to complement the machine lines already in place for the E series engines. This made the Zetland site unique in Australia at the time because it was manufacturing four-, six- and V8 engines under the same roof.

Released to the public on June 26, 1973 the Leyland dealers were inundated with people wanting a new P76 such was the success of their "Anything but Average" campaign and the media build-up in the weeks prior to the launch. Within days Leyland had orders for in excess of 2000 units with the majority being the upper better-equipped models, not what the company had planned. Some people would not wait but most did and by and large they were happy with their purchase.

There were quality issues to begin with, perfectly understandable when you consider the Zetland plant's workforce was a veritable United Nations of nationalities where English was definitely *not* the first language, where many had never worked in a factory environment before and where the engineers were learning how to design-and-manufacture a completely new car from scratch. The first six month's production quality was not good but after that when everything settled down to a steady rhythm and where component parts were available – a very real problem as GM-H, Ford and Chrysler all squeezed and black-mailed suppliers not to supply Leyland Australia – the cars off the end of the line were reasonably well made. The media, of course, created merry hell with the company and the public as it is want to do and completely distorted reality to the detriment of the company, its customers and dealers. This was so unnecessary as in point of fact the P76 was ultimately no worse in its build quality than the Kingswood, Falcon or Valiant – by world standards they were all sub-standard!

Where GM-H, Ford and to a lesser extent Chrysler offered buyers almost an open order form that allowed buyers to customise their purchase to their exact desires – a logistical nightmare of Orwellian proportions which they soon backed away from – Leyland instead offered buyers discreet packages which was easier for the buyer, more cost effective from an inventory point of view and simpler for the dealers. P76 ownership started with the Deluxe that was pretty basic and then moved up to the Super and then the Executive. Curiously the Deluxe tag was again used for the most basic model by Leyland and not for their top model as other manufacturers were doing. The Deluxe was easily recognised by its two headlight grille and inside it had bench seats front and rear, albeit quite comfortable seats because they featured Pirelli webbing and full foam padding (unlike its rivals) and apart from electric wipers and washers along with a full flow-through ventilation system had little else by way of creature comforts inside. The Super had four headlights along with bucket seats, rear seat centre armrest, colour-matched loop pile carpet, padded rear parcel shelf, padded door trims and courtesy lights in the boot, under the bonnet and in the glove box; Super buyers could order the V8 engine as an option. The top-of-the-line Executive looked like the Super (four headlights) but added a floor console in front that housed the gear selector for the standard automatic gearbox and there was a cubby under the arm rest between the front seats. Pricing began at $3250 for the Deluxe six-cylinder sedan, $3750 for the six-cylinder Super and $4525 for the V8-only Executive. Options included the V8 in the Super ($180), four-speed manual gearbox ($160), three-speed automatic ($260 on Deluxe, $100 on Super), air conditioning ($435, V8

LEYLAND
LSZ 162

VBP76

only), power steering ($150, V8 only), push button radio ($120) and reclining bucket seats cost $35 extra.

Modern Motor magazine (August 1973) published a comparison test between the luxury models from each manufacturer – Leyland P76 Executive, Holden Premier, Falcon Fairmont and Valiant Regal – with prices ranging from $4525 for the P76, $4344 for the Premier, $4484 for the Fairmont and $4447 for the Regal. Aesthetically the *MM* team rated the Leyland second – the Holden was considered the best looking – which was a refreshing comment (most so-called 'experts' in the media ridiculed the P76's styling), ranked the aluminium alloy V8 as the best engine on offer (the Holden and Ford V8s were ranked equal last!) saying "It's smooth and free-revving and gives good performance from its light weight. Better still, it has less effect on handling than the others and has better fuel economy." From a dynamic point of view the P76 again scored rather well for a first-time effort; from a pure ride point of view it was by far the best of the quartet and from a pure handling perspective it was ranked second to the Falcon and in the ride/handling compromise it again ranked second, this time to the Holden. These results were obtained using normal roads (not a race track) and on smooth bitumen the Falcon was best but on poorly sealed and rutted road surfaces the Falcon performed poorly.

In outright performance the P76 was ranked number 1 courtesy of the alloy V8 engine. Against the clock all four exceeded the magic 'ton,' the P76 running to 163.2km/h (102mph), same as the Fairmont, the Premier went to 164.8km/h (103mph) and the Regal ran to 172.8km/h (108mph) while the classic 0–96km/h (0–60mph) run had them all bunched around the 11 second mark except for the Premier which was by far the quickest at 9.8 seconds. Viewed dispassionately and in real world situations the P76 was the quickest point-to-point.

Being the luxury versions of their respective ranges interior comfort was important. All four were roomy enough for four adults to be seated on supportive seats that remained so over long distances although they felt the Regal seats were too low; the others were ranked virtually equal. On a value for money basis the P76 outranked them all.

In its January 1974 issue *Wheels* magazine announced the Leyland P76 V8 as its Car of the Year. While many critics in the media scorned the magazine for its choice it was generally accepted that the P76 did move the game on considerably from the status quo that was the Kingswood/Falcon/Valiant and for the first time offered buyers a genuine alternative. However, they qualified their announcement by saying, "But it must be made clear that it is in the V8 version that it really shows its potential." They further added, "We believe that the V8 engine turns the P76 from being a better than average car into an outstanding vehicle."

Evan Green and John Bryson entered the UDT London-Munich

Rally and decided on the P76 as their car of choice. A standard sedan was selected off the line, stripped and the body seam welded for added strength and then prepared for the long and arduous trek from London through the Sahara Desert, a competitive section on the famous Targa Florio circuit in Sicily and then through Greece, Turkey and parts of Eastern Europe before ending in Munich. Remarkably the mechanical components – V8 engine, four-speed manual gearbox, suspension, steering and brakes were completely standard – they were not modified in any way. The start in London took place on May 5, 1974 and finished on May 25.

The stretch across the Sahara was driven in unbearably hot and dusty conditions over desert tracks that pounded the body mercilessly. Perhaps to nobody's surprise they were 1800km south of Tunis when the right-hand front suspension strut pushed through the upper mount. They slowly managed to wind the coil spring back and hammered the strut top back into place and were able to continue to Tunis where a more permanent repair was carried out.

Onto Sicily and the infamous Targa Florio circuit where the P76 was the fastest competitor around the track; Green and Bryson were presented with the Targa Florio Trophy for their achievement. Only 26 cars completed the event, exactly half. The Leyland P76 was classified 13th to the joy of all concerned.

To commemorate the fine performance in Sicily Leyland released a version of the Super sedan called appropriately the P76 Targa Florio. It was a limited edition built only from July through September 1974 during which 479 were made. It was available in Omega Navy (a dark blue metallic, 319 units), Aspen Green (a medium green metallic, 80 units) and Nutmeg (a metallic brown, 80 units) with a broad white stripe

down each side, a Targa Florio decal cut out of it on the rear quarter panel and CAC alloy wheels with 185SR 14 radial tyres. All were snapped up by enthusiastic owners and are now verging on collectible.

Many years later the author met Evan Green and John Bryson and when asked about the event and their selection of the P76 Green responded by saying, "The P76 was the ideal rally car, superb balance with ample power and torque from the V8 engine." When asked if either a Kingswood or Falcon would have faired any better he commented strongly, "I knew both those cars well from my motor industry involvement over many years and I can honestly say they would never have gone the distance – the P76 was superior to them in its dynamics in every way." High praise indeed from one of Australia's greatest motoring adventurers and a proven competition driver who knew his cars.

In November 1974, not long after David Abell arrived at Zetland, the company announced it was closing its Australian operations and would henceforth be an importer of cars. The announcement did not come as too much of a surprise because the media had been forecasting it for some time. Various sage-like articles appeared in newspapers and magazines around the country blaming the collapse of Leyland Australia on the P76 but it was all a media beat-up. In actual fact Leyland Australia, through the sales of the P76 and Marina, was on the verge of breaking even financially for the first time in many years! No, the P76 was not to blame – it was all down to inept management at British Leyland in the UK and their over-commitment to the voracious banks in England. BL was losing millions of Pounds daily and when the coal miners went on strike it brought the house of cards tumbling down. Leyland Australia, along with subsidiaries in South Africa and Spain, was sacrificed to save the business in England. Ironically British Leyland had to be bailed out by the British government and was nationalised but all that did was prove just how inept management was and how intractable were the unions until stumps were eventually pulled.

Between 19,000 and 20,000 Leyland P76's were built in less than two years of production so it *was* a sales success and was going to be the springboard for a whole new range of uniquely Australian cars. At the close a very public auction of 10 Leyland Force 7V coupes took place – it was only weeks away from its public release – and the existence of a P76 station wagon was revealed. And there was going to be a brand new factory to the west of Sydney … Sadly none of these plans would see the light of day and the P76 has now become something of a collectible among enthusiasts who are now better appreciating just how good the car really was.

MINI AND MOKE

Despite the internal turmoil going on around it as BMCA management decided to convert back to rear-wheel drive cars, the ubiquitous Mini sailed on regardless. The Mini K had been released in early 1969 and was selling well; it featured for the first time on a Mini an alternator for the electrical system, something its competitors had been using for years. Local content for the Mini was said to be around the 80 per cent mark.

In August 1971 the Mini received a major facelift, literally. Badged as the Clubman, the new Mini had a longer and squarer nose that on the one hand took away some of the cheeky character of the car but at the same time updated its appearance dramatically. Opinions are still divided today, fifty years later! It was available in two versions – Mini Clubman 1100 that replaced the Mini K, and Clubman GT with the 1275cc A series engine that replaced the Cooper S. This renaming came about because of Lord Stokes' refusal to pay royalties to the Cooper family for use of their name. Such stupidity was rife in British Leyland at the time. The new nose added five-inches to the Mini's overall length; at the same time Leyland offered the car in some strikingly bright paint colours. A new dashboard was part of the upgrade and for the first time in a Mini had the dials grouped in a binnacle directly in front of the driver – hallelujah! With the GT the dash included a tachometer, another first

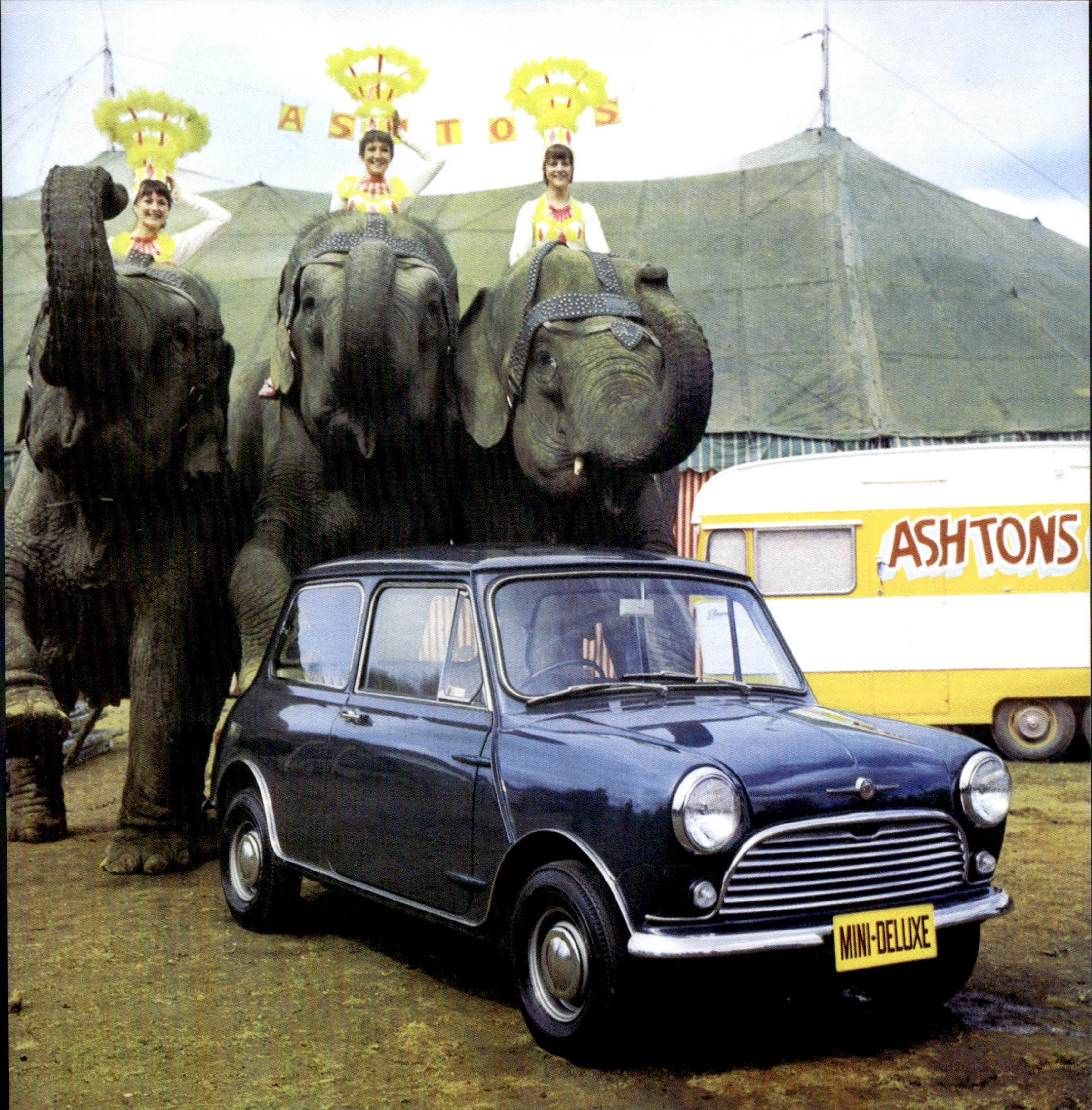
ASHTONS
ASHTONS
MINI-DELUXE

for the Mini. As well, the Clubman came with two-speed electric wipers, electric windscreen washers, centre-lock seat belts and pressure-limiting brake valves in the rear circuit.

Wheels tested a Clubman GT (October 1971) and while they thoroughly enjoyed the dynamic qualities – "the handling is exhilarating" – even after all those years but they had real issues with aspects of its interior. Of the seats they said, "They're little more than new covering on the old frames – and that can't be called anything but atrocious. The squabs are too hard, not high enough and are not raked enough." On a long night-time drive they described the journey for the front passenger as "sheer misery." Noise levels were an issue as well, being described like "sitting in a galvanised water tank with a sporty-sounding engine sending resonances buzzing through it."

Against the clock the Clubman GT reached a top speed of 156.8km/h (98mph, the Cooper S reached 155.2km/h, 97mph) and ran the 0–80, 96 and 112km/h (0–50, 60 and 70mph) sprints in 8.2, 12.2 and 16.9 seconds respectively (the Cooper S took 7.9, 11.2 and 15.4 seconds) with an overall fuel consumption for the test of 10–8.8 litres per 100km (28–32mpg).

April 1972 saw the cars rebadged, this time as Leylands. Another year on and more changes were made to the Mini and Mini S, the Clubman GT having been discontinued. The admired Hydrolastic suspension system was replaced by the original rubber cones on cost grounds, the differential ratio was raised to 3.44 from 3.65:1 (for both models) and the Mini now rode on 5.95 x 10 tyres that raised the gearing per 1000rpm from 24.6km/h (15.4mph) up to 26.8km/h (16.8mph); with the Mini S that rode on 145 x 10 radials the road speed per 1000rpm was 25.7km/h (16.1mph). The Mini S also acquired flared wheel arches, front bumper under-riders, black-painted sill panels and bright mouldings around the door window frames.

Inside were new seats with a new trim material – about time said many critics. The seats were reshaped with better cushions and their backrests folded forward for access to the rear seat; the S seats had cloth inserts. Another change was to the foot pedals – they were enlarged to take the rubbers from the Marina; carpets now graced the floors while the S had a radio as standard equipment while the three-instrument dash was retained. Prices were $2085 for the Mini and $2360 for the Mini S.

Road tests from the period showed the S to be capable of 128km/h (80mph) with acceleration from 0–80 and 96km/h (0–50 and 60mph) in 15.0 and 21.9 seconds which put it some way behind rivals like the Toyota Corolla, Datsun 1200, Honda Civic and Mazda 1300.

In September 1975 the locally produced 1098cc A series engine was replaced by an imported 998cc unit and its transmission, assembly of the rest of the car remaining unchanged. At this time the Mini S gained head restraints and a full-width boot mat. By this time sales were on the slide as the many Japanese rivals continued to undermine the marketing efforts of Leyland who were basically trying to sell a 20-year old design against far more modern designs. Consideration was given to selling the Italian Innocenti Mini with its Bertone body design and hatchback here but nothing came of that. With the closure of Waterloo Mini production was transferred to Pressed Metal at Enfield. The major difference here was the absence of the famous Rotodip process that cleaned the steel bodies of any impurities. At Enfield they developed a slipper-dip system that took the bodies through large vats of degreaser and primer before moving them on to the paint shop. The problem with this process was

that it only treated the bodies up to the waistline and not the whole body like the Rotodip process did. For Mini owners this led to corrosion issues later in the car's life.

In late 1976 Leyland marketed a limited edition Mini SS that sold for $3895 and quickly sold out. Its specification included a two-speaker audio system and alloy wheels. A further luxury edition was announced in March 1977, the Mini LS that carried a retail price of $4495. In August 1978 the LS came with the 1275cc single-carburettor engine that developed 41kW (55bhp) at 5250rpm and 93Nm (69lbs-ft) of torque at 2500rpm, and 12-inch road wheels shod with 145SR/70 x 12 radial tyres.

BMC released the Mark II Moke in April 1969 and its specifications included the 1098cc engine and full-synchromesh gearbox taken from the Mini K, a revised bonnet pressing, single taillight units, clear Perspex side screens and slightly wider wheel tracks. But the 70s saw the beginning of the age of legislation where the automobile was concerned and the Moke was unable to escape its clutches. In mid-1976 ADR27a was introduced which was the first of the engine emission regulations. To comply, the Leyland engineers adapted the air pump and charcoal canister set-up they had developed for the US market Moke Californian; 1977 saw the use of a removable grille held in place by 6 screws and the addition of separate reversing lights; 1978 saw revised bumpers designed to take some of the impact of a collision by having revised mounting points under the front sub-frame instead of on top with holes in the front panel to accommodate the brackets while in 1980 the rear bumpers had to be modified along the same lines and a new, larger square taillight unit incorporating reversing lights was fitted.

In November 1979 the Moke underwent its greatest change since the adoption of the 13-inch wheels. Of those changes by far the most significant was the introduction of zinc-coated body panels to help reduce corrosion issues. In addition the Moke was fitted with inertia reel seat belts attached to a roll bar that had been developed for the Californian, the actual seats had been redesigned for more comfort and had tilting squabs and multi-position slides. A cheaper heater/demister was fitted (it was not as good as the previous unit), there were new side screens and a new indicator/wiper/high beam/horn combination switch similar to that used in Triumphs.

In 1972 Leyland produced the Moke Californian that came from an order for 100 units from the Virgin Islands in the Caribbean and this meant that the Moke had to comply with US requirements. Powering the Californian was the 1275cc engine from the US Austin America on which all emission testing had been certified and so its specifications featured the exhaust air pump, charcoal canister vapour recovery system, catalytic converter for use with unleaded petrol and an SU HS4 (1.5-ins)

SU carburettor in place of the usual HS2 (1.25-ins) unit. Also included in the car's specifications were a repositioned (to the rear) fuel tank of just 6 US gallons (it was normally 28-litres, 6.25 imp gallons), two-speed wipers, hazard warning lights, reversing lights, independent parking and indicator lights and side reflectors.

The Virgin Island order was never delivered because the company involved went bust before the cars could be despatched. The cars were, not surprisingly, diverted for sale on the local market and released in late 1972 at a showroom floor price of $1780. Sales ended in early 1973 when the 100 units had been sold.

Another variant that Leyland marketed in the 70s was the Moke Pick-up that was released in May 1975. As was so often the case with BMC vehicles, it was a good idea spoilt by poor execution. There was no small utility type vehicle on the market at the time which meant there was a niche that Leyland could fill below the traditional Japanese utes. However, the tray hung quite a way over the rear wheels – some 60% of the load length was behind them – and the rear suspension was not strengthened in any way to keep manufacturing costs down and with the Australian penchant for overloading the handling qualities suffered dramatically. Also, within a few weeks of the Pick-up's release the 1098cc engine was discontinued meaning that virtually every one produced had the 998cc engine. Unfortunately for Leyland the Moke Pick-up never reached its sales potential – had they fitted an uprated suspension and the 1275cc engine perhaps it might have had a happier ending.

There was another unfulfilled chapter with the Moke – the 4x4 version. At least twice in its early years a 4x4 was concepted and some prototypes built for testing but it never went any further. With the ending of local production of the Mini in 1978 the Moke took on more importance and with the likes of Suzuki (Sierra) and Daihatsu coming to market with light weight 4x4's it seemed a good idea to build a 4x4 Moke variant. Two prototypes were built in late 1978 with one being shipped to Longbridge for testing. However, the decision was made to end production of the Moke in Australia and transfer its production to Portugal and so the idea of a 4x4 Moke became somewhat academic.

By October 1978 Leyland gave up the uneven struggle and stopped production of the Mini at the Pressed Metal facility on Cosgrove Road, Enfield; by then the company had built and sold 176,284 Minis. In November 1981 production of the Mini Moke ceased after building 26,142 examples in Australia.

SPORTS CARS

From April 1970 until December 1971 BMCA assembled the Mark II version of the MG Midget at Pressed Metal Corporation. It featured a black pressed metal grille and slimmer bumper bars which made it the merest of facelifts.

As for the MG B it would remain in production until November 6, 1972 when a combination of factors – very low sales volumes, a Government requirement for 85 per cent local content by 1974 – saw the inevitable decision being made by Leyland Australia management. The occasion of the last MG B rolling off the Waterloo assembly line was marked by a mock funeral.

For 1970 there was a minor facelift that included a recessed black grille, squared-off taillights, fold-down hood, smaller steering wheel, the bonnet being made from a sheet steel pressing (instead of aluminium), changes to the badges and all manual gearbox cars now had overdrive as standard. In 1971 came rubber-faced bumper over-riders, gas struts to support the bonnet when open as well as struts for the bootlid followed by head restraints.

What had been Australia's most successful sports car (from a sales point of view) was forced from our market by Government legislation even though it continued on in other international markets for another eight years.

2500
ATOMIC
SKI
RDU 996M

CHAPTER 5

AUSTRALIAN MOTOR INDUSTRIES

TRIUMPH

AMI entered the Seventies brimful of confidence, a rather different situation from a decade ago. Sales of Triumph and Rambler cars were holding up well, especially Triumph because it was now a six year-old design. And Toyota sales were rising irresistibly as the model range was widened to include a blend of locally assembled and imported models.

From March 1970 the Mark II versions of the Triumph 2000 and 2.5PI appeared in showrooms around Australia. Michelotti was again consulted on the styling and basically adapted the lines he developed for the Triumph Stag to the original sedan body. This meant a slightly longer nose by around 88.9mm (3.5-ins) and more assertive full-width grille embracing the four headlights and triangular parking/indicator lenses at the front corners. An elongated rear (by around 127mm/5-ins) with large horizontal lights set in a wider recessed panel balanced the car's new lines, the boot lid edge being chromed trimmed for effect. Inside there was a completely new dashboard padded all round with a mock wood veneer façade, the section in front of the driver containing the round Smith gauges and being curved to create a cockpit effect while all the minor functions were now on steering column stalks – indicators, hi/low beam headlight flash on the right, wiper/washers on the left. At either end of the dash was a circular air vent while in the centre were two rectangular adjustable vents making the Mark II probably the best English saloon available from the cabin ventilation point of view.

On the 2000 there were two large round Smiths dials – combination on the left, speedometer on the right – with a small clock to the left and a round dial between the two large ones containing a multitude of monitoring lights to warn the driver of any malfunction. The 2.5PI substituted a tachometer and the minor gauges were relocated to smaller units. The 2000 had a two-spoke plastic steering wheel, the 2.5PI a three-spoke unit.

With the Mark II AMI took the trouble to reposition the windscreen wipers to suit right-hand drive – something the Poms did not do – although the road wheels remained at 13-ins.

In August 1972 AMI added a revised model to the range in the form of the Triumph 2500TC. The letters stood for Twin Carburettors. Under the bonnet very little had changed apart from the removal of the troublesome fuel injection system and replacing it with twin SU HS-6 1.5-ins carburettors on the 2.5-litre six, the installation being designed here in Australia; out of sight was a Triumph GT6-spec camshaft. Power outputs were little different at 67kW (90bhp) for the 2000 and for the TC it was 74kW (100bhp) at 4250rpm with 190Nm (140lbs-ft) of torque at just 2000rpm. By comparison, the PI engine had produced 98kW (132bhp).

Wheels tested at 2500TC (July 1973) and admired the car for its easy-going nature, smoothness from the lowly-stressed six-cylinder engine,

well-suppressed road noise, almost no wind noise, the comfort of the seats and the way it would lope along at 128km/h (80mph+) without apparent discomfort. They managed a top speed of 163.2km/h (102mph) from an automatic that took 9.1, 12.8 and 17.0 seconds to dash to 80, 96 and 112km/h (50-, 60-, and 70mph) which was acceptably quick with a fuel consumption of 12.8–10.8 litres per 100km (22–26mpg). A manual TC was only 3–5km/h (2–4mph) quicker flat out and took 16.8 seconds for the dash to 112km/h (70mph).

A radio was a standard fitting – AMI learning from Toyota – in the retail price of $4349 for the manual and $4649 for the automatic.

AMI continued with the Mark II sedan that remained almost visually unchanged but nonetheless sold at a steady rate despite being an old design – it had first appeared here in Australia in 1964 – with unfashionable flat side glass. There was a certain ambience, a certain 'Englishness' about it that appealed to a conservative buyer.

In mid-1975 the 2000 version was discontinued and model nomenclature changed from 2500TC to 2500S which brought a small number of changes. A prominent 2500S badge adorned the centre of the grille and it adopted the PI dashboard complete with tachometer while the seats were now upholstered in a corded cloth for greater comfort. Again the saloon was available in either manual-with-overdrive or the Borg Warner Type 35 automatic with power assisted steering now also standard; the only really necessary option was integrated air conditioning. The S version brought 14-ins alloy wheels as standard shod with 175HR14 radial tyres and the braking system was upgraded to four-wheel solid discs. *Modern Motor* achieved a top speed of 162km/h (101mph) in their 2500S and a time of 15.0 seconds for the classic 0–100km/h 0–62mph) dash.

By the end of 1977 AMI brought its collaboration with British Leyland in England to a close in Australia which brought the Triumph chapter also to a close after nearly three-quarters of a century. The passing caused hardly a ripple in the media which was disappointing.

RAMBLER

The new decade saw AMI begin assembling the Rambler Hornet that succeeded the American here and in the US. This was one of AMC's better designs having little of the garishness of its US rivals. Its styling was characterised by the long nose-short tail look popularised by the Mustang half a decade earlier with deeply flared wheel arches and plain unadorned sides. *Wheels* magazine said of it (June 1971), "The Hornet is easily the prettiest American car in a decade, and in our opinion without doubt is Australia's best Rambler."

AMI aimed the Hornet at buyers who would consider the Holden Premier, Ford Fairmont and Fairlane, Chrysler Regal and VIP but who did not want his new car to look like the cheaper version of his neighbour.

The decision by AMI Managing Director Ken Hougham to go upmarket with the Hornet's specification levels was a smart move as pricing ex-USA meant that it could never compete in the less expensive end of the market as it did in America. The Hornet came with good quality padded vinyl upholstery for the front separate tombstone seats (made locally) and rear bench with arm rest, carpets on the floor over thick underlay, an excellent heater/demister with fan, carpeted and lined luggage compartment, footwell courtesy lights. Only an air conditioning system and radial tyres were listed as options.

The dashboard was dominated by the tall centre section that housed (from the top) dual adjustable air vents, slide controls for the heater/demister, radio and finally the ashtray and lighter. To the right was a flat hooded section that contained three round dials comprising the speedometer in the centre flanked by a clock (right) and combination dial with fuel and temperature gauges plus warning lights to the left. A matching section in front of the passenger housed the glovebox. A flat console between the front seats housed the floor selector for the automatic gearbox and a small storage cubby. Two pull-push switches to the right of the dials operate the lights and wiper/washers although the actual wipers themselves were set up for *left*-hand drive – AMI never converted them.

What surprised many people was the physical size of the Hornet but that was more an illusion created by its low height combined with very short front and rear overhangs. It was built on a wheelbase of 27476mm (108-ins) which was 76mm (3-ins) *shorter* than the HQ Holden/XA

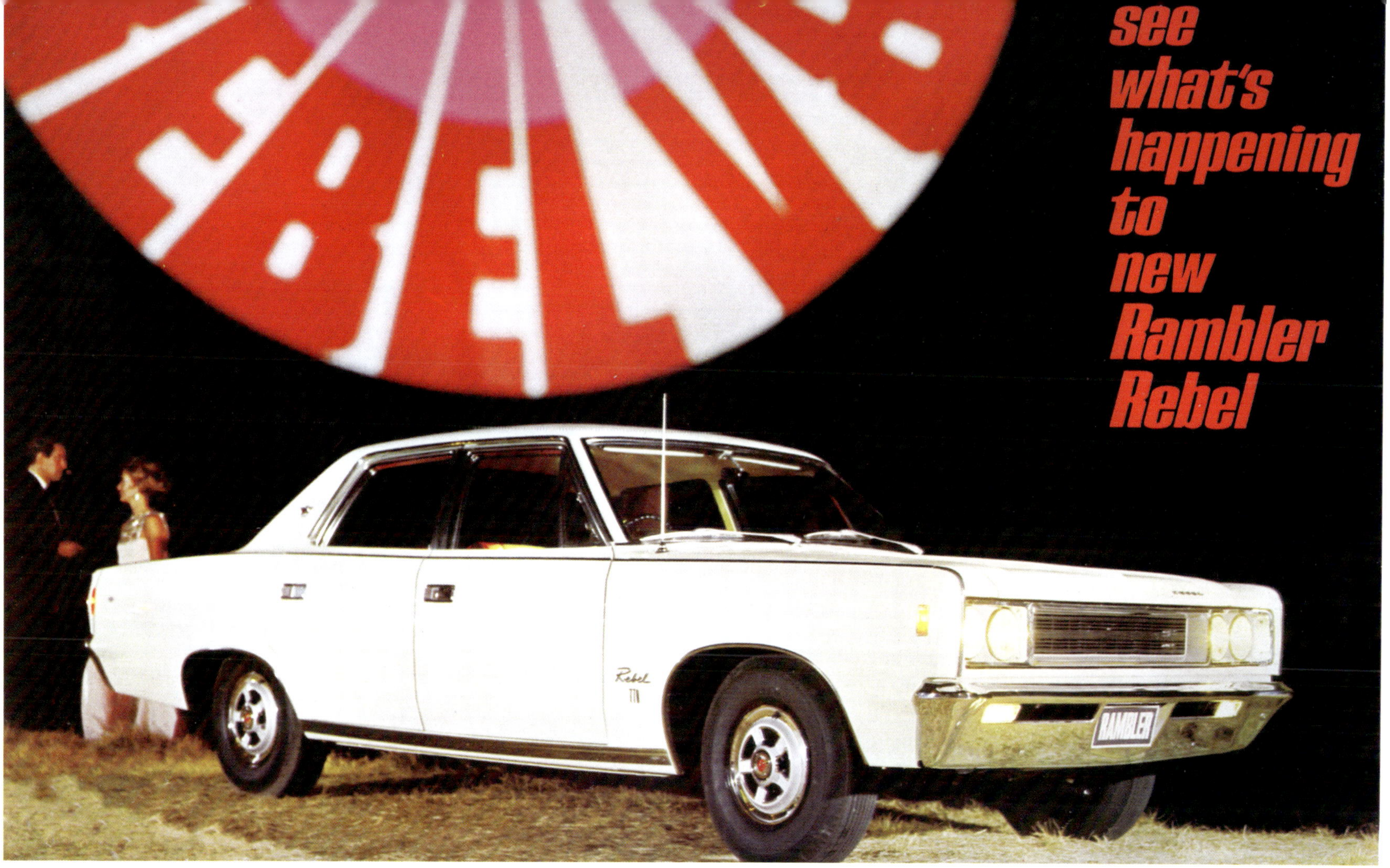
see
what's
happening
to
new
Rambler
Rebel
RAMBLER

75

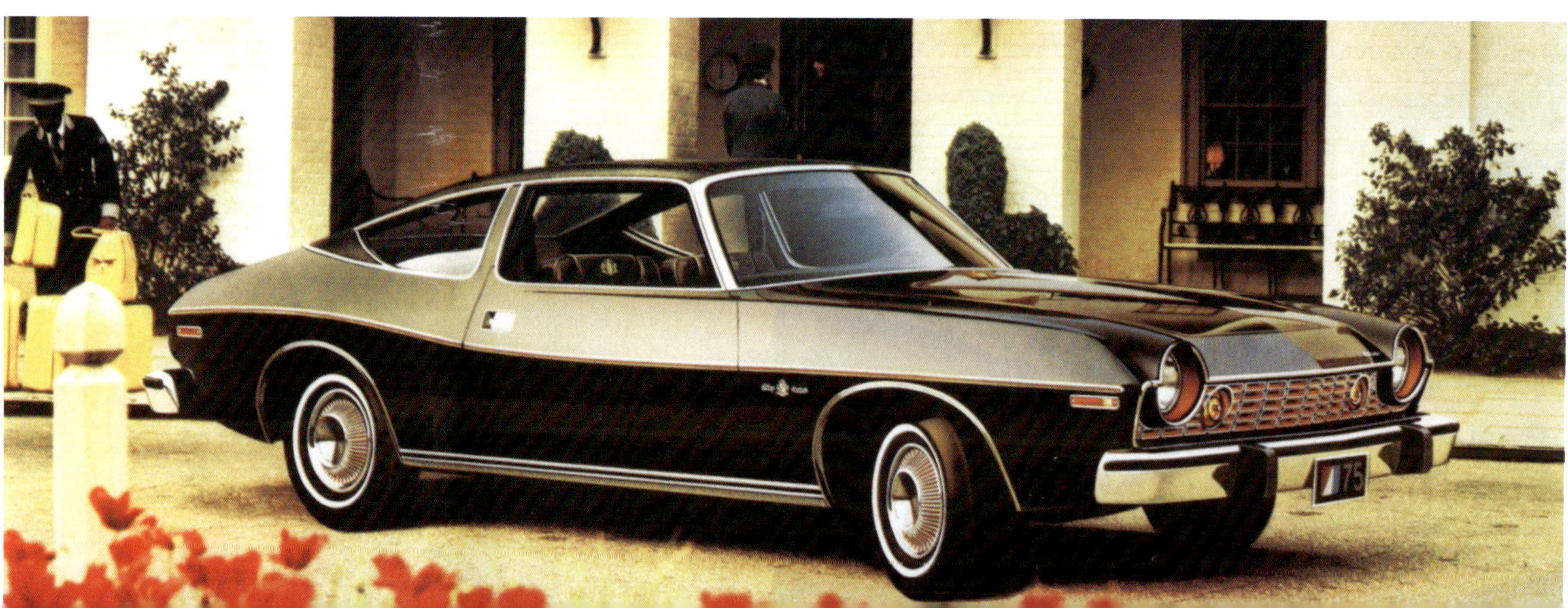

Ford/VH Chrysler and stretched to 4546mm (179-ins) in overall length by 1803mm (71-ins) in width and 1321mm (52-ins) in height; kerb weight was 1285kgs (2828lbs). In point of fact, the Hornet was about the size of the Holden Commodore that appeared towards the end of the decade.

Technically the Hornet broke no new ground – this was after all an American car – and featured a relatively new cast iron OHV six-cylinder engine of 232-cid displacement (95.25 x 88.9mm/3.75 x 3.5-ins bore and stroke) which was 3.8-litres in the new measures. Power developed was 115kW (155bhp) at 4400rpm with 300Nm (222 lbs-ft) of torque at a mere 1600rpm; the compression ratio was 8.5:1 and it used a Holley twin-throat carburettor. The only gearbox on offer in Australia was the Borg Warner Type 35 three-speed automatic, drive going via a one-piece propeller shaft to a live rear axle suspended on semi-elliptic leaf springs. At the front were upper-and-lower wishbones locating the front wheels with a coil spring and telescopic damper operating from the upper wishbone. Braking was by big front 286mm (11.25-ins) discs from the Javelin with cast iron drums at the rear plus a vacuum booster. As was often the case with American cars the recirculating ball steering system was not power assisted and consequently had more than *six* turns lock-to-lock!

Wheels and *Modern Motor* both tested a Hornet in June 1971 and both testers enjoyed the car immensely apart from the dreadful steering. *Wheels* ended by writing, "We loved driving the Hornet – it's an extremely pleasant car apart from the steering, it's smooth, quiet and comfortable." As for performance, they achieved 158.4km/h (99mph) and 155.2km/h (97mph) respectively and 0–96km/h (0–60mph) sprints in 11.7 and 12.5 seconds which was a good average return. At $4079 it found many happy owners.

The Rebel was uprated to the big 360-cid V8 engine and the ignition key was moved from the dash to the steering column where it incorporated a steering and transmission selector/ignition lock. As for the Javelin, it now featured the 390-cid V8 that developed 325bhp and would push the coupe to around 200km/h (125mph).

Late in 1971 AMI introduced a revised Hornet powered by a 4.2-litre six-cylinder engine (258-cid) with the cylinder dimensions of 95 x 99mm and on an 8.0:1 compression developed 155bhp at 3800rpm and 240lbs-ft of torque at just 1800rpm. Australian Motor Manual tested one soon after its release and noted that since its introduction the Hornet had been almost 'bug-free' but nevertheless AMI decided that along with the larger engine it would equip the Hornet with ventilated front disc brakes, redesigned seating and some minor trim changes. The engine developed the same power as before but had more torque that gave it better low speed responsiveness. The new car had a firmly sprung suspension that did allow the occasional bump-and-thump into the passenger compartment but generally the ride was pleasant and free from float. Their only real gripe was with the slow steering that need more than six turns from one lock to the other.

As for its performance, they clocked it at 158.4km/h (99mph) for its top speed and it took 11.2 seconds for the 0–96km/h dash (60mph).

Interestingly, AMC in America could supply a Hornet with their 304-cid V8 but AMI opted not to offer this engine here in Australia.

An 'all new' Matador was released in 1971 to replace the Rebel. It sat on a longer 2997mm (118-ins) wheelbase and stretched to 5235mm (206-ins) in overall length so it was quite a bit larger. The components required for right-hand drive production were, as with other AMC cars, shipped from AMC's Kenosha plant to Melbourne. The Matador was assembled in two generations: the first from 1971 to 1975, and the second from 1975 through to the end of 1976.

AMI positioned the Matador at the upper end of the market and so it came equipped with carpets, heater/demister with fan, AM radio, power windows, power steering and automatic transmission; power came from AMC's 5.9-litre (360-cid) V8 engine. Local content included paint (Toyota coded, so therefore the same colours), tyres, seating, lights and so on. Intriguingly, our Matadors had amber lenses mounted over or behind the reversing lens of the taillights and the turn signals wired into the reversing lights because the US red turn signals were outlawed here.

Our Matador, like the Rebel, used the right-hand drive dash from the Rambler Ambassador that had been produced for the US Postal Service. Despite this, the windscreen wipers swept for left-hand drive,

something AMI never corrected on Ramblers but did on the Triumphs.

Assembly continued into 1971 with only minor changes. The front parking light/turn signals received clear lenses (as opposed to amber) as did the front side marker lenses which were wired as additional turn signals. The process continued into 1972 with the biggest change being to the Chrysler A727 Torqueflite automatic gearbox, the V8 engine was now fitted with a four-barrel carburettor which gave it more power and torque and the front seat now featured individually reclining seatbacks and a centre fold-down armrest. If air conditioning was generally a standard fitting and it was an under-dash unit; also the dash was slightly modified insofar as the padding protruded more and the instruments were now white-backed as used in the 1972/73 US Matador.

The minuscule changes continued into 1974, the AMI-assembled Matadors actually being US 1973 models.

Australian Motor Industries in Port Melbourne imported 140 CKD kits of the Matador coupe from American Motors in Kenosha in 1974. Unfortunately 50 of the kits were water damaged and written off by the insurers. Of the rest, AMI assembled 80 kits into cars for sale in 1976–77 (*2 years later*!) and kept the components of the other 10 crates for spare parts. Around 1980 Toyota, who owned a big slice of AMI at the time, stopped supplying Rambler spares and shipped all the bits to a dealer in Sydney. Everything else left around the factory that was connected with Rambler was scrapped!

TOYOTA

TOYOTA

TOYOTA

TOYOTA
CORONA

QUAIL
LODGE
Matador
75

TOYOTA

AMI-TOYOTA

Toyota was on the cusp of greatness in Australia as far as market share was concerned as the Seventies began. The biggest selling small car in Australia was the Corolla 1100 and the biggest selling medium-sized car was the Corona 1600; they were outselling the four-cylinder versions of the Holden Torana, Ford Cortina and Escort and the Datsun 1000 and 1600. And despite having a smaller engine capacity the Crown was doing rather better than expected against Holden, Ford and Chrysler. For both AMI and Toyota things were only going to get even better.

A rebodied Corona 1500 arrived July 1970 and while Toyota created quite a fuss about it in their advertising it was in all honesty a body reskin over the existing mundane mechanical components. From a styling point of view it was very successful combining several interesting cues culled mostly from the Toyota Crown. At the front was a plain mesh grille sporting a bold Toyota badge, dual headlights each side with the park/indicator lights in the bumper and side repeaters almost on the front corner of the front fenders. Surrounding the grille was a grey plastic appliqué. Broad tail light units each side at the rear curved around into the rear quarter panels, the upper section housing the tail/brake lights and under the divider were indicator and reversing lights. Between them was the license plate that hinged down to reveal the fuel filler.

It was based on the RT40 floorpan and had a wheelbase of 2430mm (95.7-ins), was 4166mm (164-ins) in overall length, 1569mm (61.8-ins) wide and 1397mm (55-ins) high, kerb weight was 907kgs (1995lbs). Upper-and-lower wishbones with coil springs, stabiliser bar and telescopic dampers comprised the front suspension while the live rear axle was held up by four-leaf semi-elliptic springs also with telescopic dampers. It was plain and simple stuff, already in high volume production and so was relatively inexpensive to manufacture. But there was no adventurism in it at all.

Brakes were by way of four-wheel 228mm (9-ins) diameter drums with 116-square inches of lining area and no power boost while the steering was a recirculating ball system also with no assistance.

Interior-wise the new Corona was no roomier than the old shovel-nosed model but it did give the impression of being something of a baby Crown with its nicely upholstered front reclining bucket seats and rear bench, AMI seeming to use a better quality vinyl for its seats than Ford or GM-H. Carpet was on the floor as was the gearshift lever for the four-speed all-synchromesh manual gearbox and T-bar selector for the automatic, each door had an armrest and a powerful heater/demister was a standard fitting. The dashboard was a new design featuring three large dials in front of the driver – clock on the left, speedometer in the centre and combination dial (fuel and temperature gauges only) with warning lights on the right; to their left were the three vertical slides for the heating/demisting system, then the radio and in front of the passenger was the glovebox. The face of the dash was brushed aluminium, and the black plastic top and bottom were padded for safety reasons. At each end were adjustable air vents for the flow-through air system. The luggage space was far better utilised in this model because the spare wheel was upright in a well on the left of the boot allowing a flat and uncluttered floor area, unlike its predecessor.

On the road the Corona performed well rather than spectacularly.

The engine remained at 1490cc with power raised to 61kW (82bhp) at 5200rpm and torque to 122Nm (90lbs-ft) at 2800rpm although actual road performance was little changed.

In mid-1971 AMI released a mildly updated version that had a 1587cc four-cylinder OHV engine achieved by widening the cylinder bore from 78mm to 80.5mm and leaving the crank stroke at 78mm. Power rose slightly to 67kW (90bhp) at 5400rpm and torque was up to 133Nm (98lbs-ft) at 3000rpm. Maximum speed was 147km/h (92mph) with 0–80, 96 and 112km/h (0–50, 60 and 70mph) times of 9.7, 13.5 and 18.1 seconds respectively with fuel consumption between 11 and 8.9 litres per 100km (26 and 32mpg). Kerb weight stayed at a light(ish) 907kgs (1995lbs).

In road tests the various journalists complained about the brakes which were still non-assisted drums that required high pedal pressures, took far too long to stop the Corona from high speeds and would fade badly when used hard. And handling on the standard cross-ply tyres was sensitive to pressures. The braking issue was solved later in the year when front discs were fitted.

A Corona SE was excellent value at $2529 even if in comparison with many rivals it was a very conservative design.

Little changed until late 1973 when Toyota and AMI announced the new RT104 Corona, the car they advertised by saying "When your heart says Europe but your head says Japan." This Corona was almost the change you had because you wanted to. It appeared to be a new car but was a significant rework of the old platform insofar as it retained the upper-and-lower coil spring front suspension and semi-elliptic leaf spring rear with its live axle and stodgy non-assisted recirculating ball steering.

In Japan Toyota offered the RT104 with a variety of engines but for Australia AMI opted (wisely) for the 18R engine – a heavy all cast iron unit with a single overhead camshaft driven by a duplex chain off the front of the five-bearing crankshaft that also drove a jackshaft that operated the distributor and oil pump. Despite being a SOHC design both the intake and exhaust manifolds were on the same (left) side of the engine. Its cylinder dimensions were 88.5 by 80mm for 1968cc; it developed 89kW (119bhp) at 5500rpm and 175Nm (129lbs-ft) of torque

at 3600rpm. This output went to the rear wheels through either a four-speed all-synchromesh manual gearbox or a three-speed automatic, both with floor selectors. Braking was by a vacuum assisted disc front/drum rear system – 228mm/9-ins disc rotors, 228mm/9-ins drums – with dual circuits while the steering was still by a non-assisted recirculating ball system; road wheels were now vented and 14-ins in diameter running 165 x 14 tyres and, unusually for a Japanese car, had a simple chromed hubcap rather than a full dress trim.

The new Corona was slightly larger in dimensions than its predecessors, having a wheelbase of 2499mm (98.4-ins), overall length of 4208mm (165.7-ins), width of 1610mm (63.4-ins), height of 1397mm (55-ins) and a kerb weight of 1062kgs (2336lbs). In its styling it was a more squared-off design than previously with a typically Toyota quirky nose (although less so than on earlier Coronas) that featured dual headlights each side in prominent plastic surrounds, a plastic mesh grille between them with the large 'C' badge in the middle and the leading edge of the bonnet cut back behind the lights. At the rear were two large horizontal light units (one each side) separated by the license plate and with a thick chromed strip around them. Deep chromed steel bumpers were fitted front and rear, the front one housing the turn indicator lens.

Inside were front tombstone bucket seats (reclining on the SE) with a bench seat in the rear, floor carpets, a powerful heater/demister with the option of a fully integrated air conditioning unit – an option that an increasing number of buyers took, I might add – plus a radio and armrests on each door. For a mid-range family car of 1973 the SE version was considered to be well equipped. Besides the two sedans there was a popular station wagon available as well.

Wheels magazine published a four-car comparison between the Corona SE, Datsun 180B GL, Holden Torana 1900SL and Ford Cortina 2000XL in its November 1974 issue and it might surprise many readers to learn that the Corona SE did not fare that well! Reading the article, it becomes clear that there were two groups of cars here – the Corona and 180B in one group and the Torana and Cortina in the other. The divider was their physical size and in particular their width, believe it or not. Both the Japanese cars were narrower than their two rivals by around 100mm (nearly four-inches) which naturally affected passenger comfort.

The Corona had the crudest of suspension systems, particularly at the rear where it had an ancient live axle held up by semi-elliptic leaf springs where the 180B had a semi-trailing arm fully independent system and both the Torana and Cortina had live axles with coil springs and links. In their opinion that gave the Corona the harshest ride with poor traction on anything but the smoothest of road surfaces. The non-assisted steering was considered the heaviest of the four, the gearshift required the most push to use and it was difficult to drive smoothly in traffic. And the front bucket seats were considered poor in their padding and shaping.

Against the clock the Corona held its own as you would expect. In those early days of metrification *Wheels* used unusual segments for their acceleration runs. For instance, for the 0 – 90km/h run (56mph) they recorded 12.1 seconds for the Corona, 11.5 secs for the 180B, 11.2 secs for the Cortina and a slow 14.1 secs for the Torana. For the standing 400 metres (used to be the standing quarter mile) they recorded 18.8 seconds for the Corona, 17.6 seconds for the Cortina, 18.6 secs for the 180B and 19.7 secs for the Torana. As for top speed, the Corona achieved exactly 160km/h (100mph) at 5600rpm, the Cortina ran to 163km/h (101mph), the 180B to 158km/h (98mph) and the Torana to 155km/h (96mph).

With minor updates – new grille texture, slightly different taillights – the Corona 2000 remained on sale until the end of 1978 to be replaced by a model that I will call a hybrid – it was part Toyota and part Holden! From a styling aspect the new model was clearly a Toyota Corona and a derivative of its predecessor – there was nothing radical or different about it in any way. Inside were new seats upholstered in cloth for the top-line model, good quality vinyl for the lower versions, and a new bulky-looking dashboard that looked very Fifties with its large-sweep speedometer unit and sundry dials and controls including an oversized thin plastic-grip steering wheel.

For the first time on a Corona it featured a MacPherson strut coil spring front suspension and a four-link plus Panhard rod coil spring live axle at the rear. This was radical stuff for the arch-conservative Toyota people! Powering this Corona was not a Toyota engine but one sourced from Holden. This was all part of the need for Toyota to meet its 85 per cent local content requirements. Toyota engineers modified the engine slightly to try and gain more power and improve reliability – different valve springs, camshaft timing and a Japanese Aisan carburettor – but the reality was that it was a lost cause.

The Starfire had a cast iron cylinder block and head, the cylinder dimensions were 88.9 x 76.2mm for a capacity of 1897cc and from which it developed 58kW (77bhp) at 4800rpm. GM-H was very keen for the world to know that the Starfire four-cylinder overhead valve engine was the first such design to be manufactured in Australia and that the choice of materials – cast iron head and block, overhead valves et al – were made on sensible logical grounds. They eschewed such technicalities as overhead camshafts and alloy components to keep manufacturing simple. And cheap. GM-H was also keen to point out that the Starfire engine had absolutely no connection with the 1.9-litre Opel engine that had been used earlier. Starfire-powered Coronas were never very good property in the local used car market and have basically vanished off the face of the earth today. The collaboration with GM-Holden served its purpose for Toyota in its quest to become Number One in Australia.

In *Wheels* February 1980 was a six-car comparison test where the new Corona CS was compared with the Chrysler Sigma GL, Datsun 200B GL, Ford Cortina GL, Holden Sunbird Deluxe and the Mazda 626 Deluxe; all were contenders in the 2-litre class that was growing ever more popular. The newest of the six was the Corona. On the test track the Corona was generally outpointed by the other five cars; for

TOYOTA

example, the 0–100km/h (62mph) sprints saw the Corona CS take 15.8 seconds versus 15.4 for the Sunbird (also running the Starfire engine), 13.6 seconds for the Cortina, 13.2 seconds for the Mazda and 12.3 seconds for the Sigma and 200B. As for top speed the Corona reached 144km/h (90mph), the Sunbird ran to 148km/h (92mph), the Cortina to 154km/h (96mph), the Sigma to 160km/h (100mph), the Mazda to 162km/h (101mph) and the fastest was the 200B at 166km/h (104mph).

After a series of evaluations of various aspects of the cars' attributes and performance, the *Wheels* test team concluded where the Corona was concerned with the words: "And least but not necessarily last is the Corona. We have to ask ourselves again, how can a car that is so new, so all-different from nose to tail, a design that started with a clean sheet of paper, how can it manage to look, feel and behave so old? Admittedly the Corona sets new standards of low-to-middling-speed quietness. It's obviously well finished, is impressively comfortable at moderate speeds and is undoubtedly reliable. So is a tortoise, if it doesn't get run over while crossing the road.

"The Corona isn't all bad, of course, but it's bad enough to have fallen short of many of today's needs and standards, let alone tomorrow's … a car where time and design stood still."

Below the Corona in Toyota's carefully orchestrated marketing plan was the Corolla. By 1970 Toyota was on the second generation of the model which had rapidly carved out a significant sales niche for itself in a very short time. The second generation, the KE20, was really more of the same. It continued to be available locally only as a two-door sedan with slightly rounder, softer lines built on the same floorpan but it was 100mm (4-ins) longer and 25mm (1-ins) wider for a slightly roomier interior. In many ways it looked like a model change that had to happen even though demand for the original Corolla had not abated so it became more of the same and the sales success kept on rolling.

It was still a tight four-seater as far as accommodation was concerned but it now featured new safety items such as progressive crumple zones front and rear, anti-burst door locks, high-backed bucket seats, soft control knobs and anti-glare instrument glass on a new dashboard that was flat and full width with two round dials in front of the driver – speedometer on the left, minor dials and warning lights on the right – and the three heater/demister slides in the centre along with the radio. New for this model were adjustable air vents either end of the dash for the flow-through ventilation system. The boot was not very big(!) but the boot lid did open down to the bumper so accessing it was a doddle.

Apart from the body, pretty much all of the mechanical components were carried over unchanged; the only change was to increase the engine's capacity from 1077cc to 1166cc by widening the cylinder bore to 75mm. On a 9:1 compression and using a twin-throat carburettor the engine developed 73bhp at 6000rpm. Kerb weight was up by around 28kgs (60lbs) so the extra power made little-or-no difference to performance.

Modern Motor, January 1971 issue, compared the Corolla 1200 with the Datsun 1200 and Mazda 1300. The fully imported Mazda was by far the best equipped and finished and was the performance champion but the Corolla was not far behind in all categories. The Datsun was the poor relation in the test, slowest and the almost a 'stripper' compared with the other two. The Corolla ran to a top speed of 141km/h (88.4mph) and ran the 0–96km/h (60mph) dash in 14.8 seconds against 150km/h (93mph) for the Mazda and 13.5 seconds to 96km/h (60mph), the Datsun reaching 137km/h (86mph) and needing 15.5 seconds to 96km/h (60mph).

In concluding their searching test they said: "The Corolla is unquestionably the best-looking, and will be a sure-fire success with women and youngsters. It is very well made, finished and equipped. It's only real let-down is the brakes."

Sales momentum continued with the KE20 topping the small car sales charts through its production life, but the seamless move to the KE30 in late 1974 changed little, people continued to flock to Toyota dealerships to buy a new Corolla that now included a four-door version for the first time. The range available included a 2-door sedan, a station wagon, panel van and a Liftback coupe. Styling of the KE30 was clearly derivative of the KE20, Toyota's styling folks obviously not being too keen to move away from a formula that had seen the company build millions of the model.

Initially the KE30 continued to be powered by the 1166cc engine but the bigger body and increased weight told on its performance. Power remained at 54kW (73bhp) at 6000rpm but the car's weight had crept up to 810kgs (1785lbs) at the kerb, more if air conditioning was ordered and the automatic gearbox. And that led to the road test in the *Wheels* March 1975 road test being headed "Bigger, but Better?" Peter Robinson, then editor of the magazine, wrote "Now comes the third-generation body, and while we have few doubts that the new Corolla will be just as successful as its predecessors it's also true to say the latest version has grown something of a middle-age spread." It was nearly two hundredweight (224lbs, 102kgs) heavier than the first generation. Robinson really liked the car – its roomy and comfortable interior, the level of finish inside and out, its equipment for the price but lamented its on-road performance. This was brought sharply into focus in the September 1975 issue of the magazine where the *Wheels* crew tested the Corolla against the Holden Gemini, Mitsubishi Lancer and Honda Civic.

The Gemini was physically the biggest of the quartet with the largest capacity engine at 1584cc and not surprisingly was the heaviest at 900kgs followed by the Corolla at 845kgs, Lancer at 830kgs (but with 92bhp) and the Honda was by far the lightest at 770kgs. But it was against the clock where the inadequacies of the car's performance were highlighted. For example, on the 0–110km/h (68mph) sprint, the order was Gemini on 16.1 seconds, Lancer on 17.4 seconds, Civic on 20.4 seconds and Corolla way back on 25.8 seconds! Passing acceleration, too, was much slower than the others but surprisingly all returned around 32mpg or 8.9 litres per 100km.

But as they said in the song, help was on its way in the form of the now locally-assembled 4K-C engine where the crank stroke had been lengthened to give cylinder dimensions of 75 x 73mm and a capacity of 1290cc; on a 9:1 compression it developed 45kW (60bhp) at 5400rpm. Both the horsepower and torque readings quoted were slightly less than previously but the engine now had an air pump for emission requirements not specified before. Despite that, the 0–110km/h acceleration dash time came down to 20.5 seconds, barely competitive with its rivals but nevertheless better.

A new Corolla was waiting in the wings, announced in late 1979 in

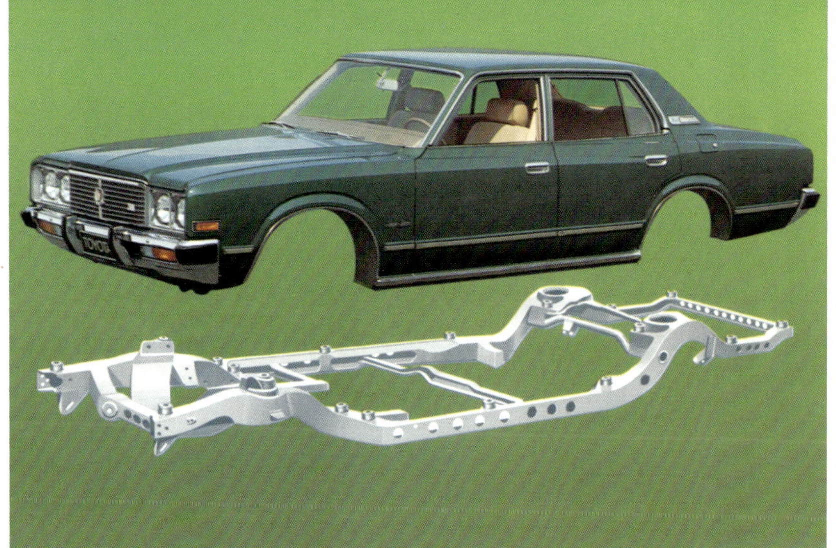

Japan but did not arrive here until mid-1980. It was the last of the rear-wheel drive Corollas powered by the K-series four-cylinder engine.

At the top of the Toyota range in Australia was the Crown, an apt name for the company's most prestigious model. Initially marketed with a 'softly, softly' approach because the executives at Toyota were unsure how Australian buyers would react to a large(ish) family sedan powered by a four-cylinder engine of just 1.9-litres capacity. As it happened, they need not have worried because Australian buyers accepted the car in meaningful sales numbers from the beginning, *despite* the engine which proved to be adequate for their motoring needs.

In April 1966 Toyota announced the Crown Six which raised many eyebrows in the local media. In place of the four-cylinder engine the company's engineers designed and developed a completely new six-cylinder engine. It was not just *any* six-cylinder engine, though. The new Crown engine was something special for its time. It featured a cast iron cylinder block topped by a cast aluminium alloy cylinder head that had a single overhead camshaft chain-driven from the crankshaft that was supported by seven main bearings. The combustion chamber was a semi-spherical type with the intake manifold and ports on the left of the head, exhaust ports and manifold on the right – it was a cross-flow cylinder head with the combustion benefits expected. With a bore and stroke of 75 x 75mm, it had a capacity of 1988cc and developed 82kW (110bhp) at 5200rpm and 158Nm (117lbs-ft) of torque at 3600rpm on a compression ratio of 8.8:1 and using a single twin-throat carburettor.

Apart from a different grille texture, discreet '2000' badges front and rear and new horizontal taillights there was little to give the game away. Acceleration times were little different from the previous four-cylinder version but top speed was up to 150km/h (94mph), quite an increase, with the most obvious difference being the creamy smoothness of the new six-cylinder engine. It certainly raised the stakes in the local market for family-sized six-cylinder sedans and at $2480 (£1240 in the old money) it was great value for money. Local assembly of the Crown by AMI started at the end of 1966.

In 1968 the RS40 was replaced by the MS50, the third generation of Crown from Toyota, and in 1971 came the fourth generation Crown and it was a rather remarkable piece of design. For such a conservative company as Toyota the Crown broke all the rules! Well, from a styling perspective at least. This new Crown carried an aggressive style. Its looks were in contrast to the previous model and to its main rival, the Datsun 240C. This new style was dominated by the body-coloured bumpers front and rear that blended into the body and no longer looked to have been 'added on.' At the front was a broad horizontal grille opening with fourteen narrow bars, the huge Crown badge in the centre and dual headlights each end, a large square indicator lens each end, chromed strips around the grille perimeter and a subtle inlet slot *above* the grille with the parking light lenses each end. At the rear was again the large bumper with wide horizontal tail light/indicator/reversing light units each side surrounded by a chrome strip.

The new styling made the Crown look bigger than it actually was because it ran on the exact same perimeter frame as its predecessor; it did

look imposing and gave an aura of being a class above its station. Inside was a new dashboard that reflected the theme of the previous Crown but this time the three dials were square although they imparted no more information than before.

AMI marketed this new Crown in two versions both of which were assembled locally – Custom and Custom SE, the latter being by far the better value and the best seller at $3799 for the four-speed manual with floor shifter and $4069 for the new Toyoglide three-speed automatic. There was only a $200 price premium over the Custom.

New, too, this time round was a larger and torquier engine; it was still a six-cylinder unit with a chain-driven single overhead camshaft but now had the cylinder dimensions of 80 x 85mm for a capacity of 2563cc from which was developed 104kW (140bhp) at 5200rpm and 210Nm (156lbs-ft) at 3600rpm. Vacuum boosted front disc brakes of 230mm diameter (9.1-ins) were now part of the Crown's specifications. Despite weighing 1314kgs (2890lbs) the Crown would run to 163km/h (102mph) with 53, 90, 131km/h (33, 56 and 82mph) available in the indirect gears (at 6500rpm!) and it would dash to 80 and 96km/h (50 and 60mph) from rest in 8.9 and 11.9 seconds which was not only competitive with the Holden/Ford/Chrysler luxury triumvirate but also with the likes of Volvo, Peugeot and the lower order Mercedes-Benz and BMWs.

In the early part of their road test *Wheels* said: "Previous Crowns were good cars for the upper-middle class, cars which reflected their apparent good taste without straining the pocket." They went on to say: "With a decent set of radial ply tyres the Crown would be just below the BMW/ Peugeot league. Who ever thought we'd be saying that about a Japanese sedan?" Old prejudices die hard!

While the Crown was very good at speed on the highways – very quiet, smooth ride, excellent directional stability – it was on the rough unsealed minor roads on which the big car excelled; nothing seemed to faze the suspension. All in all it was an ideal car for folks who drove long distances but were not necessarily 'car people.'

In early 1975 AMI launched the MS80 series Crowns, the fifth generation for the model that was really a new body over the existing mechanical components. This time the exterior styling was very conservative when compared with the previous two version. It was three boxes with various character lines included to give tension to the sheet metal. Considering the clientele Toyota/AMI were trying to attract they were undoubtedly on the right track. The new style made the Crown look dignified and solid, important for middle-class conservative buyers, characterised by a wide grille featuring six sets of vertical bars with a 30mm gap between each set. At each end were dual headlight in chromed bezels with a massive chromed steel bumper below that housed the parking and indicator lights, a repeater for the indicators being located just in front of the front wheel wells. At the back were large taillight units either side of the license plate and again, a deep chromed steel bumper.

Inside was sprawling room for up to five people, two in front on big, comfortable and fully adjustable buckets seats and three in back on the wide bench seat with a central pull-down armrest. The dash was very imposing with three large square dials in front of the driver and myriad switches either side of the steering column, audio system and heater/ventilation/air-conditioning controls in the centre. Lights and wiper/washers were on steering column stalks.

It continued to ride a 2690mm (105.9-ins) wheelbase, was 4690mm (184.6-ins) long in SE form by 1690mm (66.5-ins) wide and 1435mm (56.5-ins) high with a kerb weight of 1345kgs (2965lbs) in SE manual form, slightly heavier for the automatic and also for the fully imported Super Saloon version.

Peter Robinson, editor at *Wheels* at the time, test drove a locally-assembled Crown SE automatic and published the test in the September 1975 edition of the magazine. The heading for the article was somewhat ominous in tone, saying "CROWN … Silence isn't always golden." The sub-title read "Toyota has changed the Crown but it hasn't altered it." As was said in the article, "Ultra refined in many ways, the Crown falls down because its ride comfort and roadholding don't reach the standard expected in the mid-70s. But if you are looking for a reliable, well-made medium-sized sedan and aren't interested in brilliant dynamics … read on." A little harsh perhaps? Yes, I think so because the Crown was perfectly judged for the clientele at which it was aimed. Toyota was not looking to take buyers away from the sophisticated (read complicated) high performance European luxury saloons and was more interested in hooking buyers away from the Holden Premier, Falcon Futura and Valiant Regal buyers all of whom were being conned into thinking they were buying something special which was, from a technical point of view, not the case. The Crown SE was beautifully built, extremely comfortable, ultra-reliable and luxuriously equipped. And even at $6211 before on-roads it was still value for money.

As for its on-road performance, *Wheels* managed a top speed of 163km/h (101mph) with acceleration times from 0–90km/h and 110km/h of 13.2 and 19.6 seconds respectively and a fuel consumption of 19.3mpg. These figures were competitive with the local 'luxury' cars even though the Crown only had a 2.6-litre six-cylinder engine and 150bhp.

The MS80 would be the last Crown to be assembled locally, the operation closing down during 1978 allowing Toyota/AMI to concentrate on the fast-selling Corollas and Coronas.

CHAPTER 6

VOLKSWAGEN

Volkswagen of Australia was in decline as the Seventies dawned. The company's reliance on the Beetle was proving to be a millstone around its corporate neck as manufacturing costs rose, sales slowed and profits were squeezed to the point where the company was losing money. It had committed itself to Plan A where the Beetle was concerned and achieving that was realised as being impossible. The Type 3 range – VW 1600 sedan, station wagon and fastback – had only ever been assembled from CKD kits sent out from Germany so they were less affected by currency fluctuations and the vagaries of a Federal Labour government that chopped and changed the rules with seemingly little regard as to how they would affect the industry. In 1968 the company had repositioned itself to comply with the government's low volume plans.

VW was going through much the same process in Germany and the pain there was a hundred times worse than in Australia. What the company desperately needed was a new model to take over the mantle from the Beetle. However, the Beetle continued for the time being with minor changes such as silver painted wheels, the removal of chrome from the dash. A smaller capacity 1300cc single-port 50bhp engine in an 'economy' Beetle was introduced having the same body and ball-joint/swing axle suspension system and brakes as the 1500 and the electrical system was upgraded to 12-volts although apparently if a die-hard owner wanted it, a 6-volt system could still be supplied!

The Type 3s were more extensively updated with a squarer frontal design, bigger bumpers and tail lights along with a rear semi-trailing arm rear suspension and a Bosch fuel injection system for the engine; a 'Type 3' badge adorned the front fenders and that was unique to Australia.

Production of the Type 1 VW 1500 was discontinued in February 1971 and replaced in the marketplace by the VW Superbug S powered by the twin-port 1600cc engine (85.5 x 69mm, 1584cc) that developed 37kW (50bhp) at 4000rpm and 98Nm (72lbs-ft) of torque at 2800rpm. This engine is regarded by VW aficionados as one the finest from the company. The platform under the Superbug was all-new as was the sheet metal from the windscreen forward, the new structure including a version of the ubiquitous MacPherson strut coil spring suspension (first developed for the Type 4 of 1968) along with a sophisticated double-joint rear suspension, disc front brakes of 254mm (10-ins) diameter with solid rotors and single piston calipers, a redesigned fuel tank of 41-litres (9-gallons) capacity and a flat-lying spare to improve luggage space under the more bulbous bonnet. It was available in both manual and semi-automatic (it was similar in concept to the Porsche 'Sportomatic') forms at $2144 and $2299 respectively. The 1300 economy Beetle continued and retailed for $2085.

The best-selling Transporter received a round of improvements at this time and these included front disc brakes with solid rotors of 254mm (10-ins) diameter and single piston calipers, a rear pressure regulator in the brake circuit, wider rear track, perforated 4J x 15 wheels, twin-port cylinder heads and the oil cooler was relocated outside the fan housing to improve cooling for the number 3 cylinder, something that had been an issue for many years.

For 1972 further tweaks were applied to the Superbug S and 1300

Beetle with four sets of louvers on the engine cover, four-spoke steering wheel and ignition lock, windscreen wipers now operated from a steering column stalk, the reversing light lens was now white and there were added vents in the dash. For the Superbug there was a slightly larger rear window and US-style buckets seats with in-built headrests. Later in the year VW released a Commemorative Edition of the Superbug with floor carpets, red-wall tyres and a glovebox medallion to celebrate the Beetle passing the Model T Ford's production record – 1500 were made.

The Type 3 received the four-spoke steering wheel and reversing lights as well as better brakes and side intrusion bars in the doors while the Transporter received a modified engine carrier and gearbox mounting, larger taillights and air intakes at the rear.

In April 1973 came the Superbug L that was mechanically identical with the S but now had a curved front windscreen that shortened the front bonnet, larger round taillights – referred to by VW folks as 'elephant foot' lights – on reshaped rear fenders plus a redesigned moulded plastic dashboard with a single, deep binnacle housing the speedometer and fuel gauge, and the heating system now had a two-speed fan. Its price was $2629 compared with the 1300 Beetle that sold for $2409. *Australian Motor Manual* tested a Superbug (July 1974 issue) and published a set of figures that would have pleased any devoted VW enthusiast – maximum speed was not quoted but acceleration times were taken up to 120km/h. Never been able to do that before with a Beetle! They returned times of 11.1 and 16.4 seconds for the 0–80km/h (50mph) and 100km/h (62mph) sprints and a fuel economy in the 10–8.5 litres per 100km (28–33mpg) range. Although the quickest Beetle it was quite a bit slower than most of its Japanese rivals. The *MM* testers very much liked the Bug, particularly its ride and handling as well as the quality of construction. *Wheels* published a four-car comparison test (February 1974) between the Superbug, Renault 12, Chrysler Galant and Subaru Leone DL. They achieved a maximum speed of 133km/h (83mph) and a time of 11.7 seconds for the 0–80km/h (0–50mph) dash. What was obvious from the test was the fact that the VW was living in another world where aircooled rear engines had been the norm; the world was rapidly changing to a front-wheel drive market and the testers felt that this was the Bug's Achilles heel even though in outright terms it was a very competent car to drive.

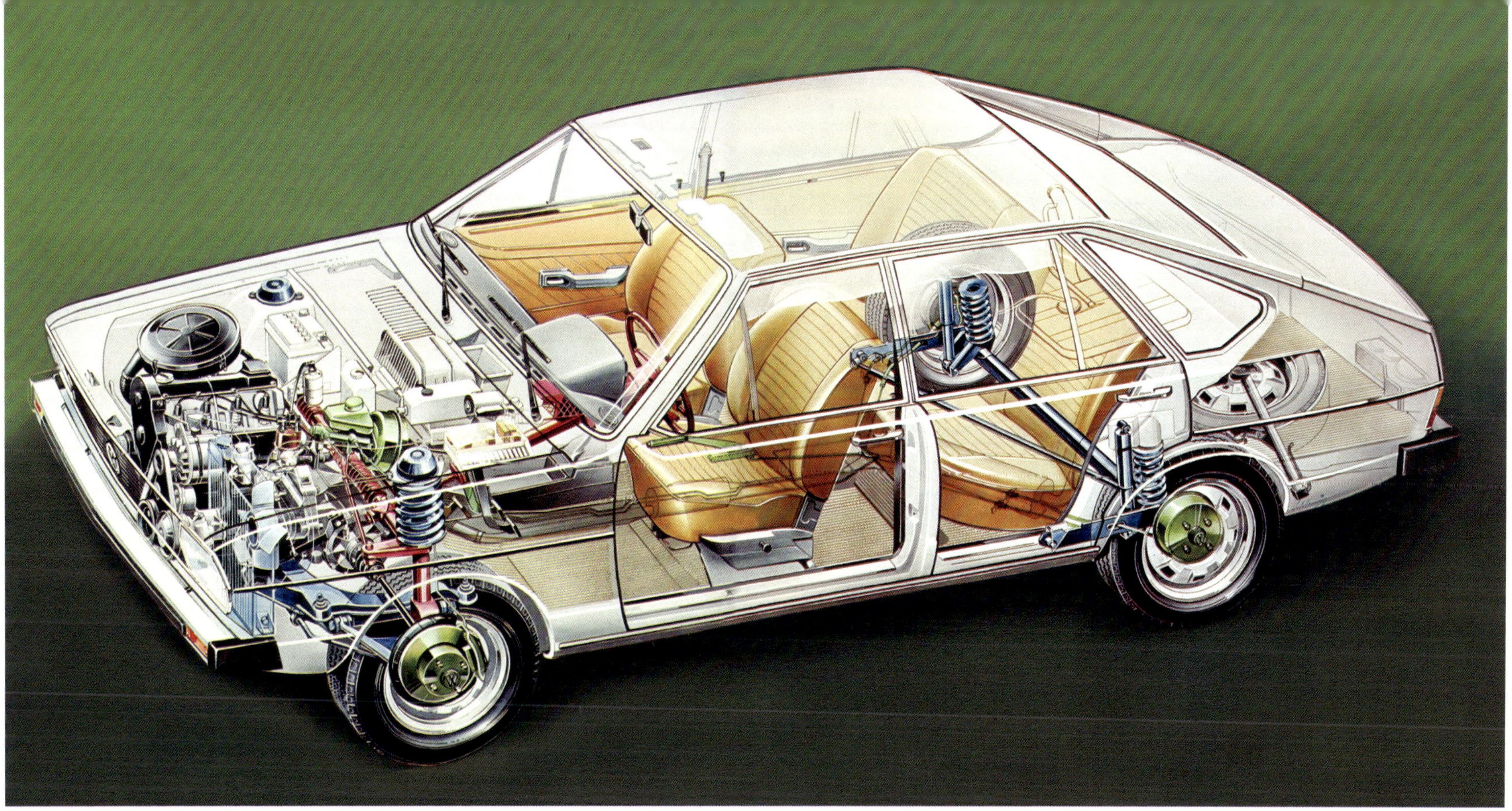

Minor updates happened with the Type 3 but with the Passat imminent assembly of Type 3 stopped in September, Australia being the first country outside Germany to assemble the Passat.

Where the Transporter was concerned, more extensive upgrades were implemented, such as a strengthened front structure to accommodate a safety crumple zone, the front brake discs were larger and the front indicator lights were moved higher up the front panel.

With new CEO Rudolf Leiding from Audi in charge in Wolfsburg the decision was made to use the new Audi 80 as the basis of the first of a new model range from VW, the Passat. It replaced the Type 3 range almost immediately upon its release in Germany. Up to the B-pillar the Passat and Audi 80 were the same but from there back the Passat was different

insofar as it was a five-door hatchback with a third window each side, large horizontal taillight units each side and rectangular headlights up front. An optional three-door body was available and it had single round headlights. Inside both were obviously close kith-and-kin with similar instrument layouts and the same minor controls with the Wolfsburg crest on the steering wheel hub being the major clue as to which car you were sitting in.

The Passat shared it mechanical arrangements with the 80 and had a watercooled in-line four-cylinder engine with a cast iron cylinder block with a five main bearing crankshaft, non-crossflow aluminium alloy cylinder head with a toothed-belt driven single overhead camshaft. Its cylinder dimensions were 75 x 73.4mm and 76.5 x 80mm giving a capacity of 1296cc and 1471cc (1300cc and 1500cc) with power outputs of 51kW (69bhp) at 5800rpm (1300) and 56kW (75bhp) at 5800rpm (1500) and torque of 92Nm (68lbs-ft) and 112Nm (83lbs-ft) at 3500rpm respectively. Unusually, the radiator was offset to the left of the engine (not directly in front as was customary) with a thermo-fan to keep temperatures under control.

Introduced with the Passat was a quite sophisticated suspension system that was shared with the Audi 80. It comprised MacPherson struts at the front with coil springs, a wide pressed steel lower wishbone for good location and a stabiliser bar. What was unique to VW Group cars from this era was the use of a negative scrub radius in the front suspension's geometry to minimise steering deflections under braking in inclement conditions. Steering was by a non-assisted rack and pinion set-up with a central take-off giving equal-length tie rods; naturally the steering column had a collapsible joint for safety reasons.

The whole engine-gearbox-suspension-steering ensemble was mounted on a separate sub-frame that was bolted up to the underbody at four points for superior NVH characteristics.

At the rear was a torsion beam axle that had short trailing arms for longitudinal location, a long Panhard rod for lateral location and

a torsion bar with the U-section of the beam to supplement the coil springs and separate dampers. Braking was by front discs and rear drums – 240mm (9.45-ins) rotors and 185mm (7.3-ins) drums respectively – with diagonally-split circuits and a vacuum booster.

Based on a completely new floorpan borrowed from the Audi 80, the Passat had a wheelbase of 2470mm (97.2-ins), was 4190mm (165-ins) long, 1600mm (63-ins) wide by 1360mm (53.5-ins) high with kerb weight starting at 860kgs (1896lbs) for the three-door and 885kgs (1951lbs) for the five-door. Externally the two cars were easily distinguishable (apart from the door count) by the 1300 having round headlights while the 1500 had rectangular headlights. The 1500 was also far better equipped having reclining front seats, cigarette lighter, clock, trip meter and a lockable fuel filler as standard. And both had the windscreen wipers set correctly for right-hand drive.

It was introduced onto the local market in February 1974 and was available as a 1300 two-door sedan, four-door 1500 sedan (a first for VW in Australia) and four-door station wagon. In June VW added the Passat TS based on the two-door body and was called a coupe by the Marketing people. The TS featured the 1471cc engine with a twin-choke Solex carburettor and tuned length exhaust manifold to develop 63kW (85bhp) and 121Nm (89lbs-ft) torque at 5800rpm and 4000rpm respectively. Inside, a small tachometer was placed between the speedometer and combination gauge with three small dials being accommodated in the centre console and the steering wheel had three aluminium spokes; tyres were 165SR13 steel radials. Pricing was from $3348 for the 1300, $3698 for the 1500 four-door and $3898 for the wagon; the TS retailed for $4048. By way of a comparison the new 2-litre Toyota Corona SE cost $3174, the Datsun 180B GL cost $2866 and a Mazda RX4 sedan cost $4078.

Wheels road tested both the 1300 and 1500 together in their March 1974 issue and wrote a glowing report about them, especially their superb dynamics that in their opinion brought a breath of fresh air to

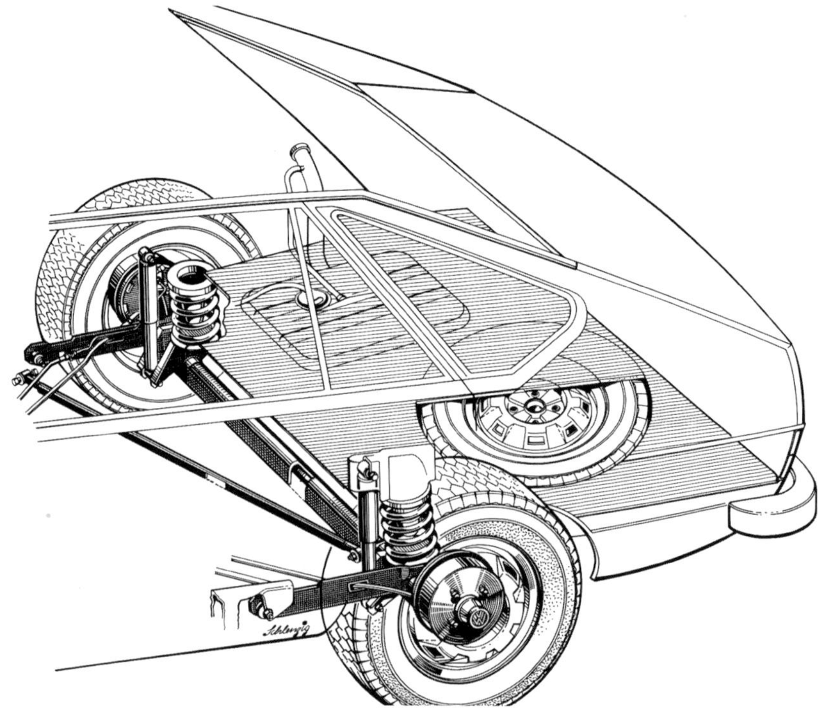

mid-sized family car motoring; there were a few glitches in the fit and finish department but the testers thought that they would be sorted as production people became more familiar with its needs. Both cars were spritely and ran to 156.8km/h (98mph, 1500) with acceleration from 0–80 and 96km/h (0–50 and -60mph) taking 9.6 and 13.8 seconds for the 1300 and 8.1 and 12.3 seconds for the 1500 with around 8.8 litres per 100km (32mpg) each giving a reasonable range from the 45-litre (9.9-gallon) tank.

As for the Passat TS, *Modern Motor's* test report from their August 1974 issue was full of praise. The tester was enamoured with the concept of the package – compact but roomy with spirited performance – that combined modern styling with excellent dynamics. *MM* managed 170.8kmk/h (106.8mph) from the TS with 0–80 and 96km/h (0–50 and 60mph) times of 8.3 and 11.3 seconds respectively with fuel economy of between 10 and 7.8 litres per 100km (28 and 36mpg) depending on how hard it was driven. Their only gripe was the price.

The folks at *Wheels* were so impressed with the Passat that it was voted Car of the Year for 1974, the first for VW in Australia.

The Superbug, meanwhile, had continued even though clearly its days were numbered. In fact, the last CKD kits arrived at Clayton in June 1975 and this last specification model featured rack and pinion steering and a charcoal canister, the front indicator lens was relocated to the front bumper and there was a bulge in the rear apron for a catalytic converter that was never fitted locally but was a requirement in the USA. The Superbug was discontinued in November leaving the 1600 Beetle to soldier on, this car often being thought of by VW enthusiasts as a 'bitsa.' Their reasoning is not without a base because it comprised the 1300 Beetle body with the torsion bar front end with disc brakes while the rear suspension, 1600cc twin-port engine with an alternator and double-joint axles came from the Superbug. Its retail price was a whopping $4140.

Salvation for VW came in the form of the Golf, a car that set the template for VW and much of the rest of the world's automobile industry for the coming decades. It was the result of collaboration between VW and Giorgietto Giugiaro from Ital Design. Giugiaro conceived the design as either a three- or five-door hatch based on a brand new front-wheel drive platform with a wheelbase of 2400mm (94.5-ins – coincidentally the same as the Beetle), overall length of 3705mm (145.9-ins), width

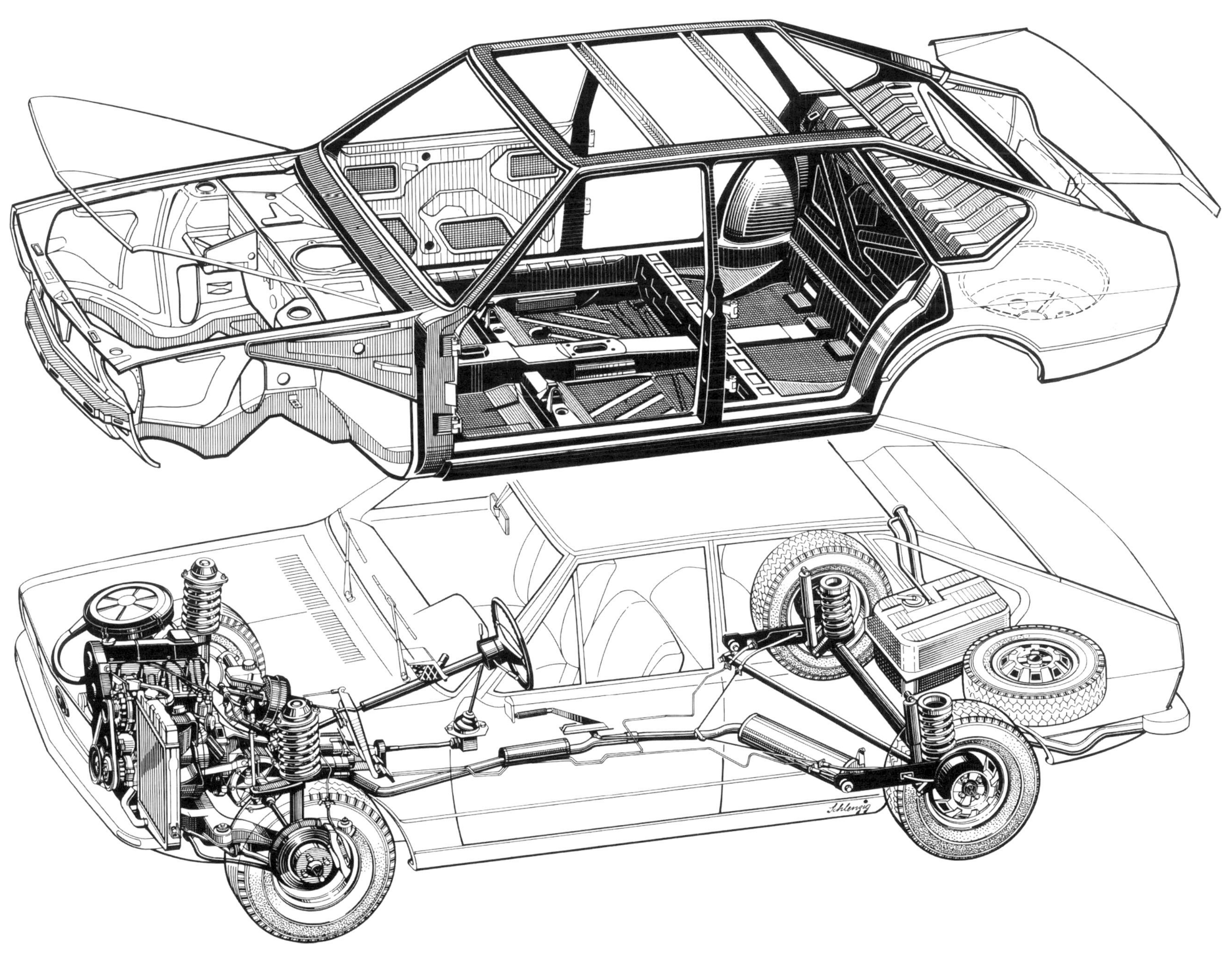

1610mm (63.4-ins), height of 1410mm (55.5-ins) and a kerb weight of 750 and 775kgs (1654lbs & 1709lbs) for two- and four-doors. From the moment it was released in Europe in May 1974 VW struggled to meet the orders such was its acceptance by the market. VW had their Beetle replacement!

The Golf was totally unlike the long serving Beetle – it had a front transverse mounted in-line four-cylinder engine with a cast iron cylinder block having a five main bearing crankshaft, an aluminium alloy cylinder head (not crossflow) with a single belt-driven overhead camshaft and it was watercooled. It was the very anti-thesis of the Beetle! Bolted end-on to the engine was a four-speed all-synchromesh manual gearbox with a stubby floor-mounted shift lever and of course, the front wheels did the driving. MacPherson struts with coil springs and a wide-based lower wishbone with negative scrub radius looked after the front suspension while at the rear was a torsion beam axle with coil springs; brakes were disc front and drum rear while the steering was by rack and pinion.

For the Australian market VW wisely decided not to offer the 1100cc version of the engine but instead offered buyers the 1588cc SOHC engine (79.5 x 80mm) with 63kW (85bhp) at 5800rpm and 122Nm (90lbs-ft) at 3200rpm using an 8.2:1 compression and a single downdraft carburettor.

The Golf was released locally in March 1976 with prices that were not inexpensive, the three-door costing $4228 and the five-door $4358. *Wheels* tested one in its April 1976 issue and opened their report by saying, "Think of the new Volkswagen Golf as just another small car and you miss the point completely." They went on to say, "This is a truly modern, truly advanced car and can be compared in ultimate terms with the Citroen GS and Alfasud. And that means it ranks as one of the finest small cars in the world." As for performance, they achieved a top speed of 156.8km/h (98mph), 0–96km/h (0–60mph) in 12.9 seconds with fuel being consumed at 8.5 litres per 100km (33mpg) or better.

To nobody's real surprise, *Wheels* voted it their Car of the Year, the second time in three years for Volkswagen.

Where the Beetle had been manufactured at Clayton the Golf and Passat followed the Type 3s and were assembled from CKD kits sent out from Germany. Following a deal being struck between Volkswagen AG in Wolfsburg and the Nissan Motor Company in Tokyo the Golf would share the production line with various Datsuns – Nissan had assumed control of Motor Producers. The last VW was assembled at Clayton in March 1977. From that time on VW reverted to full import status, a situation that remained until 1986 when the company quietly withdrew from the Australian market only to reappear several years later.

Standard Sedan

Deluxe Sedan

CHAPTER 7

NISSAN

Building on the base established in the late 1960s with the Datsun 1600 in particular Nissan was growing its market share rapidly. Not only was the 1600 winning conquest sales off the showroom floor but it had become the car to drive if you wanted to establish a rally career. Drivers like Ross Dunkerton and Greg Carr, for example, made names for themselves in 1600s.

The 1600 was assembled initially by Pressed Metal Corporation in Sydney but they were unable to meet the volumes required by Nissan and so a deal was agreed with Volkswagen to co-habit the Clayton assembly site in Melbourne. Sales of the ubiquitous VW Beetle had plummeted in the face of ever increasing Japanese competition and the VW hierarchy in Wolfsburg were keen to enter a joint agreement program. Beginning in late 1969 the assembly of the Datsun 1600 commenced at Clayton initially supplementing the numbers from PMC but gradually all assembly operations were centred in Melbourne.

For the 1970 model year the 1600 received some upgrades in interior fittings. A revised dashboard arrived with moulded plastic padding and round instruments fitted where previously a rectangular module had been. At a stroke it made the interior look better and the round dials were far easier to read although few in number – speedometer on the right, fuel and temperature dials in the smaller centre gauge and the left large dial was either blank (Standard model) or had a clock in the Deluxe. Carpet on the floor, a heater/demister, door armrests and reclining bucket seats came with the 1600 Deluxe.

Mechanically little was, or needed to be, changed. The lusty 1595cc SOHC four still produced 71kW (96bhp) at 5600rpm and drove the independently sprung rear wheels through either a four-speed all-synchromesh manual gearbox or an Aisan three-speed automatic. Aisan was a joint venture company with Mazda and Ford to produce an industry standard three-speed automatic gearbox for the small-to-medium car models in their ranges. The 1600 was available in two versions, the basic sedan at $2363 and the Deluxe at $2513 which was pretty good value compared with the Toyota Corona at $2449 for the SE (equivalent to the Deluxe), $2655 for the fully imported Mazda Capella Deluxe and $2305 for the imported Mitsubishi Galant 1300.

In its road test, June 1971, the folks at *Wheels* were impressed with the 1600's modern concept that was being copied by others, its tight body and brilliant roadholding courtesy of the fully independent suspension system that only the Morris 1500 could rival. The lack of quality in

the interior trim was their biggest disappointment. Nevertheless, they regarded the 1600 as good value for money. As for its performance, it returned a maximum speed of 150km/h (94mph), a 0–96km/h (0–60mph) time of 13.1 seconds and it consumed fuel at the rate of 11.5 litres per 100km (25mpg) on test, up to 9.5 litres per 100km (30mpg) when cruising.

At the lower end of the range was the Datsun 1000 that was available either as a two- or four-door sedan, two-door coupe and three-door wagon. Prices ranged from $1738 for the bare bones two-door standard version to $1899 for the four-door deluxe and $2145 for the imported Coupe. The 1000 struggled against the Toyota Corolla because it was smaller physically, lighter and flimsier feeling (and sounding) and its technical specification did not match up either – the cheap transverse leaf spring front suspension was not as good as the MacPherson struts of the Corolla. Mazda, too, had hit the market with its 1200 sedan in 1969 with a similar specification to the Corolla and then raised the ante in 1970 with the much better Mazda 1300 with its lively 1272cc SOHC engine.

In June 1970 Datsun announced their 1200 range – sedan, coupe and wagon – and this took over from the 1000 on the Clayton assembly line. The 1200 adopted what was to become the Japanese norm as far as specifications for a small family car was concerned with its new MacPherson strut front suspension allied to a semi-elliptic leaf spring rear live axle, recirculating ball steering, drum brakes all round and a similar-sized body. The Datsun 1200 sat on a 2286mm (90-ins) wheelbase (the Corolla's was 2336mm/92-ins), was 3835mm (151-ins) in overall length (versus 3937mm/155-ins for the Corolla) by 1496mm (59-ins) wide and 1397mm (55-ins) high with the kerb weight for the sedan (only a four-door now) of 720kgs (1568lbs). The 1200's engine followed the layout of its predecessor insofar as it had a cast iron cylinder block, aluminium alloy cylinder head, five bearing crankshaft and overhead valves. Its dimensions were 73 x 70mm for a capacity of 1171cc with a power output of 51kW (69bhp) at 6000rpm and 95Nm (70lbs-ft) of torque at 4000rpm.

The 1200's styling was pretty ordinary like most small Japanese cars of the day and its interior was similarly bland. There were thin non-adjustable bucket seats for the two front passengers and a plain and thinly upholstered bench in back for two adults or three young kiddies; boot space was minimal and compromised by the placement of the fuel tank behind the back seat. In the typical Japanese way it was quite well equipped having a push-button radio, heater/demister with two-speed fan, cigarette lighter, carpets and full wheel dress trims. No door armrests or door courtesy lights, however. The dash was a plain plastic moulding with padding around its perimeter and on the right two-thirds a shiny grey plastic section that housed the rectangular instrument pack – fan-shaped speedometer, fuel and temp one-above-the-other on the right a space for a small clock on the left – with pull-push switches for lights and wipers/washers to the right, cigarette lighter and fan to the left plus the heater slides and radio in the centre, and there were crude air vents under the dash with a control knob that was almost impossible to reach if a seat belt was being worn.

Modern Motor tested a 1200 against its rivals the Corolla and Mazda 1300 in their January 1971 issue and found it to be a nice enough car. Its engine was "the best-balanced" and it was the best-handling of the trio and was described as "the least sophisticated but was robust and well-proven" while its brakes were described as "under-fed" being drums all round (only the Mazda had front discs) and its handling was said to be such that it was "one of the best-balanced small cars currently available here." As for interior comfort they wrote that "it fails badly on comfort. The seats are hard and very upright and offer no support." At the end of the comparison test they wrote of the Datsun, "It is the plain Jane of the trio. It is utilitarian, with just a few concessions to creature comfort; it is excellent as a town commuter being easy to load and light to drive." At no time were any of the three cars referred to as exciting to drive

DAT 180

DATSUN
DATSUN

but that was not what the Datsun 1200 was all about. It produced a top speed of 137.6km/h (86mph) with 0–80 and 96km/h (0–50 and 60mph) taking 11.0 and 15.5 seconds with a remarkable 8.8–7.8 litres per 100km (32–36mpg) economy.

Meanwhile the 1600 had continued on being one of the best-selling four-cylinder cars on the market. However, in November 1972 Datsun announced the 180B to replace it. The 180B was a critical car for Nissan Australia because the company had entered it into the Government's 85 per cent local content plan so it had to be a commercial success from the outset. At the release of the 180B Nissan also announced that it would be investing over $100 million over the next few years in upgrading the assembly plant and building an engine manufacturing plant. Where the 1600's styling was simple to the point of almost being plain the 180B was the exact opposite and the media was quick to comment. Its styling was characterised by swooping lines along the body sides, a narrow window line that severely reduced visibility and styling excesses like the patterns heat pressed into the various pieces of plastic in the interior. New with the 180B were tombstone-style front bucket seats that were set quite low in the passenger compartment which meant that short drivers had problems looking over the steering wheel and out the side windows.

Interior quality looked to be OK sitting in the car on the showroom floor but out in the field it soon became an issue for buyers; it was clear that Nissan's quality at that time was not as good as its rivals, in particular Toyota's. The dash was made from hard plastics that could warp or crack in the hot Australian sun and its actual design was plain and not that attractive; there were three dials in front of the driver (they were squared-off circles) housing the speedometer in the centre, clock to the left and combination dial (fuel and temperature gauges) plus warning lights to the right. Pull-push switches were positioned along a recessed ledge under the dials – only the indicators and hi-lo beam were on the single column stalk. A glove box was off to the left with the radio and heater/demister slides in the centre. Under the dash centre were two adjustable air vents (they looked like an after-thought) that were a part of the ventilation system.

As for its physical dimensions, the 180B sat on a 2499mm (98.4-ins) wheelbase, was 4114mm (162-ins) in overall length by 1600mm (63-ins) in width and 1354mm (53.3-ins) in height, with its body weight being 934kgs (2055lbs). Its wheelbase was 50mm (2.0-ins) longer than the 1600, it was 101mm (4-ins) longer and 23kgs (50lbs) heavier. And as for the engine, its capacity was raised to 1770cc (85 x 77.9mm), the SOHC unit was now developing 78kW (105bhp) at 6000rpm and 146Nm (108lbs-ft) of torque at 3600rpm; performance was little changed from the 1600 because of the added weight. Carried through from the 1600 was the mounting of the 54-litre (12-gallon) fuel tank behind the rear seat which compromised the depth of the luggage compartment and restricted what families could carry on holidays.

In its May 1973 issue *Wheels* tested the Datsun 180B against the Mazda Capella 1600, Toyota Corona 1600 and Holden Torana 1760 in an article headed "Four Fighting Fours." In some ways the 180B was viewed as the technology leader having both a SOHC engine and independent rear suspension – the Corona had an old 1.6-litre OHV engine, the Torana's slant four came from Vauxhall and was a SOHC design with a toothed belt cam drive and cross-flow cylinder head while the Mazda had the best engine with a chain-driven SOHC with hemispherical combustion chambers and cross-flow porting. The Datsun engine, while SOHC, did not have a cross-flow cylinder head and many critics would argue that the geometry of the IRS was not well thought out such were the massive camber changes that took place under varying conditions. Criticisms of the 180B included lifeless steering, a 'dead' brake pedal and a noise level that was almost intolerable on a long drive.

With the 180B model Nissan added the availability of a locally-assembled station wagon that proved to be very popular with buyers. It was a part of the Nissan game plan to match Toyota model-for-model wherever possible. It followed the sedan in styling apart from the longer roofline and the one-piece lift-up rear door that gave access to the load space. Like the 1600 the 180B featured a MacPherson strut coil spring front suspension and semi-trailing arm independent rear suspension also with coil springs and telescopic dampers. A characteristic of the 180B was the potential to scrape its differential housing on rural roads with a high crown because when travelling with passengers in the back seat and luggage in the boot the camber of the rear wheels changed dramatically reducing the ground clearance to just millimetres. The car's handling characteristics in those conditions deteriorated dramatically, too. As for performance, the 180B would run to 164.8km/h (103mph) with 56km/h (35mph) available in first gear at 6500rpm, 94km/h (59mph) in second and a huge 144km/h (90mph) in third; this was because of the 3.70:1 rear axle ratio that gave the 180B a very relaxed long distance cruising gait.

The 180B was available in two versions, the Deluxe at $2666 and GL at $2786, the small difference being because of additional equipment, the most obvious being a radio and door armrests. In mid-1975 came

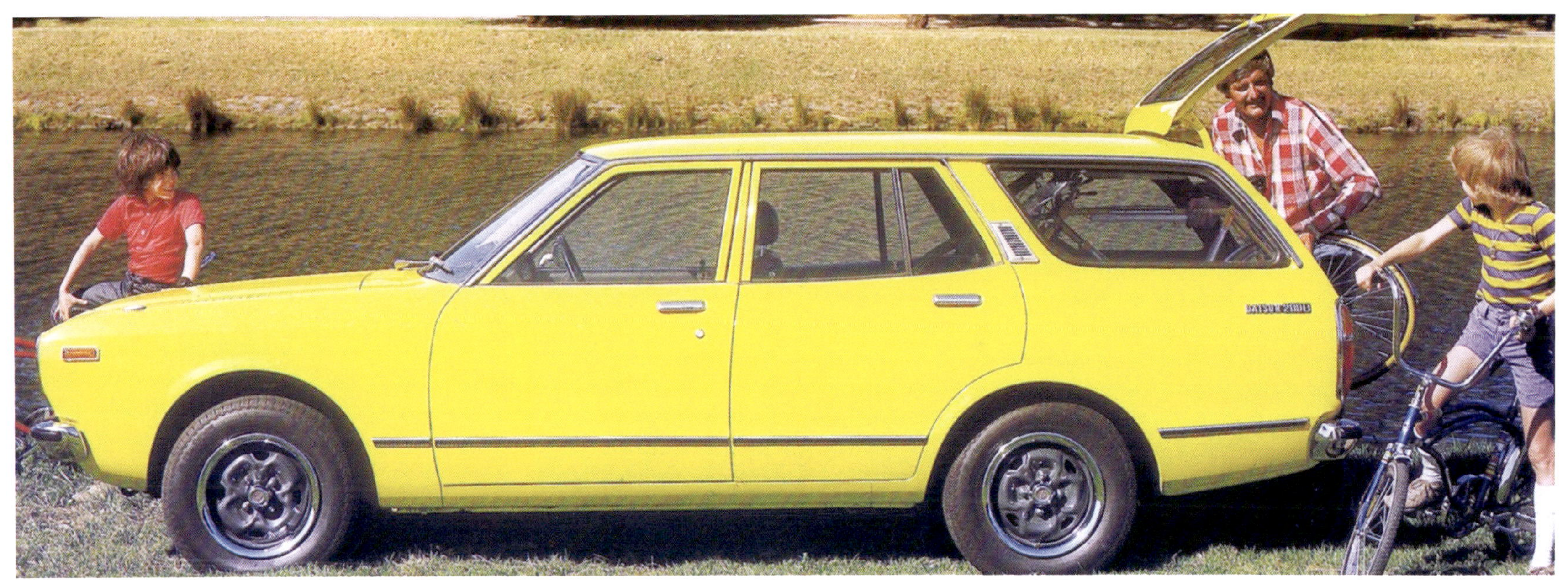

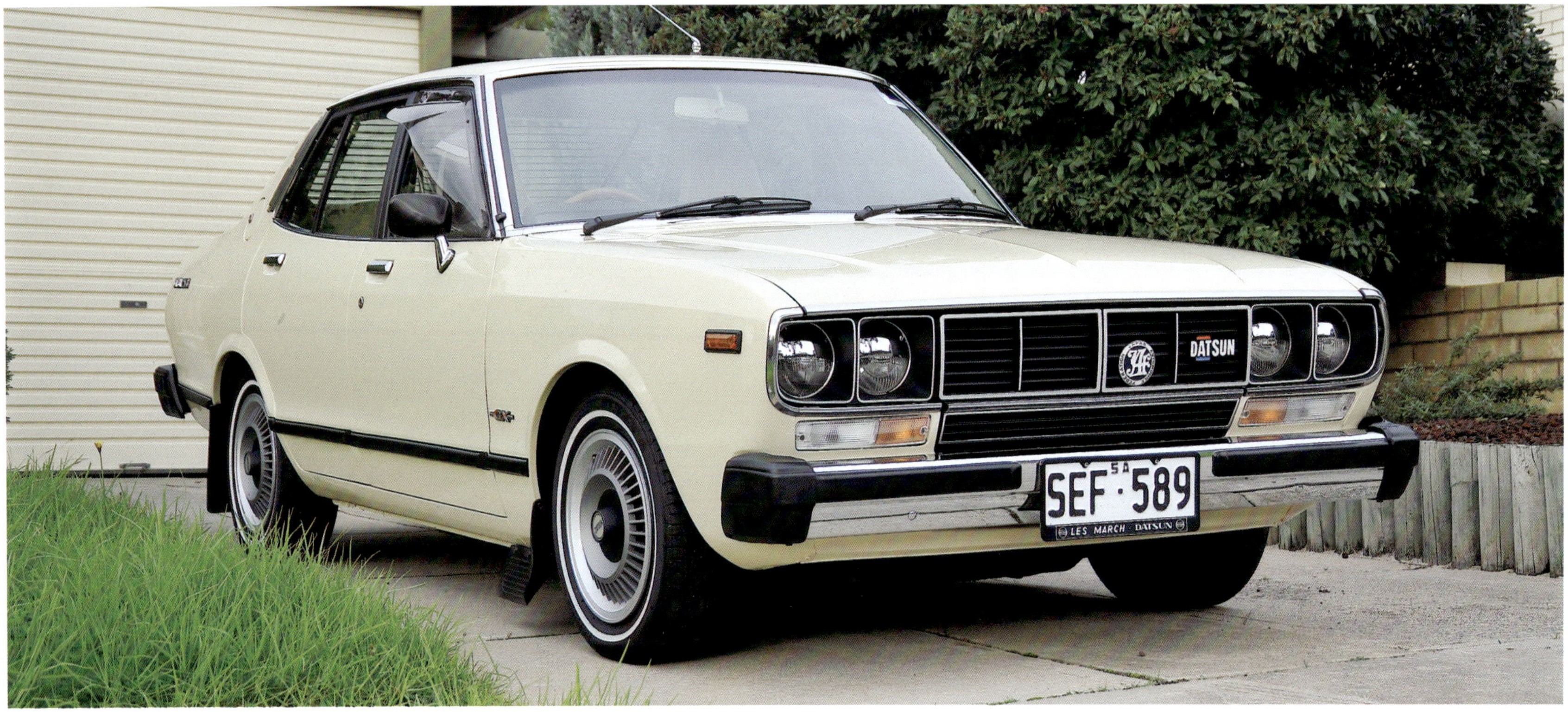
DATSUN
SA
SEF·589
LES MARCH · DATSUN

the 180B GX that was top dog in the range along with the SSS coupe but these model variants were imported, not assembled at Clayton.

The bland but ultra-reliable 1200 was replaced by the 120Y in March 1974. Like its bigger brother, it was assembled at Clayton and was available as a four-door sedan, five-door station wagon and two-door coupe. Styling of the 120Y soon garnered plenty of derision from the media and rightly so. Between them the 120Y and 180B led Nissan down a one-way street – cul-de-sac? – where the styling of their mainstream cars was concerned and this ultimately cost the company dearly.

Media opinion of Datsun cars was not high, most journalists regarded them as little more than shopping trolleys mainly because they felt and sounded tinny in their construction, had poor brakes, poor adhesion and skittishness on rough road surfaces but they did concede that they were reliable and cheap to run, specially the 1200 and 120Y. The 120Y was little more than a new (and in the opinion of many critics, ugly) body over the old 1200 components with the exception of non-boosted front disc brakes replacing the drums, stiffer front anti-roll bar and longer rear leaf springs. New box sections to cope with body deformity during a crash raised its weight by 80kgs (175lbs) and with identical power output from the engine performance did suffer.

From a size point of view the 120Y was close to the 1200, having a wheelbase of a tad over 2340mm (92-ins), overall length of 3950mm (155.5-ins) by 1545mm (60.8-ins) wide and 1350mm (53-ins) high, kerb weight being 775kgs (1705lbs) for the sedan and coupe and 817kgs (1797lbs) for the wagon. Prices ranged from $2569 for the sedan, $2715 for the coupe and $2695 for the wagon – they were slightly more expensive than the Corolla and the Mazda 1300 surprisingly.

Wheels road tested a 120Y in its May 1974 issue and initially talked about the wonderful fuel economy from the car before getting into the nitty gritty. Not far into the article they said, "Previous small Datsuns have never been particular favourites at *Wheels*, partly because they retained drum brakes and partly because they lacked comfort, had poor adhesion on wet roads and felt tinny. We have regarded them as little more than shopping baskets." The 120Y was slightly larger and heavier 80kgs (175lbs) to meet new crash requirements and yet had the same engine as the old model. As for its handling they found it was fun on smooth surfaces but the antiquated rear suspension skipped about on rougher surfaces. This was their only real gripe although there were signs of cost-cutting in the car's interior. Nevertheless, they thought it would continue the sales growth of the 1200 and on that score they were right. Against the clock it ran to 137km/h (85mph) and dashed from 0-to-80km/h (0–50mph) in 11.4 seconds; fuel economy was a remarkable 6.8 litres per 100km (41.9mpg) on test.

While Nissan were castigated by the media for their poor styling – justified – and the poor quality of the interior materials – also justified – they were no better or worse than their Japanese rivals where the technical specifications were concerned. The semi-elliptic leaf spring live axle at the rear of the 120Y was poorly located and gave a choppy ride but then so did the same axle and suspension setup under the Corolla, Mazda 1300 and Galant 1300; only Honda and Subaru had the sophistication of fully independent suspension systems in this class.

With some fanfare Nissan announced in October 1977 that the 'all-new' Datsun 200B would replace the 180B and with this car Nissan announced it was going to conquer the local four-cylinder market. The first 200B's were fully imported in sedan, wagon and coupe (the SSS) forms with the independent rear suspension from the 180B under the sedan and coupe, the wagon having a live axle with semi-elliptic leaf springs. The immediate problem for Nissan from the beginning was that the media saw the 200B as simply a 180B with twenty more problems! What was made known to the media was that Nissan in Japan had allowed the Australian engineers more freedom to engineer the 200B for local conditions. The most important of those concessions was the substitution of a live rear axle suspended by coil springs with a trailing link each side for longitudinal location and upper oblique arms for lateral location. It was primarily a local content issue for Nissan because the components for the non-independent rear suspension were all in production in Australia.

From a styling point of view – the view that the majority of buyers form their first impressions of a model – the 200B looked to be little more than a tidy-up of the uncoordinated design of the 180B. Some of the faffy stuff was gone but it still had narrow side windows, thick C-pillar and the grille was an example of the stylists not knowing how to finish the design; they opted for a design that looked like the front teeth of a buck rabbit! It retained the four-headlight arrangement and at the rear was a single three-lens taillight unit each side.

Again Nissan offered the 200B in a range of models, from the Deluxe at $5700, the GL at $5920 and GX at $6215 and later came the SX sedan at $6340; the 200B wagon came in Deluxe and GL formats. It was very close to the 180B in dimensions and therefore roominess inside was unchanged. Passengers in front sat on tombstone-style locally-made bucket seats and there was a bench in back best suited to two people, perhaps three kids, the upholstery being a hard, shiny plastic that was undoubtedly cheap. It was certainly not very comfortable on any long journey.

A new dashboard came with the 200B. It had no pretence of curving around the driver to give a cockpit effect but had a control area that stretched across two-thirds of the dash with three recessed round dials in front of the driver – speedometer in the middle, combination dial on the right with fuel and temperature dials plus some warning lights and a blank to the left that could be used for the optional tachometer. To the right was a tiny cubby for coins and off to the left was the push-button radio, clock and a bank of four warning lights, all surrounded by a silver plastic that looked gauche. Under the centre of the dash were the slides for the heater/demister and two-speed fan plus two more air vents to supplement those either end of the dash; an integrated air conditioning system was an option but the airflow through the vents was poor. Indicators, hi/lo beam change with the light switch (twist) on the end was on the right of the steering column while the two-speed wipers and washers were operated by a switch on the left of the column. All were within finger-tip reach. And the ignition switch-cum-starter now incorporated a steering lock.

On the road the 200B was one of the quicker two-litre cars on the market, its enlarged engine – 1952cc from a bore and stroke of 85 x 86mm – developing 69kW (93bhp) at 5600rpm and 152Nm (112lbs-ft) of torque at 3200rpm. These figures are only marginally different from the original Datsun 1600! *Wheels* carried a five-car comparison test in its March 1978 edition – it compared the 200B (an imported one with the IRS) with the Corona , Sigma, Cortina and Sunbird – and had few kind words about the 200B. They felt that even though the 200B was new it looked old-fashioned in its styling and especially its interior. On the performance side of the argument, they said, "The trouble is the Datsun is so noisy and harsh that you need to be completely unsympathetic to the engine and car to achieve to performance figures quoted." They went on to say, "Performance there is, but unless you wear ear plugs it's not useable and even a simple down change from fourth to third gear for extra passing power brings on a roar and vibrations that come up through the floor and accelerator." And when discussing the car's handling and roadholding they were very critical of the steering and added, "The 200B moves around on the road while the steering does its best to make precision something that other cars possess. It is a tiring car to drive fast and has nothing to offer the keen driver."

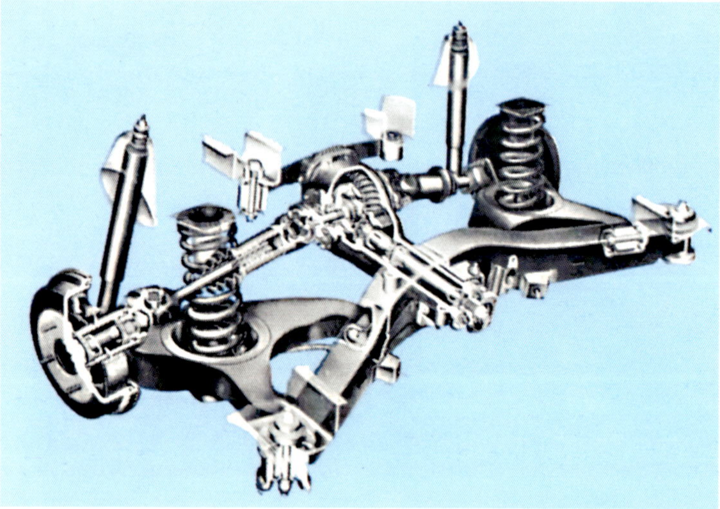

Against the clock the 200B recorded a maximum speed of 156km/h (97.5mph) at 5600rpm – they took the engine out to 7000rpm for first and second, the noise must have been deafening! – where the Corona ran to exactly the same speed, the Sigma was marginally the fastest with the Cortina and Sunbird trailing behind.

Despite the panning by the media the 200B very quickly became the top-selling 2-litre family sedan on the market so clearly the dynamic deficiencies targeted by the press had little bearing on the buying public. Nevertheless, Nissan management was stung by the criticisms and instigated a program to improve the 200B. The results of the first part of the program arrived in November 1979, a little more than a year after the car had been announced. Externally there was little to show apart from a new plastic moulded grille with deep-set dual headlights each side, different wheel trims and new more substantial bumpers front and rear with plastic end-caps.

However, it was vital that Nissan attack the major criticisms of noise and vibration, something that the rival Chrysler (nee Mitsubishi) Sigma was very good at mainly because of the balance shafts within the engine. By this time Nissan was manufacturing the 200B's engine locally so there was a huge investment at risk. Vibration from the engine was being exacerbated by road noise being transferred into the passenger compartment. To cure this Nissan fitted a mass dampener to the front cross member supported by rubber springs tuned to absorb the engine's vibration and the rear engine/gearbox mounting point was redesigned to minimise the transfer of noise and vibration.

The media really spoke out about the uncertain handling of the 200B – it had a tendency to wander from the straight ahead and was slightly unpredictable when cornering where its rivals were not – and the steering was lifeless. By retuning the suspension bushes and revising the calibration of the dampers they were able to achieve better control of the rear axle and a new variable ratio recirculating ball steering box improved the steering characteristics. At the same time Nissan specified new slimmer and lighter front disc calipers and modified the brake servo for a smoother action.

Inside the rear seat squab was changed to a moulded foam construction that improved headroom and helped reduce noise transmission. Cloth was the standard seat material now with vinyl available as an option on the GL. Thicker one-piece carpets were used front and rear to also assist with noise mitigation. In addition, the steering wheel was slightly smaller in diameter and was now of the soft-feel type with simulated stitching, the rear window now had electric heating to demist it, the ignition now had a small light timed with the door courtesy lights, a trip meter was now included in the speedometer and the GX had a 7 second delay when in the intermittent setting for the wipers.

The SX model was continued over – it had proven to be surprisingly popular when you consider it was a cosmetic dress-up package only, not a performance option – with a blacked-out grille and new ABS bumpers

that incorporated a subtle air dam underneath plus new wire spoke alloy wheels. A wagon was an option in the 200B and it was equipped to the same level as the GX sedan; and the SSS hardtop was discontinued.

In late 1977 Nissan replaced the 120Y with the Sunny, a new name here but a familiar one from Japan. It was essentially a new suit over old bones; the plain, bland styling of the Sunny was panned by the media but, as with the 120Y and 200B, again it was no inhibitor to sales. The model range continued with a four-door sedan, station wagon and coupe. Size-wise it was pretty much line ball with the old 120Y, sitting on a wheelbase of 2340mm (92.1-ins) and stretching 4190mm (165-ins) in overall length with its kerb weight being just 907kgs (2000lbs).

Inside was a neat dashboard with three round dials in front of the driver, bucket seats in front and a bench in back plus a small luggage space at the rear. Like its predecessor it was economical to own and run but it was an uninspiring car in almost every way.

By late 1978 Nissan had transformed its Australian operations. They had recruited Lloyd Beck from Holden and he had overseen the growing of the business. The company had invested $35 million in a new engine plant at Dandenong, $12 million had been invested in the Clayton assembly plant, $20 million for tooling from local suppliers and $5 million in new buildings and there was still a state-of-the-art paint shop to come. On a two-shift basis the plant could produce 135,000 engines a year or 100,000 on a single-shift system; according to management at Nissan Australia there was an export market of 50,000 engines to Japan, Malaysia and New Zealand. By late 1979 it was planned that cylinder heads, crankshafts and camshafts would be manufactured in the plant, the cast iron cylinder blocks coming from the Chrysler foundry at Lonsdale south of Adelaide. Using two shifts Clayton could produce 350 cars a day, 200 on a single shift.

In October 1978 Nissan released the Datsun Stanza to much acclaim from the media. After all, Nissan wanted us to believe they were recreating one of the company's more successful periods it enjoyed with the Datsun 1600. In their eyes, the Stanza was a modern day interpretation of that iconic car. Physically the similarities are obvious – the 1600 had a wheelbase of 2420mm (95.3-ins), the Stanza's was 2400mm (94.5-

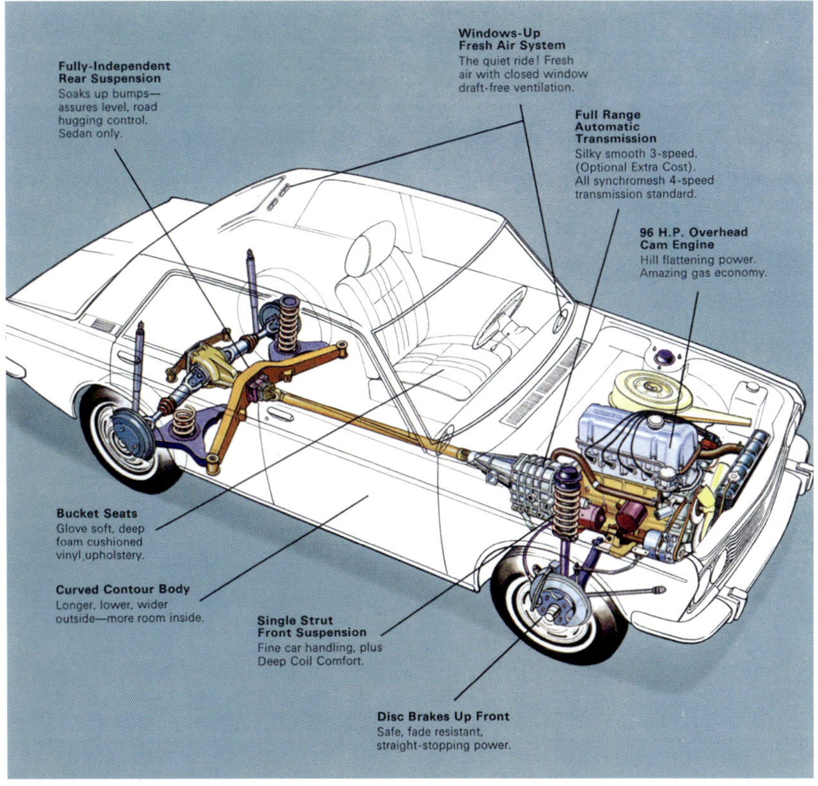

1600
DELUXE

ins), overall length of the 1600 was 4064mm (160-ins), the Stanza was also 4064mm (160-ins), width was 1559mm (61.4-ins) against 1600mm (63-ins), height was 1409mm (55.5-ins) against 1389mm (54.7-ins) and there was around 23kgs (50lbs) difference in weight with the 1600 weighing 932kgs (2051lbs) and the Stanza 954kgs (2100lbs).

Mechanically it was a 1600 clone apart from the rear suspension – the 1600 as everyone knows had a semi-trailing arm independent suspension with coil springs and telescopic dampers (hence why it was often called "the poor man's BMW1600") – where the Stanza had a similar live axle with four links and coil springs like the 200B. Engine-wise the two cars shared the SOHC 1595cc unit that developed 71kW (96bhp) at 5600rpm and 135Nm (100lbs-ft) of torque at 3600rpm although the Stanza unit was locally made and detoxed for the ADRs, drove through a four-speed all-synchromesh manual gearbox with slightly different ratios (the Stanza's first three ratios are slightly lower) to a 3.7:1 rear axle; brakes were disc/drums for both with the Stanza having a booster as standard, recirculating ball steering and 13-ins steel rims wearing 6.15 x 13 crossply tyres on the 1600 and 155SR x 13 steel radials on the Stanza.

Both cars' styling was boxy as you would expect, the 1600's plain and simple while the Stanza's was contrived as was the way with Datsuns at the time. Both were comfortable four seaters, five at a pinch and again, the dashboard for the 1600 was plain and simple, that in front of the Stanza driver looked a little like that in the 200B and looked 'bitty' and uncoordinated.

Wheels conducted a full road of the Stanza (February 1979) and opened the article with the following comment: "Optimistic magazine writers periodically see a car like the Honda Accord as the beginning of a general improvement in Japanese car design. Then someone releases a car like the Datsun Stanza – economical, probably trouble-free but utterly pedestrian – and their hopes are dashed." That would have got the attention of the executives at Nissan Australia!

The *Wheels* folks went on to say, "The Stanza is not the car the 1600 was when it was new. In its time, the Datsun 1600 offered a horde of features that one could not take for granted in opposition cars. It had an independent rear suspension system that people tended to compare with that of the small BMWs. It had MacPherson strut front suspension, front disc brakes, an engine with a single overhead camshaft and twin-throat carburettor, a good power to weight ratio and gearing that allowed 130km/h cruising across Australia. All in 1968."

Editor Robinson was critical of the Stanza in three main areas: noise and vibration, body construction and suspension shortcomings and managed to have audience with senior Nissan executives to discuss the car's flaws, a most remarkable response from Nissan. In was, in many ways, a repeat of the issues that plagued the 200B a couple of years earlier.

As for its performance on test, they managed a top speed of 158km/h (98.7mph) with 51km/h, 87 and 133km/h (32mph, 54 and 83mph) at 6500rpm in the indirect gears with acceleration times of 7.3 secs for the 0–70km/h (44mph) run, 11.0 secs for the dash to 90km/h (56mph) and 16.8 secs to 110km/h (68mph).

From a local assembly point of view Nissan saw out the decade struggling to maintain a viable market share on the back of the 120Y and 200B. During the latter part of the decade the company began taking steps towards manufacturing more of their cars locally with both the Stanza and 200B being powered by the locally-manufactured SOHC engine and the Sunny using an imported unit. These cars were supplemented by the fully imported 240K sedan and coupe, the 240 and 260Z sports coupes and the luxury 240C. They did not realise it but there were tough times ahead for Nissan.

VOLVO

CHAPTER 8

THE NICHE PLAYERS

By this time there were two companies, both Melbourne-based, who were assembling multiple franchises. We have already dealt with Australian Motor Industries (AMI) for whom Toyota was by far their largest client. The other company was Motor Producers Limited, formerly Volkswagen Australia Limited. Volkswagen AG owned Motor Producers from 1971-through-1976 when they sold it to the Nissan Motor Company. However, with the downturn of the economy and the shift away from the traditional English and European marques to new Japanese makes and models, Volkswagen of Australia (VWoA) reverted to assembling Golfs and Passats rather than manufacture them locally as they had done with the Beetle. To help pay the rent they went into partnership with Nissan who was looking to expand its presence in Australia and also with Volvo who was at that time dominating the luxury European end of the market.

VOLVO

The Swedish company was well-known in Australia having been imported by several State distributors since the early 1960s. Initially the only model available was the Volvo 122 which came as a two- or four-door sedan and there was also a station wagon but very few of them were imported. This model quickly established a reputation for toughness and sportiness that endeared it to enthusiast motorists who enjoyed spirited motoring and the occasional rally.

In August 1966 Volvo released the new 144 in Europe which arrived in Australia in April 1967 as a full import. It was a much larger car with a larger body of more contemporary style than the 122 but used almost all of its running gear even if it was modified for the new car. It was built on a wheelbase of 2603mm (102.5-ins), was 4635mm (182.5-ins) long by 1727mm (68-ins) wide and 1448mm (57-ins) high with a kerb weight of just under 1182kgs (2600lbs) for the sedan, slightly heavier for the 145 station wagon. Under the bonnet was the reliable Volvo B18 in-line four-cylinder OHV engine that had a bore of 84mm and a stroke of 80mm for a capacity of 1781cc. Using a single Zenith-Stromberg-type carburettor and an 8.7:1 compression it developed 63kW (85bhp) at 5000rpm and 147Nm (108.5 lbs-ft) of torque at 3000rpm. A twin SU carburettor version was available in the 144S that developed 85kW (115bhp) at 6000rpm and 4lbs-ft more of torque. In some ways it was a little like Grandpa's axe – if it ain't broke don't

fix it. Volvo chose to go with what they already had for an engine rather than invest in something new like BMW had done three years earlier and most of the Japanese manufacturers were doing.

To say that the 144 was a major break with Volvo's past would be something of an understatement. It was a big sedan (and wagon) that had a presence because of its size. The cabin was large and very roomy for up to five adult passengers and visibility was uninterrupted due to the vast glass area – large windscreen up front, big window at the rear and six side windows. Aerodynamics was not on the roster for the stylists, the 144 having a big, bluff front with a pressed aluminium grille flanked by a single headlight and parking light each side, the indicators being an orange lens on each front corner. The body sides were unadorned apart from a full-length character line highlighted by a discreet chrome strip. At the rear were vertical taillights either side of a recessed panel that carried the rear license plate light and model badges; the boot lid opened from the top of that panel which meant loading heavy cases for example required some physical effort.

Inside were twin front bucket seats with an adjustable lumbar support (a Volvo first) and a bench in back, the floors were carpeted and the dash was a bulky-looking piece of art with perimeter padding enclosing the rectangular instrument cluster, various pull-push switches and three vertical rotary wheels that controlled the very effective heating/demisting system; in front of the passenger was a grab handle. Actual dials included a strip speedometer with a movable red pointer to remind the driver of a particular speed limit plus fuel and temperature dials. At the time Volvo made a big deal out of the total odometer which read to 1 million kilometres – this was in recognition of the fact that many Volvo owners exceeded the previous 100,000km odometer reading! It spoke volumes for the ruggedness of Volvo engineering and the longevity of the cars.

Carried over, albeit in slightly modified form, was the upper-lower wishbone front suspension with coil springs, ball joints, telescopic dampers and a stabiliser bar while at the rear was a live axle and coil springs with longitudinal support arms and torque arms to control sideways movement. Braking was by four-wheel discs and dual triangulated circuits with a vacuum boost and dual reducer valves in the rear circuits to prevent rear wheel lockup. Steering was by a cam and peg system and the steering column was collapsible. Wheels were 4.5 x 15 ventilated steel shod with 165S 15 radial tyres. The rugged four-speed all-synchromesh manual gearbox now had a direct floor gearshift lever and the optional Borg Warner 35 automatic had a floor selector.

Volvo laid claims to a whole raft of safety 'firsts' with the 144. We have already mentioned the collapsible steering column and divided brake circuits but three-point safety belts were standard as were radial tyres and the rust-proofed all-steel body was designed with built-in crumple zones.

At the end of 1968 the 144 was made available with the B20B engine which was a 2-litre unit that enabled Volvo to better compete with the likes of BMW, Rover 2000, Triumph 2000 and Mercedes-Benz in Europe where this engine size was extremely popular. Power rose only 3bhp (to 118bhp) and torque was increased to 166Nm (123lbs-ft) at 3500rpm. A running change came in early 1971, not long after local assembly of the 144 began when a slightly different three-section black grille was fitted that featured the traditional Volvo slanting spear across it. At this time buyers who desired real luxury – metallic paint, leather seats, wider wheels, driving lights, heated rear window, automatic gearbox and so on – could order the 144 Grand Luxe (later shortened to GL) and this version was only available with the 96kW (130bhp) Bosch fuel injected engine that had previously been the preserve of the 1800 coupe.

Volvo Australia had been established on July 1, 1970 and initiated negotiations with VW Australia to assemble the 144 locally. The first Australian-assembled Volvos rolled off the Motor Producers Limited line in late 1971. Incidentally, Volvo was the last company to be accepted by the Federal Government to participate in the local assembly plan.

Dealers were able to source their stock from either Motor Producers – non-metallic paint cars – or if a buyers wanted a metallic paint colour then the car would be imported. Equipment levels pretty much matched those from Sweden so it was only a paint-type issue for buyers. Phased-in at this time was an electrically heated rear window and flow-through ventilation.

1971 also saw the introduction of the 142, a two-door version of the

sedan which was surprisingly successful given that Australian motorists have never been great supporters of the configuration. Introduced at the same time were new wheels and the B20E engine with Bosch D-Jetronic injection system.

Modern Motor tested a 144 Grand Luxe (April 1971) and came away impressed. The car's ability to cruise over long distances in complete comfort for the driver and passengers – the front seats were described as being "orthopedically correct" – which combined with the superb stability of the car, its excellent road manners and powerful brakes made for reassuring driving no matter what the conditions. They achieved a maximum speed of 173km/h (108mph) with a 0–96km/h (0–60mph) time of 12.8 seconds with 10.5 litres per 100km (27mpg) for one trip, not bad at all for a luxury sedan weighing more than 1182kgs (2600lbs). The interior was roomy and the boot huge with the spare wheel upright to one side.

During 1972 a number of improvements arrived including flush-fitting exterior door handles, minor revisions to the dashboard, new centre console and a shorter gearshift lever for manual transmission cars.

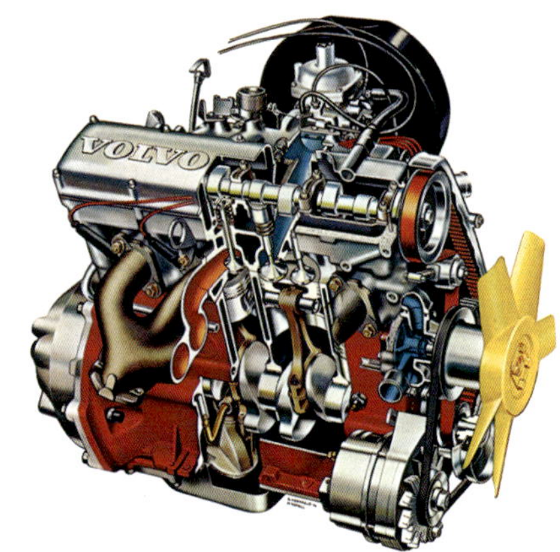

In early 1973 Volvo again updated the 144, this time to a one-piece plastic grille still with the traditional spear, larger amber indicator lenses on each front corner, restyled rear with much larger multi-lens taillight units and a new dashboard with round instruments in a raised binnacle, rocker switches replaced the former pull-push type and the ventilation system was redesigned. A year later the B20 engine had been switched to Bosch's new K-Jetronic fuel injection system – there was no power or torque gain – and the fuel tank was moved forward closer to the rear axle for better protection in a rear-end collision and large rubber-faced bumpers appeared for the first time. The only other change of note was the deletion of the quarter vents in the front windows and the wipers had been transferred to sweep towards the driver for better visibility in inclement weather.

Late in 1974 the 140 series was replaced by the 240 series. This was the first (and only) major redevelopment of the original theme and was influenced by research learned from the Volvo Experimental Safety Car (VESC) from the 1972–73 period. In simple terms the 240 was the 140 with a new nose but there was far more to it than that. All the sheet metal forward of the bulkhead was new and the styling reflected the VESC with its broad expanse of bonnet that sloped down to a rearward sloping plastic grille with the Volvo spear, single headlights each side and indicator/parking lights at each corner, and there were those huge bumpers designed to cope with the 5-mph requirements in America. It was not pretty but it was functional. The rest of the 240 was pretty much carry-over 140.

Under the sloping bonnet, however, huge changes (for Volvo) had been wrought. Gone was the upper-and-lower wishbone front suspension to be replaced by a MacPherson strut system with a wide-based pressed steel lower wishbone and a rack and pinion steering system accompanied the new suspension as did new inner panels to locate the struts. The new suspension system brought a wider front track of 1420mm (55.9-ins) (plus 74mm/2.9-ins) and the kerb weight had risen to 1280kgs (2811lbs) for a GL sedan. And finally, the wheels were reduced to 14-ins diameter with 175SR14 radial tyres fitted as standard.

Developed out of the B20 engine was a new B21 engine with a capacity of 2127cc from its dimensions of 92 x 80mm. It was available in two forms – B21A that developed 72kW (97bhp) at 5000rpm using a single Zenith-Stromberg carburettor, and as a B21E using Bosch L-Jetronic fuel injection system and a solid-state ignition system that developed 92kW (123bhp) at 5500rpm. Included in the B21's specifications were

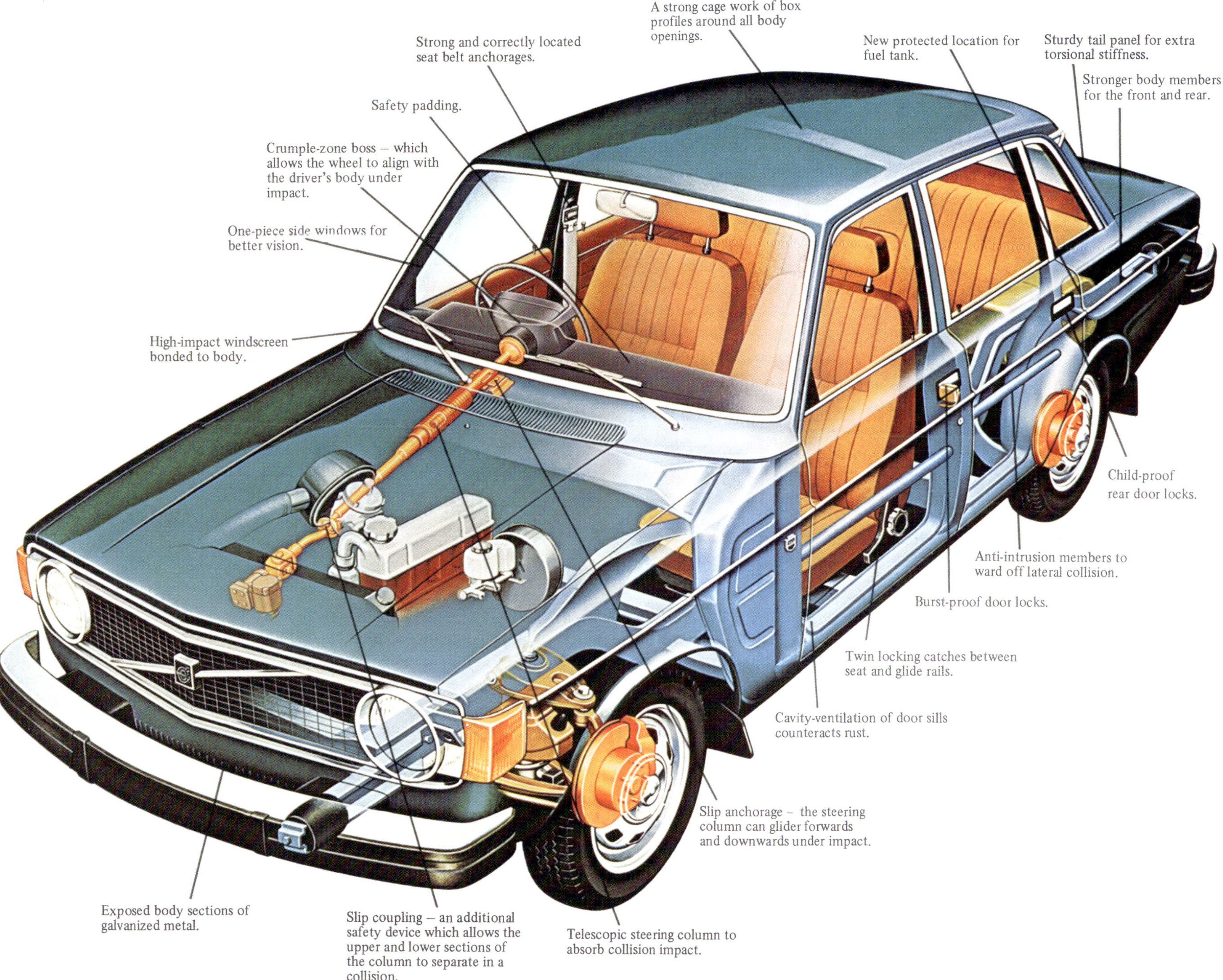
A strong cage work of box profiles around all body openings.
Strong and correctly located seat belt anchorages.
New protected location for fuel tank.
Sturdy tail panel for extra torsional stiffness.
Stronger body members for the front and rear.
Safety padding.
Crumple-zone boss – which allows the wheel to align with the driver's body under impact.
One-piece side windows for better vision.
High-impact windscreen bonded to body.
Child-proof rear door locks.
Anti-intrusion members to ward off lateral collision.
Burst-proof door locks.
Twin locking catches between seat and glide rails.
Cavity-ventilation of door sills counteracts rust.
Slip anchorage – the steering column can glider forwards and downwards under impact.
Exposed body sections of galvanized metal.
Slip coupling – an additional safety device which allows the upper and lower sections of the column to separate in a collision.
Telescopic steering column to absorb collision impact.

an aluminium alloy crossflow cylinder head and a toothed-belt driven single overhead camshaft.

In a full test published in *Modern Motor*, writer John Crawford opened with the words, "We said in our pre-release impressions of the new 244 that our previously critical opinion of Volvos has changed. It has – but after a full test on the 244GL we believe it still has a way to go. The new range is vastly improved – but vast improvement doesn't always mean perfection. Ride, handling, comfort, performance and safety are better – but some not enough." Volvo's message to the market was safety, safety, safety with few compromises and it did sell cars for the company, no doubt about that. However, in comparison with other European cars like the Saab 99, Peugeot 504 and 505, BMW 520/528, Rover 3500, Citroen CX and so on it still had a way to go. "Body roll," said *MM*, "was quite dramatic and yet the ride was only marginally improved despite the all-new MacPherson strut front suspension." They liked its ability to cover long distances quickly and quietly but with the proviso that some road rumble and vibrations crept inside. It was very stable under all conditions, the steering was precise and the brakes powerful. An oddity that remained with the 244 automatic was a transmission shudder taking off under power – it seemed to be a 'feature' of the model for some strange reason.

Both *Wheels* and *MM* managed a top speed of 154km/h (96mph) for an automatic DL, 158km/h (99mph) for a manual, with the 0–110km/h acceleration runs taking 17.7 seconds with the auto, 15.1 seconds for the manual. Both magazines opined that people who were real drivers would probably not understand or appreciate the Volvo's dynamics – they'd be far happier with a Peugeot 504/505 or BMW 520/528 – but for those who appreciated a long service life coupled with great reliability and a tremendously solid feel then the Volvo 244 made eminent sense. At $7395 for the DL auto it was not inexpensive for a car that had few standard fittings inside when a Peugeot 504 auto retailed for $6439 or $6785 for the Ti injection version.

Released simultaneously was the new Volvo 264 that used exactly the same body as the 244 because its new V6 engine was short enough to fit in the same engine bay. The previous top Volvo, the 164, had a unique front clip to cater for the long in-line six-cylinder engine. The 264's V6 was part of a collaboration between Peugeot, Renault and Volvo – it was badged the PRV engine – and was a radical departure for Volvo. Badged as the B27E, it was an all alloy unit with a 90-degree Vee, a forged four bearing crankshaft, 'wet' cylinder liners and a Bosch L-Jetronic injection system. Its bore and stroke were 88 x 73mm for the unusual capacity of 2664cc. On an 8.7:1 compression ratio it developed 103kW (140bhp) at 6000rpm and 204Nm (150lbs-ft) of torque at 3000rpm.

The most obvious exterior clue as to its identity was the different nose that featured a separate chromed grille flanked by large rectangular headlights and the taillights wrapped around the corners slightly; all other exterior features were shared with the 244 as was the interior. The seats were upholstered with leather and the dash had the same instrument binnacle, centre outlet vents for the ventilation/air conditioning system and centre console with the controls for heating/demisting/air plus radio and clock. Standard equipment for the Australian market included integrated air conditioning, power steering, electric windows, AM/FM audio system, headlight washers/wipers, full carpeting, reclining front seats with lumbar support, seat belt warning lights and daytime running lights.

A 264 was quieter than its 244 sibling because of the nature of its V6 engine that was both smoother and quieter than the sometime coarse B21E unit. Road tests by local magazines seem not to have been undertaken (rather surprising) and the only article I could find came from *The Autocar* in England where the 264 was compared with its engine-sharing rivals, the Peugeot 604 and Renault 30TS. They recorded a maximum speed of 166km/h (104mph) versus 168km/h (105mph) for the 604 and 177km/h (111mph) for the 30TS. A 0–96km/h (0–60mph) time of 12.7 seconds against 11.9 and 11.7 seconds was recorded and fuel economy on the test worked out at 15 litres per 100km (18.6mpg)

for the Volvo and the Peugeot and 14 litres per 100km (20.2mpg) for the Renault. In summary the general feeling from the three testers rated the 264 last in quietness when cruising, last again in terms of ride and handling – "it lacks the ability to cope with serious undulations and rough road sections which shows up the limitations of wheel travel and relatively soft damping" – and they felt it rolled too much . Ergonomically all three were classed as very good (for the period) and interior comfort was similarly very good. When pushed for a decision they opted for the one of the French cars and opined the appearance (especially the front) of the 264 was something that they could not live with.

For the rest of the decade the 244/245 and 264/265 continued to be assembled at Clayton with only minor changes, the most noticeable of which was the use of the 264 grille and square headlights on the 244/245 from 1977. To give some idea of how successful Volvo had been, in March 1983 the 50,000th locally assembled Volvo rolled off the Clayton assembly line. Volvo eventually wound down its car assembly operation in 1988 after assembling around 65,000 cars, the last car being a 740GL. From then onwards the company reverted to full importation.

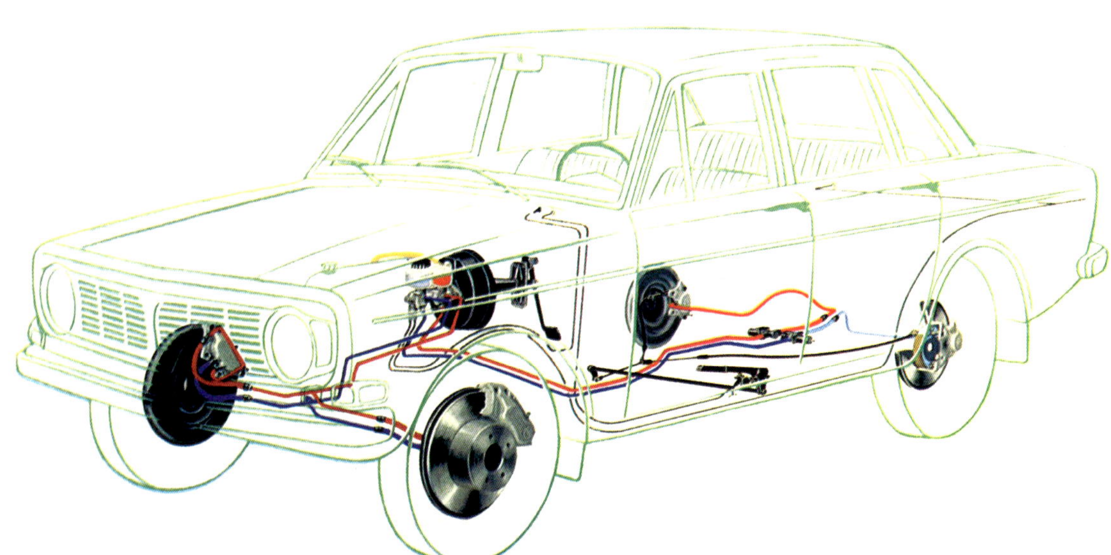

RENAULT

The company entered the 70s with some confidence and with two models in its range – the rear-engined and ancient R10 and R10S plus the ultra-clever R16 in normal and TS formats. The 16 had in a very short time established itself as one of the best family sedan-hatches ever and it had proven itself by winning rallies consistently driven by Bob Watson in particular. At this time, further investment had taken place at the Heidelberg West (suburb of Melbourne) factory with the installation of a new electrophoresis anti-corrosion painting process that had been developed by ICI BALM but it must be said that in the very early days there were a number of paint quality issues which were soon overcome.

The R10 acquired a locally sourced Bosch alternator early in 1970, making it one of the last cars to use the old DC generator. In May the uniquely Australian 10S model appeared that featured the European 8S engine with its Weber twin-choke downdraft carburettor, alternator and revised dash with round VDO speedometer, tachometer and fuel gauge plus a delete option matt black stripe along each side and S badges front and rear.

In November 1970 the company introduced the brilliant new R12 to replace the 10. Like the 16, it was the result of some creative thinking by Renault's engineers in France but it must be said that as good as it was, the 16 was still a more versatile design. By Renault's standards the 12 was almost conventional! It established a template for Renault that would last for many years and would be found in various forms under a wide range of models in the future. From Renault Australia's point of view, they entered it in the Government's Plan B and the aim was for 50 per cent local content by May 1971.

The R12 stood on a 2438mm (96-ins) wheelbase – it was the same both sides – and was 4343mm (171-ins) overall (it was actually 5-ins *longer* than the 16) by 1638mm (64.5-ins) wide and 1435mm (56.5-ins) tall with a useful 12.5 cubic feet boot at the back with a flat floor and the spare located upright on the right. It was recognisably a Renault from the front because of the square headlights set either side of a plain horizontal bar plastic grille with the chromed U around the corporate diamond logo. Like the 16, the new 12 spent considerable time in the company's wind tunnel where its design was honed to give a good Cd and excellent stability in windy conditions. An unusual point of its styling was the small ridge across the rear of the roof that did two things – raised the roofline for more head room in the back seat, and helped air separation as it flowed over the car. Interestingly, both the 16 and 12 had full side windows (no quarter windows in the front glass) and yet the glass was flat at a time when curved door glass was becoming common.

Mechanically it was partly carry-over but mostly new. The oldest part was the engine, a wet sleeve in-line four-cylinder OHV unit that could trace its roots back to the 4CV engine of 1948 and had evolved through the 8 and 10. Initially it had a bore and stroke of 73 x 77mm for a capacity of 1289cc but in May 1971 a slightly smaller version – 71.9 x 77mm, 1251cc – was built for Australia only; the reason for this was bureaucratic and was part of the rules of the small volume assembly plan – there had to be a 25 per cent difference in engine capacity between models in a range and so the 12's engine was reduced from 1289cc in Europe to 1251cc for Australia to keep it spaced apart from the 1470cc capacity of the 16's engine. It meant that power output was reduced slightly to 45kW (60bhp) at 5250rpm and torque to 95Nm (70lbs-ft) at 3000rpm using a Solex 32 EISA downdraught carburettor and a mild 8.5:1 compression.

Where the 16's engine was behind the gearbox, up against the bulkhead, the 12's engine was way out front overhanging the front wheels as Audi was doing at the time; the four-speed all-synchromesh gearbox and differential were behind with a floor gearshift for the driver. The front suspension was independent by upper and lower wishbones with wide coil springs acting on the upper wishbone and into a small turret under the bonnet, a little like a MacPherson strut. At the rear was a pressed steel beam axle located centrally by a pivoted triangle and longitudinally by trailing links, the suspension being by coil springs and telescopic dampers; braking was by a disc front/drum rear system with a single circuit but for 1972 came a dual-circuit system and in 1974 a vacuum booster was added while the rack and pinion steering remained non-assisted.

Inside was a moulded plastic dashboard with a shiny plastic face surrounded by ribbed moulded plastic; the deep glovebox lid was a part of the dash top and in front of the driver were three round dials with deeply hooded surrounds to eliminate reflections – Jaeger speedometer with no trip meter was in the centre flanked by a combination unit on the right with dials for fuel and volts plus a bunch of warning lights and a blank for a clock (if fitted) to the left.

The instrumentation was changed in May 1971 to locally-made VDO dials with a printed circuit panel, the actual instruments remaining as they were but with a 'Fasten Seat Belts' warning light now in the third dial. In 1972 with the release of the 12GL a tachometer replaced the clock in the left dial.

On the right hand end of the dash was a large pointy control for the heater temperature; off to the left were switches for heated rear window plus a spare and under them were the slides for directing the air up or down and the heater fan speed. For smokers there was a cigarette lighter. Like the 16, the air entered the interior through a full-width grille at the base of the windscreen with three levers to direct it either onto the face of the driver and passenger or to the windscreen for demisting. It was effective but crude compared with what the Japanese were offering. And there was no provision for integrated air conditioning.

At first the 12 was available only in TL trim that had many French-sourced components including left-hand drive wiper sweep and a Ducellier distributor albeit with a special dust cover. From local sources came the alternator, battery, vinyl seat and door trim, floor carpets and paint. At the end of the year *Wheels* magazine announced the Renault 12 as its 1970 Car of the Year, the second such award for Renault. Comments in the January 1971 issue said, "It is a good performer with

a bonus of incredible fuel economy and general economy-of-operation. It has a built-in long service guarantee – low maintenance, component longevity and extended servicing periods.

"It is one of the most comfortable cars of our time – combining excellent interior seating, appointments and ventilation with superb ride and ease of driving control."

As for its performance, on test *Wheels* achieved a maximum speed of 142km/h (89mph) with 0–80 and -96km/h (0–50 and 0–60mph) times of 10.1 and 14.9 seconds, 48–80km/h (30–50mph) time of 5.3 seconds in second gear, 6.5 seconds in third and 11.3 seconds in top gear; economy was in the 10–8.4 litres per 100km (28–34) range. For a car that weighed 880kgs (1940lbs) at the kerb and had only 45kW (60bhp) these figures were most commendable.

During 1971 several improvements unique to Australia were incorporated into the 12 – articulated wiper arm on the driver's side that swept right to the A-pillar (never adopted by the 16 because of insufficient space at the rear of the engine bay), electric windscreen washers to replace the European plunger type, the boot floor mat was a plastic/felt item and the summer/winter airflow slides were deleted. Further Australianisation took place with locally-sourced window glass, VDO instruments including a 'Fasten Seat Belts' light, wiring loom, exhaust system, radiator, dampers, Bosch starter motor and distributor, anti-roll bars and coil springs.

At this time the 16 came in for the Australianisation treatment as well with local Bosch starter motor, alternator, distributor and coil, Lucas rectangular headlights (replacing the expensive Cibie units), Smiths heater with fan and radiator, Monroe dampers, Preslite wiper motor and in the 16TS, VDO instruments; the 16TL retained the original Jaeger strip instruments.

From May 1971 came new larger taillights for the 16 TL and TS that incorporated reversing lights and a black embellisher strip between the light units and the TL received the 1565cc engine but with the original non-crossflow cylinder head.

Renault released the 12 GL sedan in June 1972 which had improved interior comfort and equipment plus brighter paint colours; upholstery was in the then fashionable all-black vinyl that extended to the door trim panels and the roof headlining with the seat part made from a perforated tan vinyl plus one or two other colours, stick-on strips were applied to the body side crease for protection from opening doors in car parks as well as GL badges and it wore Dunlop SP44 red-line radial tyres. Two months later followed the 12 TL Station Sedan that retained the Jaeger instruments for the moment.

The 16 was re-specified from January 1972 to comply with various ADR requirements, getting head restraints on the front seats, new seats and trim, break-away interior mirror and a dual-circuit braking system. On the 16TS the same equipment was added and in August 1972 came the availability of the 16TSA, a TS fitted with a three-speed automatic gearbox. It retained the Jaeger instruments because the transmission indicator was located in the base of the tachometer.

For 1973 the reversing lights on the 12 were positioned vertically alongside the taillight units on the sedan and the hand brake was relocated between the bucket seats on the floor, new combined armrest/door pulls were fitted to the doors of the GL, a vacuum-servo unit was part of the dual-circuit braking system and self-adjusting rear drum brakes were fitted to the 12 station sedan.

A modified 12GL arrived in May 1974 that had a Weber twin-choke carburettor, the engine specifications being roughly similar to the European 12TS although still with the 1251cc capacity engine. Inside, locally-made tombstone seats were fitted with perforated vinyl facings and a 12GL station sedan became available that had all the sedan fittings apart from the Weber carburettor, and its roof was strengthened to accommodate a chromed roof rack. The boomerang steering wheel hub returned and the Bosch alternator was a 40 amp unit replacing the previous 30 amp version. And locally sourced Uniroyal 180 steel belt radial tyres were standard.

At the same time the 16TS received the tombstone seats, lost the front centre armrest but retained the oddments bin between the front seats, locally produced Uniroyal 180 steel radial tyres were standard and the driving lights were relocated onto a locally-source badge bar. At the end of 1974 a batch of 16TS Specials was produced that featured cloth faced upholstery, metallic gold paint, electric front windows and a radio/cassette deck.

For the 1975 model year Renault Australia initially marketed the 12TL and 12GL in sedan and station sedan formats with an automatic gearbox option coming mid-year. For this model year the local company adopted the French market mechanical specifications. This meant that both the TL and GL gained the 12TS (in France) 1289cc engine with a twin-barrel Weber carburettor, full French Jaeger instrumentation including a tachometer, heated rear window, hazard warning lights and 'kangaroo' headlights. These were QI bulbs set into the lower section of the headlight reflector and added an enormous amount of light for night-time driving giving the driver time to spot the kangaroo in time before colliding with the unpredictable animal.

The difference between a TL and GL was in the interior trim – the TL had low-back seats with separate head restraints, single colour trim with co-ordinated carpets and door trims; the GL had two-tone trim, perforated coloured facings with black side facings, head lining and door trims, colour co-ordinated carpets and combined armrest/door pull on the front doors and inertia reel seat belts as required by the ADRs.

Styling-wise not much changed apart from the grille having a U-shaped piece of chrome around the Renault diamond, and there was an upgrading of equipment generally. The most popular model was the

DRIVE-IN CINEMA
RENAULT 12

1978 RM 92

RENAULT 18 Diesel

RENAULT

GL which featured a full-length thin side protection strip along each side, rubber-faced bumper over-riders front and rear and a GL badge on the front fender.

From May 1975 the 16 received front inertia reel seat belts, hazard warning flashers and evaporative emission controls (ADR 27) as well as a matt black plastic grille, black wiper arms and new diamond pattern hubcaps. The TS received a new steering wheel with drilled holes in the aluminium trim, French Jaeger instruments and Cibie headlights units replaced the previous Australian Lucas units and now had a hydraulic beam height adjustment controlled by a rotary knob on the dashboard; the new headlights incorporated the 'kangaroo' halogen bulbs lights that replaced the previous separate Cibie driving lights.

In October 1976 the Renault 12 became the Renault 12 1.4 to signify an increase in engine capacity which was necessary to meet ADR 27A. Its bore and stroke were now 76 x 77mm for 1397cc, power rising slightly to 49kW (66bhp) at 5750rpm and torque to 103Nm (76lbs-ft) at 3500rpm. Visually there was a new plastic grille with a chromed surround, new bumpers front and rear with the indicator/parking lens in the front bumper that also had rubber buffers attached, 1.4 badges, new larger tail lights and the air extractor vents in the C-pillar were repositioned. Equipment levels matched that of the previous GL. Despite the capacity increase and slight power rise top speed remained at 144km/h (90mph), still good for a relatively large sedan (and wagon) powered by a relatively small engine.

Inside was a completely new dashboard with a broad binnacle in front of the driver containing three large round dials – speedometer, tachometer, combination – with superb graphics, a four-spoke steering wheel with thick padded rim, under dash parcel shelf, console with a clock and heater/demister slides in the middle along with three switches and cigarette lighter.

What had increased, and significantly, was the price, from $2398 in 1972 up to $5136 in 1976! However, people still bought the 12 because even at that price it represented good value for money.

The final rendition of the 12 was badged as the Virage and this arrived in Renault showrooms in February 1978 and would last until April 1980 when the new Renault 18 was announced. In simple terms the Virage was a French-sounding name applied to a mildly restyled 12 1.4, that restyling being in the form of another new grille this time with four round headlights and not much else. Compared with its mainly Japanese rivals – Chrysler Sigma, Datsun 200B, Toyota Corona for example – the Virage was a very old design but it only showed in the flat side glass where everybody else now used curved glass. It was still a roomy sedan with a superb ride, easy handling, great stability in windy conditions and excellent brakes. In straight line performance its rivals were quicker but as cruising cars there was little or no difference between them.

In mid-76 Renault released a limited edition (250 units) Special whose specifications included tinted banded laminated windscreen, tinted side and rear windows, optional metallic paint, Gordini-styled wheels, AM/FM radio with centre roof aerial and buyers had the option of manual or automatic gearboxes. The 16 range was discontinued in late 1976 with no direct replacement; this was because of the investment required to meet upcoming ADR requirements such as ADR 27A engine emissions, side impact bars and child restraint anchorage points given the relatively small volume of sales. Stocks were sufficient for sales to run through much of 1977.

Renault enjoyed an excellent reputation and good sales through the 70s, especially of the 12 and the 16 until it (the 16) was discontinued and never really replaced. It was a remarkable and versatile family hatchback that has gone down in Australian motoring folklore and deservedly so. Remarkably Renault travelled through most of the Seventies on the back of the 12 and 16, but particularly the 12 and its several variants. The cars that replaced them were the 18 and 20 which arrived on dealer's floors late in 1979 and neither really struck a chord locally with the result that Renault closed the West Heidelberg factory in July 1981.

Part of Renault's deservedly strong reputation in the late 60s and through the 70s was earned in rallying. Bob Watson and Jim McAuliffe won the 1970 Australian Rally Championship and the Victorian Rally Championship driving a Renault 8 Gordini. In Western Australia Rod Slater and John Large won the 1970 Rally Championship driving one of the Harry Firth-modified Renault 16TSs; and Bruce Collier and Lindsay Adcock came second in the 1970 New South Wales Rally Championship in another Renault 8 Gordini.

Renault Australia prepared and entered four 16TSs for the Ampol Trial of 1970. These were new cars, not the 1969 cars recycled. The engines were blueprinted and balanced by Repco and installed by Renault but for some unfathomable reason once the engines were run-in the cylinder head bolts were not checked for tension. This resulted in the cars continually experiencing engine problems throughout the trial and literally 'blew' any chance of success. The crews for the factory cars were Bob Watson with Jim McAuliffe, Bruce Collier with Lindsay Adcock, Mal McPherson with Roger Bonhomme and a three-person crew consisting of Sue Ransom, Marcia Tuckey and Vivian Hellewell. A fifth 16TS was privately entered and finished …

The Renault 8 Gordini continued to be the rally car of choice for Bob Watson teamed with Andy Chapman who came second to Colin Bond in a Torana GTR XU-1 in the 1971 Australian Rally Championship while Mal McPherson with Roger Bonhomme took out the Victorian Rally Championship. In South Australia Tom Barr-Smith with Rob Hunt won the Rally Championship in a standard 16TS.

The 1972 season was more of the same with Chuck Mora and Colin Abbey winning the South Australian Rally Championship in a standard 16TS with Tom Barr-Smith and Rob Hunt taking out second place in a new Renault 12 Gordini. Over in the west Rod Slater and John Large took out the Western Australian Rally Championship in another 12 Gordini. The 12 Gordinis were fully imported left-hand drive cars that were converted to right-hand drive at the factory using 12TL components while the engines were special 1596cc 160bhp units built from kits ex-Renault France and assembled by both Renault Australia in Melbourne and Bob Collier in Sydney.

PEUGEOT

This conservative French manufacturer surprised the world with the release of the 504 in September 1968. It confounded the critics and was a major departure from the well respected 404. Only the engine and gearboxes were carried over – everything else was all-new as the advertising people like to say. The European critics were so impressed that they voted it the 1968 Car of the Year.

Styling for the 504 was carried out by Pininfarina in Turin with assistance from Peugeot's own stylists who were mainly responsible for the interior design. Apart from being a larger car – up another class in Europe – the 504 brought unusual trapezoidal-shaped headlights to the market at large and a chamfered boot line at the rear with flush-fitting multi-lens light units either side; and the 504 brought curved side glass to Peugeot for the first time. Amazingly the 204 and 304 that preceded it had flat side glass even though the rest of the world was rapidly going over to curved glass.

The 504 sat on a long 2743mm (108-ins) wheelbase (up from the 404's 2642mm/104-ins) and stretched 4496mm (177-ins) overall by 1689mm (66.5-ins) wide and 1455mm (57.3-ins) high; weight initially was 1150kgs (2524lbs). From a physical point of view, it was bigger and more accommodating than its 404 sibling, Volvo 144, BMW 2000 (and later 520), Rover 2000 or 3500 or the Triumph 2000/2500 and was less expensive than all of them. It broke the mould for the middle-class car buyers in Europe and that carried over to Australia.

Although the four-cylinder in-line XM engine was carried over, it was bigger in capacity than for the 404 engine. Peugeot's engineers had taken it out to 1796cc with a bore and stroke of 84 by 81mm and as in the 404 offered it in two versions – with a single Solex carburettor that produced 65kW (87bhp) at 5500rpm and Kugelfischer fuel injected with 72kW (96bhp) at 5600rpm. The XM continued Peugeot's long standing tradition of having a cast iron cylinder block with a five main bearing forged crankshaft and replaceable 'wet' cylinder liners, a cross flow aluminium alloy cylinder head with hemispherical combustion chambers, overhead valves operated by pushrods from a side camshaft and the whole assembly reclined at 45-degrees to the right in the engine bay. Like all French cars, the engine bay looked messy even if all service points were easily accessible – it would take the Japanese to show the rest of the world that an engine bay could look attractive …

Like the 404, the 504's steering was by a non-assisted rack and pinion system and the brakes were now four-wheel vacuum boosted discs with 272mm (10.7-ins) diameter solid rotors front and rear, the hand brake operating on a small drum inset into the rear rotors and there was a pressure limiting valve in the rear circuit. But the most significant aspect of the 504's specification was the suspension system which continued with the MacPherson struts at the front but there was a completely new rear independent system comprising massive pressed steel semi-trailing arms pivoted by rubber bushes on a substantial cross

504
50

member with large coil springs as the suspension medium. People knew the 404 was world-class but once they drove a 504 there was simply no comparison!

With the 504 the Peugeot engineers devised a new and different way of mounting the mechanical components to the body. The engine was bolted to the gearbox which in turn was bolted via a hollow torque tube to the differential unit, the two being connected by an alloy steel driveshaft contained within. Included in this unit was the independent rear suspension.

Inside it was neat without being ostentatious. The dash had a wide, hooded binnacle in front of the driver with three equal-sized round dials within and from there it stretched straight across to the passenger's side, there was a padded dashtop with an unusual air vent in the centre of it. It had two vents within that could be slid out by about 50mm (2-ins) and the gills of the vents were angled to direct airflow to either the driver or passenger. Tiny supplementary vents were at either end of the dash for airflow over the side windows. Below the centre of the dash was another section that housed the four slides that controlled the efficient heating/demisting system as well as the cigar lighter and ashtray; a console between the under-dash and floor had provision to house the sound system. Carpets covered the floor and the seating was by superbly comfortable adjustable bucket seats in front that featured wind-up and wind-down head restraints, a wide bench with centre armrest in back and the boot was surprisingly roomy.

It took nearly two years for the 504 to arrive in Australia. There were two reasons for this – huge demand in Europe and the need to prepare the factory at West Heidelberg to assembly it from CKD packs. Its release locally was on June 2, 1970. Initially Continental and General planned to run the 404 alongside the new 504 because there was still a strong demand for the older (and cheaper) model. However, they and Peugeot ran afoul of the Government's idiot bureaucrats who deemed that the two models were insufficiently different to be classified separately! Their engine capacities had to be at least 25 per cent apart but at 1618cc and 1796cc they would never pass that needless test. As a result assembly of the 404 stopped in June 1970 and because Renault Australia were unable to immediately increase local content to 45 per cent they were required to pay import duty on all the imported parts for the 504, increasing the retail price from $3535 to $3835.

Modern Motor tested a 504 in its August 1970 issue and was mightily impressed as their introduction said, "Outstanding value for money, superb comfort and brilliant ride more than compensate for its too modest performance." Through their commentary of the car they eulogised about the extreme silence of the interior, precise manual gearshift, the comfort of the seats, the brilliant stability over rough roads, powerful all-disc braking system and so it went. Carps included the flimsy-feeling plastic of some of the controls and 'cheap-looking' plastics of the dash and the lack of outright get-up-and-go although this was negated somewhat by the car's brilliant handling. They published a top speed of 152km/h

(95mph) – pretty damn good for a 1.8-litre engine pulling a 1230kg (2700lbs) sedan – with acceleration times of 10.6 and 15.5 seconds for the 0–80 and 96km/h (0–50 and 60mph) sprints, with 11.4-litres per 100km (25mpg) fuel economy. And at $3475 they thought it a bargain although that would soon change.

From December 1971 the engine was upgraded to 2.0-litres in capacity by widening the cylinder barrels from 84mm to 88mm and leaving the crank stroke at 81mm; actual capacity was 1971cc and along with a twin-choke Solex carburettor power rose to 73kW (98bhp) at 5600rpm with torque now at 160Nm (118lbs-ft) at 3000rpm. These changes took the 504 (now with the letters GL added to its name) a little further upmarket and in many ways it was competing with Fairlane and Statesman with its supreme ride and handling qualities and improved performance – 157km/h (98mph) maximum speed, 0–96km/h (0–60mph) in 11.8 seconds, 11.6 – 9.5 litres per 100km (24–30mpg) economy – and $4145 price tag for the manual, $4695 for the *Automatique.* With the availability of the 2-litre engine Peugeot took the opportunity to introduce the 504Ti version with its mechanical Kugelfischer injection system. Power was increased to 82kW (110bhp) at 5600rpm and torque was up to 177Nm (131lbs-ft) at 3000rpm plus the final drive ratio was raised from 3.88 to 3.79 for more relaxed cruising and, because of the extra power, no loss of performance. Against the clock the Ti was able to run to 170km/h (106mph), do the 0–96km/h (0–60mph) dash in 11.3 seconds and return 13 – 10 litres per 100km (22–28mpg) economy. It was regarded by *Wheels* and other critics as one of the world's best long distance cruising family cars and rightly so.

With the upgrade to 2-litres came several other changes. The expensive French Cibie trapezoidal headlights were replaced by dual 5-ins round Lucas lights set into a chromed surround that was the same shape as the former lights – incidentally, the headlight beams, particularly on high beam, with the four-headlights was vastly superior – and the locally-sourced Borg Warner Type 35 three-speed automatic became available and extractor vents appeared on the C-pillar for the flow-through ventilation system.

In 1973 locally-made high-backed bucket seats replaced the earlier

French type, the hand brake was relocated to between the seats as part of a new console incorporating provision for twin speakers, the seat belts featured fixed inner buckles, the windscreen wiper sweep was increased (but they still swept the wrong way!) and the exhaust system was modified to eliminate an annoying interior resonance at certain engine speeds. For 1974 the fuse box was positioned under the dash on the driver's side, the speedometer now had metric graphics, tombstone front buckets (very similar to those in the Renault 12 and 16) made their appearance, there was now a heated rear window and there was additional lining in the boot.

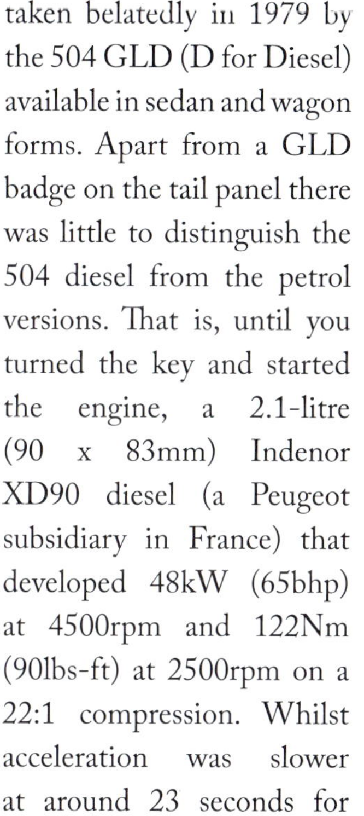

1975 saw this mild progression continue. New this year were recessed exterior door handles replacing the former push button type, revised door locks, a soft feel steering wheel, inertia reel seat belts (as per ADRs), evaporative emission controls on the engine, standard push button radio and certain items that were of Australian Bosch manufacture were replaced by French components – the distributor was now a Paris Rhone item, the starter motor was a Ducellier and the coil was now from SEV.

During the year Peugeot announced the locally assembled 504 LTi (for Luxury Touring *internationale*) that was available only with the Borg Warner three-speed automatic transmission, Kugelfischer fuel injection, tinted side glass, tinted band windscreen, sliding steel sunroof, stereo radio/cassette player, QI high beam lights, a carpeted luggage compartment and metallic paintwork. The same year saw the introduction of the 504 Familiale station wagon to replace the much-admired 404 Familiale. As before, the wagon's wheelbase was extended by four-inches – up to 2844mm (112-ins) – so that three rows of seats could be fitted and the well-proven torque tube rear suspension using a live rear axle suspended by *four* large coil springs – two each side – and heavy duty dampers replaced the independent system used on the sedans.

By 1976 the 504Ti had been dropped from the range, its place being taken belatedly in 1979 by the 504 GLD (D for Diesel) available in sedan and wagon forms. Apart from a GLD badge on the tail panel there was little to distinguish the 504 diesel from the petrol versions. That is, until you turned the key and started the engine, a 2.1-litre (90 x 83mm) Indenor XD90 diesel (a Peugeot subsidiary in France) that developed 48kW (65bhp) at 4500rpm and 122Nm (90lbs-ft) at 2500rpm on a 22:1 compression. Whilst acceleration was slower at around 23 seconds for the 0–100km/h dash it would cruise happily at 120km/h (75mph) – its maximum under ideal conditions was around 135km/h (84mph) – and was particularly frugal in its consumption of fuel at up to 7.5 litres per 100km (38mpg). It retailed locally for $13,475 compared with the 504 petrol at $10,990. And the GLD soon had a following of keen people who loved it for its ruggedness, reliability and relaxed character, particularly in rural communities.

With the petrol-engined 504 there were changes, too, because of

ADR 27A. The engine's compression ratio was reduced to 8.0:1 and it was fitted with twin single-choke Solex carburettors and revised ignition timing; inside 'keyhole' style tombstone front seats replaced the earlier solid ones and if a buyer specified air conditioning the unit was Peugeot-sourced rather than from Renault Australia.

Through 1977 and 78 very little appeared to have happened apart from a black slatted grille with two chromed horizontal bars and a stylised Lion emblem, a new range of colours, a laminated windscreen (something the Japanese manufacturers had been fitting as standard for some time!) plus a radio aerial positioned on the roof above the interior mirror and the seat upholstery was now a cloth material.

The 504 in GL and GL Special format quietly slipped onto the market without fanfare – the car was nearly a decade old in Australia – and it now was powered by the XN1 engine that had an 8.8:1 compression and had reverted back to a single twin-choke Solex carburettor. Inside, the seats were sourced from France and had separate head restraints.

In its August 1979 issue *Wheels* compared the 504 GL with the Volvo 244 GL, Alfetta 2000L and Fiat 132 2000 – a group of European sporting and luxury sedans well above the plebeian Sunbird, Cortina, Sigma, Corona and 200B but well below exotics like the Mercedes-Benz 230E, BMW 520i and CX Citroen. As for its price, the 504 started at $10,690 but the test car cost $11,065 fitted with a better quality audio system, tinted glass, laminated windscreen and cloth seats. Even though it was a decade old (only the Volvo was older) the 504 set the standards for ride and handling. Power and torque outputs were least for the Peugeot at 73kW (98bhp) at 5200rpm and 170Nm (124lbs-ft) at 3500rpm which surprised the testers as this was the revised 2-litre OHV engine with a new cylinder head to go with a revised camshaft. As they commented, "It's a stayer, not a sprinter" after the performance runs where the 504 finished third – top speed of 162km/h (101mph), 0–100km/h (0–62mph) acceleration in 13.0 seconds, 60–90km/h (38–56mph) in third gear took 7.0 seconds – behind the Volvo and Alfetta. On the subject of ride, they said, "The Peugeot is outstanding on moderately rough roads where its all-independent suspension soaks up disturbances and transmits little of them to the interior."

In conclusion they selected the Alfetta as the winner with the Peugeot second commenting "it's a damn good car and still comes close to being the ideal concept for an Australian family car."

Peugeot continued with the 504 until the end of the decade when it was replaced in October 1980 by another model that would go on to write its own history – the 505 – but that is a story for another day.

BOLWELL

Through the 1960s Bolwell established a reputation as a quality supplier of fibreglass bodies and chassis kits for enthusiasts to assemble for themselves using donor engines – usually grey Holden – and various other mechanical components. Campbell Bolwell, the main man behind these activities, was aware that the quality of some of these assembly operations was less than ideal. Starting with what were so eloquently described as 'backyard specials' in the late '50s Campbell and his brothers Graeme and Winston gradually refined what they made and sold. In 1962 they released the Mark 4 which was a Lotus 11-style car powered by a Cortina engine until the Corolla K engine became available and one or two even had a grey Holden motor squeezed under the bonnet. Production of the Mark 4a included ten or so gull-wing coupes that were not particularly attractive but are now prized collectables. A little later came the Mark 4b that was far more streamlined. By late 1964 they had released the Mark 5 which was a fibreglass-bodied coupe with a faintly Jensen Interceptor-like style, especially the large rear window. It rode on a Bolwell-designed-and-made backbone type chassis built from rust proof light gauge steel panels welded together. The package that enthusiasts bought incorporated the foot wells, front and rear inner guards, transmission tunnel, luggage compartment, cockpit sides and floor.

It was sold as a kit with the company offering to build owners a complete car but only 2 or maybe 3 were ever factory-built out of the 75 made.

Next came the Mark 6 – a one-off Group A sports racing car with a 192-cid Holden red six mid-mounted – and then the Mark 7 in March 1967 which became the most numerous of all the Bolwell models. In some ways the styling of the Mark 7 was a template for the future Mark 8, aka Nagari. It featured low sweeping lines starting from an oval-shaped grille opening and recessed single headlights and ended with a fastback sloping rear window which some owners converted to an opening hatch. Significantly the Mark 7 was designed around Holden components exclusively and the engine in particular where either the grey or new red motor would drop straight in. If an enthusiast owner had the wherewithal a 289- or 302-cid Ford V8 could be accommodated and not the new Holden V8s because there were installation problems. The factory prototype was fitted with a Triumph 2000 four-speed manual gearbox although most of the 'production' cars were fitted with Holden's own four-speed gearbox. Some Ford components crept into the specifications, items like wiper motor, horn, interior light, brake and clutch master cylinders, interior air vents while the headlights were supplied by Lucas, the taillights came from the Toyota Crown and front parking lights were from the Morris 850. Pilkington Glass manufactured the laminated windscreen to Bolwell's specifications.

Sports Car World carried a full test in its March 1967 issue and was stunned by its performance, handling and style, in fact they headed their test with the words "Brain Snapping Bolwell." Bystanders noticed the car and out on the road they found its handling to be exhilarating saying "it tracked beautifully at highway speeds with totally neutral behaviour." It ran to a top speed of 200km/h (125mph) although the average was only 190km/h (119mph), it despatched the 0–80 and 0–96km/h (0–50 and 0–60mph) acceleration runs in a mere 6.0 and 8.5 seconds respectively, ran though the quarter mile in 15.9 seconds (fastest was

Bolwell Nagari
V8

15.0 seconds) and when cruising sipped fuel at the remarkable rate of 10 litres per 100km (28mpg); with a kerb weight of just 805kgs (1770lbs) such performance figures should not surprise.

During its six-year production run (1967–72) Bolwell made around 400 units (all but a handful being kits) which interestingly enough made the company Australia's fifth largest vehicle manufacturer!

The most famous of all Bolwells was released in January 1970 – the Nagari; its name was an Aboriginal word that meant 'flowing.' Work on its design and construction began in early 1969 with the intention of it being a fully-built production car and not a kit. The basis of the Nagari (nee Mark 8) was the 14-gauge steel backbone chassis similar in concept to the Mark 7 (but far stronger) which in turn had been influenced by that from the Lotus Elan – Graeme had worked at Lotus after graduating from university. As to its physical dimensions, the Nagari sat on a 2286mm (90-ins) wheelbase, was 4013mm (158-ins) overall by 1676mm (66-ins) wide by 1041mm (41-ins) high, the wheel tracks being 1432mm (56.4-ins) at the front and 1498mm (59-ins) at the rear.

Initially it was intended for the mechanical units to be sourced from Holden – Bolwell had in fact expected to be able to do a deal with GM-H – but because Holden was keen to produce their GTR-X sports coupe based on Torana components they refused to supply Bolwell and so Graeme approached Ford who were only too happy to supply their Windsor 302-cid V8 engine (and the 351-cid as an option) and four-speed all-synchromesh 'top loader' four-speed manual gearbox fully assembled as a package and delivered to Bolwell's factory. After about chassis #50 Bolwell installed the new Borg Warner four-speed manual gearbox which was a much more pleasant 'box to use. As received at Bolwell the engine had an Autolite carburettor but this was replaced by a Holley 500 two-barrel. Ford also supplied their Falcon rear axle assembly – it had an 8-ins differential from the compact Fairlane – complete with 254mm (10-ins) drum brakes. Graeme and Campbell Bolwell designed their own rear suspension comprising twin trailing arms locating the axle longitudinally with oblique torque rods for lateral location, the actual suspension being by adjustable coil-over-dampers from Monroe-Wylie. Up front were upper-and-lower wishbones fabricated in-house as had been Bolwell's tradition with coil springs and telescopic dampers.

Other technical items of interest included the use of a shortened Austin 1800 rack and pinion steering system mounted behind the front wheel centre line. Many owners later replaced the 1800 unit with a rack from the Torana and repositioned it in front of the axle line. Brakes were Falcon-sourced front disc rotors and calipers, the rotors being ventilated and 286mm (11.25-ins) in diameter with a PBR44 vacuum booster and split front-rear circuits. Wheels were Bolwell-designed alloys, 14 x 6 shod with Avon 185 x 14 radial tyres. Under the boot floor was an XP Falcon station wagon 55-litre (12-gallon) fuel tank.

Fitted over the chassis on the rudimentary 'production line' at the factory – the chassis sat on 'dollies' and were hand-pushed from one station to the next during the production process – was the one-piece fibreglass body already painted. The Nagari design was drawn by Campbell Bolwell and like its predecessors owed something to the Mark 7, Jaguar E-Type and the Toyota 2000GT as well as Lotus. It was low and lithe with good aerodynamic properties and was obviously stylish – it certainly caught the eye.

The interior was quite a conservative design having a padded top over a fibreglass base and grained vinyl trim on the fascia. Instrumentation comprised large diameter Stewart Warner speedometer on the right, tachometer on the left with smaller gauges for coolant temperature, ammeter, fuel level and engine oil pressure. Space for a sound system was available in the centre while a row of toggle switches (4 of them) was lined up on the centre console with the ignition switch closest to the driver, the steering wheel had a wide hub and three drilled alloy spokes and there were large air vents (sourced from the Cortina) at either end of the dash and the padded dashtop was similarly sourced from a Mark II Cortina. Seating was made in-house. From chassis #80 the toggle switches were replaced by Jaguar-style piano-key style units.

With 164kW (220bhp) at 4600rpm available from the 302-cid V8 and with the whole assembly weighing less than a ton (2040lbs) or around 950kgs in today's measure, the Nagari was quite a spectacular performer. *Sports Car World* tested a coupe in the November 1971 issue and the writers were amazed at the combination of performance and price of $6200. As they wrote, "Just try and buy anything comparable within a couple of grand of that figure!"

Against the clock the Nagari ran to 208km/h (130mph) at 5000rpm with 75, 108 and 154km/h (47, 68 and 96mph) available in the lower three gears, times of 5.5, 7.2, 9.3 and 11.7 seconds for the 0–80, 96, 112 and 128km/h (0–50, 60, 70 and 80mph) sprints and a standing quarter mile time of 14.9 seconds. If an owner fitted the optional 351-cid V8 with 216kW (290bhp) the acceleration times were even quicker!

Interestingly it appears that a small number was built with a Holden six-cylinder engine and at least one with a Cortina GT four-cylinder engine. Do any of these still exist I wonder?

Bolwell introduced the Nagari Sports in 1972 to add to the prestige and sales of the model. As with its coupe brother, the convertible was a stunner.

During the same year several modifications were made to the Nagari chassis to accommodate the physically larger Cleveland V8 engine that Ford was now building locally which required repositioning of some brackets as well as widening the bay and the fitting of a new bonnet with a distinctive bulge to clear the bigger engine. Also, MG B parking/indicator lights replaced the original Cortina units and there was now a collapsible steering column with a flatter steering wheel.

One enthusiast owner fitted a Ford GT HO 351-cid Cleveland V8 to his Nagari and allowed *Sports Car World* to test drive it. Despite a recalcitrant condenser in the ignition system they found it would dash through the quarter mile in 14.1 seconds and go from a standstill to 160km/h (100mph) in less than 15 seconds. No actual top speed run was attempted but a reasonable guesstimate by the tester said it should see 240km/h (150mph) when the engine was on full song.

As the 1970s progressed more and more Australian Design Rules became law and meeting them was causing problems within the automobile industry. It was less of a problem for companies like GM-H and Ford who could amortise the cost of compliance over many thousands of units but for Bolwell that was impossible. Towards the end of 1974 the company ceased production of the Nagari and sought to expand other areas of its burgeoning business. Exact production records for the Nagari no longer exist but a best guess estimate is around 100 coupes and 18 roadsters were built over a four year period.

Today these cars are very collectable and not inexpensive.

WILLYS

The story of Jeep in Australia was basically one of decline during the 70s. At the end of the 60s Shute Upton Engineering in Brisbane became involved in manufacturing the chassis for the Overlanders and would remain linked to Willys Motors Australia for several years.

The locally assembled model range consisted of the CJ5 and CJ6, but the numbers were tiny. Shute Upton ceased making chassis in August 1971 and with that local assembly wound down.

Another name change came through in 1970 after the American Motors Corporation acquired Kaiser Jeep and renamed the company the Jeep Corporation. Sales dwindled to the point where in 1973 they totalled less than 100 units; in mid-1974 Willys Motors Australia ceased operations with the importation and distribution of products being taken over by LNC Industries who formed a subsidiary called Jeep Australia Pty Ltd and announced lofty sale predictions whereby they would achieve 10 per cent of the 4WD market within a year. Needless to say this bold prediction was never realised …

LAND ROVER

Apart from moving the headlights into the front wings on all models and shallower sill panels very little changed on a Land Rover as it entered its fourth decade. Some months later the rear wheel arches were reprofiled to accommodate chains on the larger 9.00 x 16 tyres that were available on the 2769mm (109-ins) models.

The Series IIA came along in the late 60s and in 1971 came the Series III which was virtually indistinguishable from the IIA. The most obvious difference was the replacement of the traditional wire mesh grille by a plastic one. With competition for sales increasing around the world – the arrival in numbers of competition from Japan – Land Rover updated the interior in the Series III. Until now the instruments on the dashboard had been located in the centre of the dash; now the instrument cluster was in front of the driver for both left- and right-hand drive vehicles and the dash itself was now a moulded plastic unit in line with world-wide safety requirements.

Mechanically, the III now had a full-synchromesh gearbox and the long wheelbase cars had a new Salisbury rear axle in which the differential housing and axle case were one piece. Along with these changes there were upgrades for the engines in the form of five main bearing crankshafts that increased the rigidity of the engine-gearbox unit and the axles and wheel hubs were strengthened. Little else changed during a production run that lasted from 1971 until 1985. In 1979 Land Rover offered the 3.5-litre alloy V8 engine as an option.

Apart from minor upgrades to its specification little seemed to change during the 70s on local Land Rovers. Small scale production and assembly continued at Pressed Metal in Sydney. Life for the iconic four-wheel drive from Britain rolled blissfully onwards …

EPILOGUE

At the end of the Seventies the local motor industry executives must have breathed a huge sigh of relief as, industrially, things began to settle down. No longer were employees downing tools and walking off the job for little or no reason and wage demands had eased substantially. This was *despite* rampant inflation throughout the decade – sound familiar?

But life was still a struggle for the local manufacturers as tariffs began to be lowered in a deliberate move by the Federal Government to create what they dubbed "a level playing field!" What nonsense! That action was the beginning of the end of manufacturing here in Australia in *all* sectors, not just the automobile industry.

By the 1980s Holden was riding high on the backs of the Commodore, Statesman, Torana/Sunbird and Gemini and was about to embark on the J-car program that brought us the front-wheel drive Camira while, across town at Broadmeadows, Ford had stayed with the larger-bodied Falcon and took market leadership from Holden. Ford was about to drop its English connection where Escort and Cortina were concerned and replace them with mildly modified Mazda 323 and 626. Ironically, Ford soon had market leadership in the small and medium-class cars with those two models. Warranty claims at the dealership level had never been so low …

What nobody could foresee coming was the Button Plan of 1984 that was allegedly designed to make the local car industry more efficient by significantly reducing the number of models manufactured in Australia. This led to hasty and dubious cross pollination of models where, for example, a Toyota Corolla became a Holden Nova, the Toyota Corona became a Holden Apollo and the Holden Commodore became the Toyota Lexcen. Over at Ford, they derived the rebadged Nissan Pintara as a Corsair and the Falcon ute wore Nissan badges. The plan failed in its objective and was quietly dropped but it caused much damage to the industry.

There were even discussions between the Federal Government and industry representatives about a common four-cylinder, locally manufactured engine to be used by several manufacturers but that too came to nothing. The government folks were surprised by the outcome. That's was how little they knew about the rivalries between the manufacturers! If the Federal Government had stopped meddling with tariffs *and* the industry it is entirely possible that we might still have a viable local car manufacturing industry today. After all, Australia was one of the few countries in the world where a car could be conceived and manufactured from the drawing board to the production line. We had some very talented designers and engineers here in Australia, but sadly that talent has now gone overseas.

MODEL SPECIFICATIONS 1970–79

Year	Make	Price $	Engine	Capacity	BHP	Torque lb-ft	Trans	Wheel-base inches	Length inches	Weight	Max speed mph	0–50 mph	Econ-omy mpg
1970–73	Austin X6 Tasman/ Kimberley	$2830 T m $3166 K m	6-cyl SOHC	2227cc	102/5500 115/5500	116/3500 118/3500	4-sp man/3-sp auto	108.13	174.58	2572 2613	 104	10.0 9.8	20–25 21–26
1970–74	Bolwell Nagari (Mk VIII)	$6200 coupe $6800 conv	V8 OHV	4958cc (302) 5735cc (351)	220/4600	300/2600	4-sp man	90	158	2040	130	5.5	19–22
1970–71	Chrysler Valiant VG Pacer Pacer Hardtop	$2686 $3483 Regal $3748 V8	6-cyl OHV V8 OHV	4014cc (245) 4014cc Pacer 5192cc (318)	165/4400 185/4600 230/4400	235/1800 240/2000 340/2400	3-sp man, 3-sp auto	108 112	192 199	2890 2890 2880	102 112 112	8.0 5.8 6.6	19–22 20–24 16–21
1970–71	VIP by Chrysler VG	$4332	6-cyl OHV V8 OHV	4014cc (245) 5192cc (318)	165/4400 230/4400	235/1800 340/2400	3-sp auto	112	196	 2980	 110	 6.8	 16–22
1971–76	Chrysler Valiant VH, VJ, VK	From $2895 Regal from $3685	6-cyl OHV, V8 OHV	3523cc (215) 4014cc (245) 4345cc (265) 5192cc (318)	140/4400 165/4400 203/4800 230/4400	200/1800 235/1800 262/2000 340/2400	3-sp man, 3-sp auto	111	192	3120 3230	 102 112	 7.6 7.1	 17–22 15–19
1976–81	Chrysler Valiant CL, CM	$5712 CL $7275 Regal $6265 CM $7947 Regal	6-cyl OHV, V8 OHV	4014cc (245) 4345cc (265) 5192cc (318)	165/4400 203/4800 230/4800	235/1800 262/2000 340/2400	3-, 4-sp man, 3-sp auto	111	192	 3157	 109 109	 9.9 8.9	 17–22 16–20
1970–72	Chrysler Valiant Pacer VG, VH	$2998 VG $3235 VH	6-cyl OHV	4014cc (245) 4345cc (265)	195/4800 218/4800	n/a 273/3000	3-sp man	108 111	192	2890 3161	112 116	5.8 6.2	20–24
1971–78	Chrysler Valiant Charger VH-CL	XL $3195 770 $3625	6-cyl OHV, V8-cyl OHV	3523cc (215) 4014cc (245) 4345cc (265) 5192cc (318)	140/4400 165/4400 203/4800 230/4400	200/1800 235/1800 262/2000 340/2400	3-sp man, 4-sp man, 3-sp auto	105	179	 3061	 107	 6.8	 17–22
1971–78	Chrysler by Chrysler	$4895 (265) $5095 (360) Hardtop same	6-cyl OHV V8-cyl OHV	4345cc (265) 5880cc (360)	203/4400 255/4400	262/2000 360/2400	3-sp auto	115	197	3370 3570	106 115	8.0 6.5	14–21 13–19
1971–73	Chrysler Charger E37/E38 E48/ E49	R/T $3395 E38 $3975 E49 $4320	6-cyl OHV	4345cc (265)	248/4800 280/5000 302/5600	306/3800 310/3700 320/4100	3-, 4-sp man	105	179	3090	 126 134	 6.4* 6.1*	 18–22 16–24
1972–1977	Chrysler Galant sedan, s/wagon	GA $2268 GB GC $3445 GD	4-cyl SOHC	1289cc 1597cc	87/6300 100/6300	66/4000 101/4000	4-sp man, 3-sp auto	95.3 95.3	160 165.4	1920 1960	95 94	8.0 8.9	27–32 28–34

Year	Make	Price $	Engine	Capacity	BHP	Torque lb-ft	Trans	Wheel-base inches	Length inches	Weight	Max speed mph	0–50 mph	Econ-omy mpg
1977–85	Chrysler Sigma sedan, s/wagon	GE $5918 GH	4-cyl SOHC	1597cc 1995cc 2655cc	 86/5200 73kw/4500	 145N·m/2400 184N·m/2500	4-sp man, 3-sp auto	99	169	 2398 2442	 99 99	 9.0 8.7	 23–28 21–26
1974–77	Chrysler Centura	$3740 $3900	4-cyl SOHC, 6-cyl OHV	1981cc 3523cc(215) 4014cc (245)	120/5700 140/4400 165/4400	129/3500 200/1800 235/1800	3-, 4-sp man, 3-sp auto	105	180.5	2480 2680 2680	105 114	8.5 8.0	22–30 20–25
1970–74	Datsun 1200 sed, coupe, wagon	$1885 $2058 Dx $2295 Coupe $2115 s/w	4-cyl OHV	1171cc	69/6000	70/3600	4-sp man, 3-sp auto	90	151	1568	86	11.0	31–38
1968–72	Datsun 1600 sed, wagon	$2363	4-cyl SOHC	1596cc	96/5600	100/3600	4-sp man, 3-sp auto	95.3	162	2006	91	9.3	30–32
1974–77	Datsun 120Y sed, coupe, wagon	$2778 sed $2934 coup $2913 wag	4-cyl OHV	1171cc	69/6000	70/4000	4-sp man, 3-sp auto	92	155	1705	94	12.2	30–34
1977–82	Datsun Sunny	$5399 sed $6600 coup $6650 wag	4-cyl OHV	1171cc	69/6000	70/4000	4-sp man, 3-sp auto	92	165	2000	90	12.4	29–34
1972–77	Datsun 180B	$2570 Dx $2690 GL	4-cyl SOHC	1770cc	105/6000	108/3600	4-sp man, 3-sp auto	98.4	166	2205	103	9.1	28–32
1977–81	Datsun 200B	$5410 DX $5630 GL $6050 SX	4-cyl SOHC	1952cc	94/5600	152N·m/3200	4-sp man, 3-sp auto	98.5	168	2398	98	9.0	26–30
1972–76	Datsun Stanza	$5360 GL $5600 GX	4-cyl SOHC	1596cc	96/5600	100/3600	4-sp man, 3-sp auto	94.5	160	1991	98	9.2	26–32
1970–72	Dodge Phoenix	$6500 $6850	V8 OHV	5210cc (318) 6266cc (383)	230/4400 270/4400	340/2400 390/2800	3-sp auto	120	214	3750 3875	104 108	7.9 7.7	12–18 10–16
1970–72	Ford Cortina Mk II	$2072 240 $2202 440	4-cyl OHV	1599cc	75/5000	97/2500	4-sp man, 3-sp auto	98	168	1960	78	13.3	30–35
1970–72	Ford Cortina GT Mk II	$2672	4-cyl OHV	1599cc	93/5200	97/3600	4-sp man	98	168	1870	90	9.9	24–32
1972–73	Ford Cortina Mk III TC, TD	$2425 1600 $2510 2000 $3035 6XL $3525 XLE	4-cyl OHV 4-cyl SOHC 6-cyl OHV	1599cc 1998cc 3300cc (200) 4100cc (250)	93/5200 102/6000 130/4600 155/5000	07/3600 112/3500 190/2000 240/1600	4-sp man, 3-sp auto	101.5	168	2171 2310 2550 2580	102 106 112	8.1 8.7 7.9	24–30 18–26 17–26

Year	Make	Price $	Engine	Capacity	BHP	Torque lb-ft	Trans	Wheel-base inches	Length inches	Weight	Max speed mph	0–50 mph	Econ-omy mpg
1973–79	Ford Cortina TE, TF	$5383 L $5818 GL $7613 Ghia	4-cyl SOHC, 6-cyl OHV	1998cc 3300cc (200) 4100cc (250)	102/6000 130/4600 123/3700	112/3500 190/2000 212/2400	4-sp man, 3-sp auto	101.5	172	2675	105	6.5	18–22
1970–80	Ford Escort	$2130	4-cyl OHV, SOHC	1298cc 1998cc	75/5400 94/5200	91/2500 109/3800	4-sp man; 3-sp auto	94.5	157	2034 2150	89 102	7.4	32–38 26–30
1970–80	Ford Escort GT	$2350	4-cyl OHV	1298cc	75/5400	91/2500	4-sp man	94.5	156	1736	96	8.5	25–31
1970–73	Ford Capri	$2630 $2880 XL $3230 V6 GT	4-cyl OHV, V6 OHV	1599cc 2994cc	75/5000 144/4750	97/2500 192/3000	4-sp man, 3-sp auto	100.8	169	2068 2375	102 112	10.0 7.9	26–30 20–25
1970–72	Ford Falcon XY	$3412 GL	6-& V8 OHV	3268cc (200) 4085cc (250) 4946cc (302) 5751cc (351)	130/4600 155/4000 240/5000 250/4600	190/2000 240/1600 305/2600 355/2600	3-sp man, 4-sp man, 3-sp auto	111	185	3003 3070	98/102 124	9.4 6.1	16–22 14–19
1972–77	Ford Falcon XA, XB, XC	$2805 base to $3825 F'mont	6-cyl OHV, V8 OHV	3277cc (200) 4085cc (250) 4946cc (302)	130/4600 155/4000 240/5000	190/2000 240/1600 305/2600	3-, 4-sp man, 3-sp auto	111	185.5	3047 3260	93 104 109	9.8 8.7 7.3	18–22 18–24 15–20
1970–72	Ford Falcon XY GT	$5643	V8-cyl OHV	5751cc (351)	300/5400	380/3400	4-sp man, 3-sp auto	111	184	3360	126	6.8	15–20
1969–72	Ford Fairlane ZC ZD	$3141 ZA $3590 ZA V8 $3910 ZC	6- & V8 OHV	3277cc (200) 3610cc (221) 4095cc (250) 4736cc (289) 4946cc (302) 5749cc (351)	121/4400 135/4400 200/4400 195/4800 230/4800 290/4800	190/2400 208/2400 282/2400 282/2200 305/2600 385/3200	3-sp auto	116	196	3215 3224 4572	104.5 99.0 115	8.9 9.5 5.5	16–22 18–22 14–18
1972–78	Ford Fairlane ZF, ZG, ZJ	$4720	6- & V8 OHV	4095cc (250) 4946cc (302) 5750cc (351)	200/4400 260/4600	355/2600 305/3200	3-sp auto	116	198	1757	109	7.5	12–16
1973–76	Ford LTD, Landua	$7770	V8-cyl OHV	5800cc (351)	290/5000	380/3200	3-sp auto	121	203.8	3950	122	7.0	13–18
1972–76	Ford Falcon GT	XR $3890 XT $4050 XW $4250 XY $5643	V8-cyl OHV	4736cc (289) 4934cc (302) 5751cc (351) 5751cc (351)	220/4800 230/4800 290/4800 300/5400	305/3200 310/3800 385/3000 280/3400	4-sp man	111	185	3136 3304 3360	123 129 127	6.3 6.4 6.8	17–22 18–22 15–21
1970–73	Hillman Hunter, Hunter Royale, GT, Hustler	$2171 $2698 Roy $2638 GT $2378 Hust	4-cyl OHV	1725cc	94/5200 94/5200 94/5200	107/4000 107/4000 107/4000	4-sp man, 3-sp auto	98.5	168	2050 2050	94 95	8.3 7.4	27–32 28–32

Year	Make	Price $	Engine	Capacity	BHP	Torque lb-ft	Trans	Wheel-base inches	Length inches	Weight	Max speed mph	0–50 mph	Econ-omy mpg
1967–69	Holden Torana HB	$1795 $1951	4-cyl OHV, OHC	1157cc 1598cc	56/5400	67/3000	4-sp man, 3-sp auto	95	162	1750	83	12.8	30–36
	Holden Gemini sedan, coupe, wagon	$3144 $ $	4-cyl SOHC	1584cc	85/5000	135N·m/4000	4-sp man, 3-sp auto	94.6	163	2030 1987 coupe	103	9.8	28–36
1970–72	Holden Torana LC	$2050 $2515 S $3168 GTR $3455 XU-1	4-cyl OHV, SOHC; 6-cyl OHV	1157cc 1599cc 1897cc 2260cc (138) 2638cc (161) 2638cc GTR	69/5800 100/5400 95/4600 114/4400 125/4800	68/4200 XX/2800 120/1600 157/2000 150/2800	4-sp man, 3-sp auto	95.8	177	2446	92	9.8	22–32
1972–75	Holden Torana LJ	$2370 1.3 $2510 1.6 $2595 2.25 $2810 2.85 $3260 GTR $3559 XU 1	4-cyl OHV, SOHC; 6-cyl OHV	1256cc 1599cc 2262cc (138) 2834cc (173) 3310cc (202) 3310cc (202)	62/5400 80/5500 95/4600 118/4400 135/4400 190/5600	71/3600 96/3200 120/1600 168/2000 200/4000	4-sp man, 3-sp man, 3-sp auto	95.8 95.8 100 100 100 100	162 162 173 173 173 173	1886 2055 2294 2338 2422	80 85 95 97 120	13.6 12.0 10.9 10.5 8.4	26–36 25–34 19–24 19–23 15–21
1975-	Holden Torana LH Sunbird, Hatch	$4359 Plus 4	4-cyl OHV	1897cc	100/5400	116/3600	4-sp man; 3-sp auto	102	177	2446	94	9.8	24–30
1971–74	Holden HQ	$2215 Belmont $2359 Kingswood $2760 K/w SS $3295 Premier	6-cyl OHV V8 OHV	2826c (173) 3313cc (202) 4144cc (253) 5044cc (308)	114/4400 135/4400 185/4400 240/4800	194/2000 262/2400 315/3000	3-sp man, auto	111	186	3024	98 110	8.9 7.5	19–24 16–24
1971–76	Holden HQ Monaro LS GTS 4-d GTS 350	$3185 $3645 $3815 $4740	6-cyl OHV V8 OHV	3313cc (202) 4144cc (253) 5044cc (308) 5729cc (350)	135/4400 185/4400 240/4800 275/4800	194/2000 262/2400 315/3000 360/3200	3-, 4-sp man, 3-sp auto	111	187.5	3020	114 125	6.3 6.2	16–20 11–16
1971–78	Statesman, Caprice	$4085 $4660 DeV	6-cyl OHV, V8 OHV	3313cc (202) 4144cc (253) 4965cc (308) 5729cc (350)	135/4400 185/4400 240/4800 275/4800	194/2000 262/2400 315/3000 360/3200	3-sp auto	114	198	3029 3416	97 107	8.9 7.8	15–22 18–26
1978–80	Holden Commodore	$6513 base $7813 SL $10513 SL/E	6-cyl OHV V8 OHV	2850cc (173) 3300cc (202) 4142cc (253)	64k/4000 71k/3800 87k/4000	198N/2200 213N/2200 271N/2200	3-sp; 4-sp man; 3-sp auto	105	186	1219 1224 1365	98 106	12.1 9.4	18–24 15–20

Year	Make	Price $	Engine	Capacity	BHP	Torque lb-ft	Trans	Wheel-base inches	Length inches	Weight	Max speed mph	0–50 mph	Econ-omy mpg
1973–74	Leyland P76	$3250 Dx $3750 Sup $4524 Exe	6-cyl SOHC, V8 OHV	2623cc 4416cc	121/4500 192/4250	165/2000 285/2500	4-sp man, 3-sp auto	111	194.3-ins	2820	91 105	10.1 6.7	20–24 16–22
1963–80	MG B	1365	4-cyl OHV	1798cc	94/5300		4-sp man	91	153	2016	105	9.5	24–30
1971–76	Mitsubishi Galant sed, wagon	$2726 GA $3771 GC	4-cyl SOHC	1597cc	100/6300	101/4000	4-sp man, 3-sp auto	95.3	160	1960 2068	95 95	8.9 9.6	30–36 24–30
1976–80	Mitsubishi Sigma sedan wagon	$5116 $5826 GL $6280 SE	4-cyl SOHC	1597cc 1995cc	55k/4800 64k/5200	116n/3200 145n/2400	4-sp man, 3-sp auto	99	176	2660	99	11.1	23–28
1972–74	Morris Marina Sedan coupe 4-cyl 6-cyl	$2590 sed $2350 Coup $2775 TC C	4-cyl OHC, 6-cyl OHC	1485cc 1746cc 1746cc TC 2623cc	62/5500 78/4800 90/5200 110/5500	77/2500 99/3000 104/3400 145/3000	3-, 4-sp man, 3-sp auto	96	163	2029 2029 2237	93 98	12.6 8.5	26–32 21–28
1973–78	Morris Mini Moke Clubman Clubman GT	$1550 Mok $1950 Cl $2502 GT	4-cyl OHV	1098cc 1275cc	50/5100 78/5800	60/2500 80/3000	4-sp man, 4-sp auto	80	120	1316 1428	73 78	16.9 14.0	45–50 38–45
1962–70	Mini-Cooper Mini-Cooper S Clubman GT	950 $2457 S $2036 $2657 GT	4-cyl OHV	997cc 998cc 1098cc 1275cc	55/6000 55/5800 50/5100 78/5800	55/3600 55/3000 60/2500 80/3000	4-sp man	80	120 125	1400 1610	88 77 98	9.6 12.4 9.4	30–38 34–38 30–38
1973–74	Leyland P76	From $3250 From $3430	6-cyl OHC, V8 OHV	2623cc	121/4500 192/4250	165/2000 285/2500	3-, 4-sp man, 3-sp auto	111-ins	192	2820 2838	91 105	8.8 6.7	18–24 15–22
	Mini Moke	$ $1510	4-cyl OHV	998cc 1098cc	50/5100	60/2500	4-sp man	80	128		70	12.9	
1969–72	Morris 1500, Nomad	$2318 $2443 Nom	4-cyl OHC	1485cc	73/5500	81/4000	4, 5-sp man, 4-sp auto	93.5	146	1952			
	MG Midget	$2670	4-cyl OHV	1275cc	65/6000	72/3000	4-sp man	80	126	1603	102	8.8	26–32
1963–72	MG B	£1395	4-cyl OHV	1798cc	95/5500	110/3000	4-sp man, 3-sp auto	91	154	2072	103	8.3	22–28
1970–80	Peugeot 504 sed, Station wagon	$3475 $4698 GL $4695 Ti $13,475 ‘79	4-cyl OHV	1796cc 1971cc 1971cc inj 2112cc D	87/5500 98/5600 110/5600 65/4500	108/3500 124/3200 131/3000 90/2500	4-sp man, 3-sp auto	108 112 S/w	174 187 s/w	2524 2632 2614 2816	97 105 106 85	8.8 7.9 8.0 12.8	21–30 22–30 22–26 24–32

Year	Make	Price $	Engine	Capacity	BHP	Torque lb-ft	Trans	Wheel-base inches	Length inches	Weight	Max speed mph	0–50 mph	Econ-omy mpg
1971–78	Rambler Matador	$6699	V8 OHV	5882cc (360)	245/4400	365/2600	3-sp auto	118	206	3584	114	8.6	16–19
1976	Rambler Matador X Coupe	$12,000	V8 OHV	5882cc (360)									
1970–75	Rambler Hornet	$4099 $4412	6-cyl OHV	3802cc (232) 4229 (258)	155/4400 155/3800	222/1600 240/1800	3-sp auto	108	179	2828 2830	101 99	8.4 8.3	20–26
1968–74	Rambler Javelin		V8 OHV	5604cc (343)				110	192				
1969–72	Renault R10, 10S	$2082 $2128 S	4-cyl OHV	1108cc	50/4900 60/5000	65/2500 65/3000	4-sp man	89.5	165	1736 1740	81 93	12.8 10.6	32–38 31–37
1967–77	Renault 16	$2582 GL $2930 TS	4-cyl OHV	1470cc 1565cc	63/5000 90/5750	78/2800 88/3500	4-sp man	104/106	166	2304 2337	87 106	11.4 8.8	26–33 22–30
1972–79	Renault 12	$ $3940 GL	4-cyl OHV	1250cc 1289cc	60/5250 68/5500	70/3000 72/3000	4-sp man	96	171	1940 1980	89 98	10.1 10.4	28–36 33–42
1978–80	Renault Virage	$6440 sed $6990 s/w	4-cyl OHV	1397	65/5750	76/3500	4-sp man, 3-sp auto	96	173	1980 2200	90 90	12.8 13.0	28–34 28–34
1971-	Statesman, Statesman De Ville, Caprice	$6450 (DeV)	V8 OHV	4965cc	240/4800	315/3000	3-sp auto	114	198	3308	107	7.8	17–21
1969–79	Toyota Corolla	$2049 $2199 SE	4-cyl OHV	1166cc	73/6000	74/3800	4-sp man, 3-sp auto	92	155	1618 1680	88 87	10.0 10.4	34–38 34–38
1969–74	Toyota Corona	$2299 $2499 SE	4-cyl OHV	1587cc	82/5000 90/5400	87/2500 98/3000	4-sp man, 3-sp auto	95	159	2016 1906	83 93	13.3 9.7	28–35 26–33
1974–80	Toyota Corona sed, station wagon	$3198 $3373 SE $3749 wag	4-cyl SOHC	1968cc	119/5500	129/3600	4-sp man, 3-sp auto	98	166	2420	97	9.5	23–28
1969-80	Toyota Crown	$2999 $3299 SE $3799 SE	6-cyl SOHC	1988cc 2253cc 2563cc	 115/5200 140/5200	 127/3600 156/3600	3-sp man; 3-sp auto	106	183	2810 2762 2890	94 97 104	10.3 10.1 8.9	21–30 22–27 20–25
1970–75	Triumph 2000 Mk II 2500, 2.5PI, 2500TC, 2500S	 $4859 (PI) $4699 (TC)	6-cyl OHV	1998cc 2498cc 2498cc (PI) 2498cc (TC) 2498cc (S)	 132/5450 100/4250	 152/2000 140/2000	4-sp man, 3-sp auto	106	171	 2682 2514	 112 104	 8.7 9.1	 20–25 21–27
1972–75	Volvo 144/145	$3995 $4515 DL $5395 GL	4-cyl OHV	1986cc	90/4800 90/4800 130/6000	119/3000 107/3500 119/3000 130/3500	4-sp man, 3-sp auto	102.5	182.5	 2716 2576	 99 108	 10.3 9.5	 20–26 23–28

Year	Make	Price $	Engine	Capacity	BHP	Torque lb-ft	Trans	Wheel- base inches	Length inches	Weight	Max speed mph	0–50 mph	Econ- omy mpg
1970– 75	Volvo 164, 164TE	$5849 $	6-cyl OHV	2980cc carb 2980cc inj	145/5500	163/3000	3-sp auto	106	185	2840	102	7.9	22–26
1975– 1980	Volvo 244/245	$7535 DL $8275 GL $8490 DL w	4-cyl SOHC	2127cc carb 2127cc inj	97/5000 123/5500		4-sp man, 3-sp auto	103.9	192.8	2811			
1975– 80	Volvo 264	$13050	V6 SOHC	2664cc inj	140/6000	150/3000	3-sp auto	103.9	192.8	3125	104	9.4	18–24
	VW 1302S 1600L	$2144 $2629	4-cyl OHV boxer	1584cc	60/4400	78/3000	4-sp man, 3-sp auto	95.3	163	1918 1958	80 83	13.4 11.7	26–32 26–32
19xx- yy	VW Type 3 sed Station wagon Fastback	$ $2549 $	4-cyl OHV boxer	1584cc	65/4600	87/2800	4-sp man, 3-sp auto	94.5	171	2240	83	12.9	28–34
1974-	VW Passat LS, wagon	$3598 1.3 $3968 1.5 $4298 TS $4168 s/w	4-cyl OHV	1296cc 1471cc 1471cc 1471cc	60/5800 75/5800 85/5800 75/5800	67/3500 84/3500 89/4000 84/3500	4-sp man, 3-sp auto	97.3	165	1896 1950 2006	97	7.7	30–34
1976	VW Golf	$5351 LS 35540 LS 5	4-cyl OHV	1588cc	75/5500	82/3200	4-sp man/3- sp auto	94.5	147	1771	97	10.5	30–36

These acceleration times are for 0–100km/h (0–62mph)

SELECTED PRODUCTION DATA

Make and Model	Production Dates	Number made
Morris Marina sedan & coupe 4- & 6-cyl	March 1972 – December 1974	30,007
Austin Tasman & Kimberley	November 1970 – December 1972	c. 15,000
Leyland P76	May 1973 – November 1974	18,007
Leyland Mini		
MG B	1970 – 1972	4,231
Chrysler Valiant VG	March 1970 – May 1971	46,374
Chrysler Valiant VH	May 1971 – March 1973	67,800
Chrysler Valiant VJ	April 1973 – September 1975	90,865
Chrysler Valiant VK	October 1975 – October 1976	20,555
Chrysler CL	November 1976 – October 1978	36,672
Chrysler CM	November 1978 – August 1981	16,005
Chrysler by Chrysler sedan	1971 to 1978	9986
Chrysler by Chrysler Hardtop	1971 to 1974	474
Chrysler Valiant Charger VH	1971 to 1973	17,990
Chrysler Valiant Charger VJ	1973 to 1975	10,509
Chrysler Valiant Charger VK	1975 to 1976	1,625
Chrysler Valiant Charger CL	1976 to 1978	1,822
Chrysler Valiant Charger R/T, E37/38, E48/49	1971 to 1973	1300
Holden HT	June 1969 – July 1970	183,402
Holden HG	July 1970 – June 1971	155,787
Holden HQ	July 1971 – October 1974	485,650
Holden HJ	October 1974 – August 1976	176,202
Holden HX	August 1976 – October 1977	110,669
Holden HZ	October 1977 – April 1980	154,155
Holden Commodore VB	October 1978 – March 1980	95,906
Holden Torana LC	September 1969 – February 1972	74,627
Holden Torana LJ	February 1972 – May 1974	81,813
Holden Torana LH	May 1974 – December 1975	70,184
Holden Torana TA	May 1974 – March 1975	11,304
Holden Torana LX	December 1975 – February 1978	65,977
Holden Torana UC	February 1978 -	53,008
Holden Gemini TX	February 1975 – December 1976	43,099
Holden Gemini TC	December 1976 – March 1978	17,256
Holden Gemini TD	March 1978 – September 1979	42,396
Holden Gemini TE	September 1979 – February 1982	70,567
Holden Gemini TF	February 1982	28,326
Ford Falcon XY	1970 – 1972	118,666
Ford Falcon XA	1971 – 1973	152,609
Ford Falcon XB	1973 – 1976	220,765
Ford Falcon XC	1976 – 1979	150,707
Ford Falcon XD	1979 – 1982	206,974
Ford Fairlane ZD	September 1970 – January 1972	12,797
Ford Fairlane ZF	March 1972 – November 1973	17,306
Ford Fairlane ZG	November 1973 – May 1976	19,556
Ford Fairlane ZH	May 1976 – May 1979	22,982
Ford LTD	August 1973 – June 1979	13,171
Ford Cortina Mk II	1970 – 1971	14,306
Ford Cortina TC	1971 – 1974	45,714
Ford Cortina TD	1974 – 1976	37,181
Ford Cortina TE	1976 – 1980	93,075
Ford Capri	1970 – 1972	10,250
Ford Escort Mk I	1970 – 1975	60,616
Ford Escort Mk II	1975 – 1980	78,116
Datsun	1970 – 1979	432,772
Peugeot	1970 – 1979	17,489
Renault	1970 – 1979	46,889
Volkswagen	1970 – 1979	84,948
Volvo	1971 – 1979	47,489

Notes:

1 Peugeot numbers include the 504 and 505 models; no separate breakdown was available.

2 Renault numbers include the 12, 16 and 18 models, again no separate breakdown was available*. See table below.

3 Volkswagen numbers include the Type 1 Beetle, Type 2 Kombi, Type 3 range, Passat and Golf.

4 Volvo numbers include the 140/160 series followed by the 240/260 series; no breakdown was available.

5 MG and Mini production numbers provided by Craig Watson, editor of *The BMC Experience* magazine.

6 Datsun figures include locally assembled models (1600/180B/200B; 1200/120Y/Sunny) as well as imported 240K, 240/260C, 240/260Z.

RENAULT PRODUCTION IN AUSTRALIA

Year	Number	Year	Number
1970	4,434	1976	4,938
1971	5,964	1977	2,075
1972	6,024	1978	1,076
1973	5,317	1979	1,239
1974	7,076	TOTAL for the Decade	45,371
1975	7,228		

Figures supplied by Regie Renault, Paris, France

PRODUCTION FIGURES CHRYSLER BY CHRYSLER

CH Sedan and Hardtop	**1971**	**1972**	**1973**	**TOTAL**
Six cylinder 265 Sedan	241	132	19	392
Six-cylinder 265 Hardtop	38	38	-	76
V8-engined 360 Sedan	892	1439	314	2645
V8-engined 360 Hardtop	268	125	5	398
CJ Sedans (265 & 360-cid)	**1973**	**1974**	**1975**	**TOTAL**
	2381	1732	545	4658
CK Sedans (265 & 360-cid)	**1975**	**1976**	**TOTAL**	
	152	718	870	
CK/CL Sedans	**1976**	**1977**	**1978**	**TOTAL**
	319	954	148	1421
TOTAL Sedans:	**9986**			
	Hardtops:	**474**		
Grand TOTAL:	**10,460**			

AUSTRALIAN MOTOR INDUSTRIES: TOYOTA PRODUCTION FIGURES

Year	Corona	Crown	Corolla	Total
1970	7,914	6,114	7,665	21,693
1971	10,216	5,032	8,869	24,027
1972	9,010	4,242	8,409	21,661
1973	12,260	4,191	9,582	26,033
1974	12,665	4,655	10,723	28,043
1975	16,818	2,646	14,726	34,190
1976	18,674	2,540	18,502	39,716
1977	20,018	1,440	15,694	37,152
1978	22,605	1,380	18,664	42,649
1979	20,587	1,079	25,337	47,003
	150,767	**33,319**	**138,171**	**322,257**

REGISTRATION FIGURES FOR AUSTRALIAN MADE OR ASSEMBLED CARS

**Figures provided by Robert Simpson, gleaned from Australian Motor Manual and the Bureau of Statistics*

Marque	1970	1971	1972	1973	1974	1975	1976	1977	1978	1979
Austin	11,311	6,896								
Chevrolet	84	41	17	45	150	72	55	25	25	29
Chrysler	53,878	50,734	40,220	45,675	44,356	46,300	43,986	39,644	45,200	50,558
Datsun	19,989	27,035	29,897	42,592	46,430	54,700	54,946	50,547	56,824	49,812
Ford	92,040	92,914	111,091	102,957	109,087	101,981	104,304	100,228	100,259	104,831
Holden	139,834	140,257	124,751	131,239	107,845	113,809	119,015	106,676	117,813	131,691
Leyland			22,356	27,794	21,966	8,864	6,532	6,015	5,610	1,451
MG	1,321	883								
Morris	17,127	13, 594								
Nissan							8	12	19	30
Peugeot	1,694	1,223	1,480	1,527	2,024	2,328	2,090	1,543	1,757	1,823
Pontiac	165	63	18	29	88	22	25	17	22	28
Rambler	839	1,073	657	486	254	263	289	214	15	
Renault	5,039	4,708	5,930	6,743	6,569	6,313	4,873	3,237	1,807	1,670
Statesman		2,624	3,818	4,603	5,125	4,921	1,021	742		
Toyota	26,171	26,049	27,775	40,060	48,983	56,603	57,314	56,921	61,991	55,589
Triumph							3,177	2,895	2,437	315
Volkswagen	12,995	14,661	10,697	9,815	7,927	9,755	9,889	4,184	2,905	2,120
Volvo	1,031	2,007	3,073	4,754	6,400	7,401	6,762	5,123	5,640	6,329

PICTURE CREDITS

The Gavin Farmer Library Collection: Pages 6, 7, 8, 9, 15, 16, 17, 24, 25, 27, 28, 29, 30, 31, 33, 34, 35, 38, 45, 46, 52, 53, 54, 55, 56, 57, 58, 59, 60, 61, 62, 63, 64, 65, 66, 67, 68, 69, 70, 71, 72, 73, 74, 75, 76, 79, 81, 82, 84, 86, 88, 89, 90, 91, 92, 93, 94, 95, 96, 98, 100, 102, 103, 104, 105, 106, 107, 108, 109, 110, 111, 112, 113, 114, 115, 116, 117, 118, 119, 121, 123, 124, 126, 127, 128, 130, 131, 132, 134, 136, 137, 138, 139, 140, 142, 144, 145, 146, 147, 148, 149, 150, 151, 152, 153, 154, 155, 156, 157, 158, 160, 161, 162, 163, 164, 165, 166, 167, 168, 169, 170, 171, 172, 173, 174, 175 (upper), 176, 177, 178, 179, 180, 181, 182, 183, 184, 185, 186, 187, 188, 189, 190, 191, 193, 198, 200, 201, 202, 203, 204, 205, 206, 209

Holden: Pages 10, 11, 13, 14, 18, 20, 21, 22, 23, 26, 32, 36, 39, 40, 42, 43, 44, 46, 47, 48, 49, 50, 51

Bob Taylor: Page 175 (lower)

Renault: Pages 194, 195, 196, 197

ABOUT THE AUTHOR

Gavin Farmer has had a lifetime involvement with motorcars one way or another. He bought his first car magazine – *Modern Motor*, September 1959 – while in high school and this began a collection of magazines, books and model cars that occupy a special place in his life today.

He is one of Australia's leading motoring historians and has regularly contributed to such prestigious publications as *Automobile Quarterly, Collectible Automobiles, The Automobile, Bimmer, Sports Car International* and others around the world. In addition he has written many books relating to the post-war Australian motor industry which can be seen by going to the ILINGA BOOKS website at www.ilingabooks.com.au.

From the 70s through to the 90s he worked in the automobile industry in various roles from manufacturing, sales and public relations before turning his talents to writing. His original professional training was for teaching but he was looking for wider challenges in life. To this end he has been a State Manager for a multi-media educational publisher as well as a company that marketed computerised dispensary systems.

All the while he was adding to his knowledge of automobiles, the industry and the many new technologies. A colleague once described him as a "barefoot engineer!"

A man who is passionate about the automobile and its history, Gavin lives with his wife on a small property in the beautiful Adelaide hills where he enjoys occasional drives in his newly restored and quite rare Subaru FF-1.

INDEX

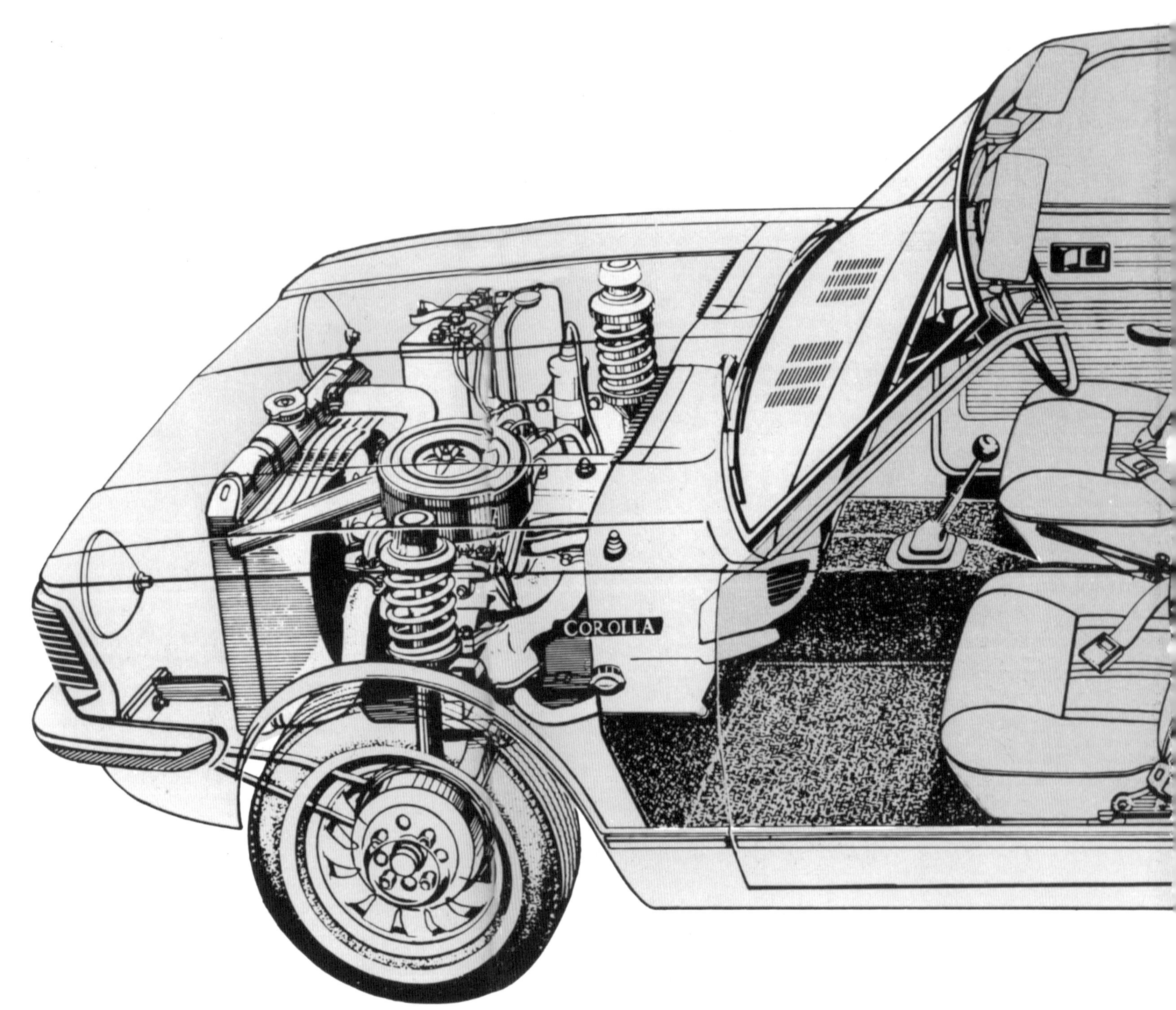
COROLLA